The X Window System and Motif

A Fast Track Approach

The X Window System and Motif

A Fast Track Approach

Jan D. Newmarch
University of Canberra

ADDISON-WESLEY PUBLISHING COMPANY

Sydney • Wokingham, England • Reading, Massachusetts
Menlo Park, California • New York • Don Mills, Ontario
Amsterdam • Bonn • Singapore • Tokyo • Madrid
San Juan • Mexico City • Paris • Milan • Seoul

Acquisitions Editor: K. Andrew Semmens
Production Editor: Susan Lewis
Cover Designer: John Windus
Printer: Globe Press, Australia

First printed 1992

National Library of Australia Cataloguing-in-Publication Data
Newmarch, J. D. (Jan Dennis).
    The X Window System and Motif: A fast track approach.

    Includes index.
    ISBN 0 201 53931 4.

    1. X Window System (Computer system). 2. Motif (Computer
    program). I. Title.

    005.43

Library of Congress Cataloging-in-Publication Data
Newmarch, Jan.
    The X Window System and Motif: A fast track approach / Jan
    Newmarch.
      p. cm.
    Includes index.
    ISBN 0-201-53931-4
    1. X Window System (Computer system) 2. Motif (Computer
    program). I. Title.
    QA76.76.W56N59 1992
    005.4'3--dc20   92-25196
                                     CIP

Preface

The X Window System is a networking window and graphics system from the Massachusetts Institute of Technology (MIT). It can run on a large number of hardware platforms and a number of operating systems. This ability to run across different systems has made it very attractive to use in heterogeneous environments and it has been adopted as a standard windowing system by a substantial group of computer manufacturers.

With the ever-increasing popularity of graphical user interfaces, and the major role that the X Window System is going to play in this application there will be a great demand for application programmers who know at least the basics of X Window programming. This book will interest those people who want to get around the X Window System quickly—students who may be studying the X Window System and Motif as a component of a course and professionals who want to get the feel of the X Window System and Motif to decide if it is worth further exploration.

What is involved in learning about the X Window System and Motif? We assume that you know the C programming language and have at least some experience with C programming in the Unix environment. The first component of the X Window System is the environment itself. You will need to learn what tools are available in the X environment and how to use them. The next component is the library of X Window routines called Xlib. The application programmer needs to learn the way around this function library. Xlib is designed to give a general purpose set of windowing functions. In contrast to many other window systems, this set of functions does not enforce a particular style of interaction, or look-and-feel. To get a particular style you either have to design and implement it yourself using Xlib, or use a toolkit that has already been built for it.

The toolkit that looks likely to become standard is the Motif toolkit from the Open Software Foundation. This gives a look-and-feel similar to that of IBM's Common User Access, as exemplified by Microsoft Windows 3 and Presentation Manager.

How do you gain familiarity with these three components? It can be a daunting task: the manual pages for the standard X environment and for the Motif window manager run to over one hundred and sixty pages; Xlib contains nearly four hundred functions and macros; to use any of the major toolkits requires use of a set of functions called the Intrinsics, and there are one hundred and ninety of these; the Motif toolkit has over two hundred functions in it. To fully explain the use of each of them is also a huge task: books on Xlib typically run to over five hundred pages; on the Intrinsics to over four hundred pages; and on Motif, to about five hundred pages.

This book takes the fast-track approach: how little do you need to know to productively work with the X Window System? Surprisingly little—this book is less than two hundred and fifty pages long.

Despite this fast–track approach, the book does not cut corners. There are many realistic examples dealing with the major concepts of X and Motif. Obviously the depth, range and detail on any topic is restricted, but we cover enough to allow you to build fully functional applications.

The structure of the book is as follows: it is divided into three parts, the first on the X environment, the second on Xlib and the third on Motif. Within each part, the material is presented in two stages: how to do the easy things which are just enough to get going, and then how to use more sophisticated mechanisms to improve things. Individual chapters reflect this in the first two parts, but the third part is more spread out.

The book has a comprehensive set of exercises which expand upon and explore the material in the text. Most of these exercises are quite short. There are also two major projects, one in Xlib and one in Motif. These require the use of most of the techniques discussed in the text and can be extended by using material covered in the exercises.

The book aids the use of X and Motif in two further ways: first, real manual entries are used, because if you go further in this area much time will have to be spent with the programmer's reference manuals. Second, common problems (and actual bugs) and methods for dealing with them are discussed.

Does this mean that the other books and manuals are overdoing it? Not at all. The X Window System is a very large system and an exhaustive treatment requires that volume of documentation. However, the exhaustive treatment is not needed until you begin to run into problems and limitations with the more basic parts. You will not be able to avoid the reference manuals and frequent reference to the larger volumes will always be needed. Even then, if you can get access to UseNet or a feed to the electronic news group `comp.windows.x` and its subgroups, you will find discussions of aspects of X Window that are often not in the books or reference manuals.

One controversial decision made in this book is the use of the Motif toolkit. There are a number of toolkits available with competing claims: the Athena toolkit is freely available, and with source code; the OpenLook toolkit is being promoted by members of Unix International (including Sun Microsystems and AT&T); Motif gives a look-and-feel similar to that of IBM's Common User Access. In the GUI 'wars', it is the look-and-feel argument that swayed the author: to see people move from a PC to a Unix system and sigh with relief as they see a familiar window system is justification enough.

Note that in the format of this book, programs and program terms are always shown in a typewriter font `like this`. Functions and macros are always given with brackets following them as in `f()`. Many of the examples are developmental programs, in which relatively small changes are made to earlier programs. In such cases revision bars are placed to the side of the page to show the changed lines, similar to the bar to the left of this sentence.

The programs in this book can be fetched using anonymous ftp from export.lcs.mit.edu (18.24.0.11) as /contrib/newmarch.tar.Z. For those who do not have access to the Internet, copies are available on 5 1/4 or 3 1/2 inch disks (MS–DOS format) from X Window S/W, Computer Services, University of Canberra, PO Box 1, Belconnen, ACT 2616, Australia. The cost, including postage and packing, is A\$20 within Australia and US\$20 outside Australia.

This book grew out of short courses offered both to students at the University of Canberra and to business organisations. It has benefited from the input of all who attended the courses. The referees of this book made many useful and constructive suggestions which led to many improvements. The referees include Kee Hinckley, Niall Mansfield, Thomas Berlage, Brian Lovell and David Wilson. Thanks are also due to the many people who contribute to the Motif news group on the Internet, and in particular to Kee Hinckley for setting up and maintaining the electronic mail feed to this group. I have learnt a lot from all of these people. The staff at Addison-Wesley have helped guide this book along from the beginning. The Ken Tate Scientific Editing Service did a very thorough edit of the text, and Anaconda Graphic Design gave the style guidelines. The book was produced using Interleaf on a Sun SparcStation, which gave me a very high quality environment in which to work. During the writing of this book I spent three months in Malaysia, and would like to thank Komputer Sistems Sdn. Bhd. for the loan of a Sun SparcStation during this period.

Contents

Figures

Programs

PART I

The X environment

Part I examines the X Window System from the user point of view. It begins by describing the history and model of X and how X can be used. Some tools available under X are then described. In addition it examines ways in which the user can control and customize the X environment. You will learn how to control the behavior of individual applications from the command line, and by the 'resource database'. Finally, some common window managers are discussed, as well as how they give global control over applications in a configurable way.

Chapter 1

Basic concepts

This chapter examines the history of the X Window System and how this gave rise to a particular client / server model. Some of its consequences and uses are discussed.

1.1 History

X is a window system that grew out of the Athena Project at the Massachusetts Institute of Technology (MIT). MIT had (and still has) a large number of different computers, all running under different operating systems. The Athena Project attempted to link them together in such a way that they all became accessible over the network and, where possible, each computer could become a *network resource.*

Many of the machines only supported character-based terminals. There were, however, a number of graphics machines capable of high quality display. The Athena Project was able to take advantage of the character-based machines, but not the graphics features of the graphics machines—graphics remained an individual non-sharable resource. In order to run a graphics application, the user had to sit down in front of one of these machines and run the application, see the output and give mouse and keyboard input direct to that computer. The X system added the graphics capability as a network resource so that an application could prepare graphics at any location on the network and both deliver them to, and receive input from, any suitable piece of hardware elsewhere on the network.

This allows, for example, the following:

- A person can sit in front of a Sun workstation using its keyboard and mouse and seeing graphics on its display. The actual application could be running on a vector processor elsewhere in the network.
- Similarly, a user on a PC with a graphics card and mouse can interact with a database program on a mainframe.

- A demonstration program executing on one machine can be displayed on a number of graphics display terminals.
- A graphics workstation can access a number of different machines simultaneously, displaying results in a suitable form.
- A user can pop up a dialog window on someone else's terminal.

The name X follows on from W—a window system invented at Stanford University. It has nothing to do with the X in Unix.

X is now up to version 11.5 (just released at the time of writing). The previous version 11.4 is just being shipped in commercial systems. The earlier version 11.3 should still be common. The versions are often referred to as X11R3, X11R4, etc. The MIT X Consortium is responsible for any future development of X. This consortium includes many of the big names of computing: IBM, DEC, Hewlett Packard, Sun, AT&T, Microsoft, Borland, etc. Control of X finally resides with MIT, rather than with any of the individual manufacturers, so it is guaranteed to remain a non-proprietary product.

X has become the *de facto* standard windowing system in Unix environments, with major window systems developed on top of it by Sun and AT&T on the one hand, and by DEC and Hewlett Packard on the other.

1.2   Server model

X works on a client/server model. A client is any application running anywhere on the network. The server is a graphics display terminal. The client and server run as separate processes in a multiprocess environment. Many people find the terminology confusing in that 'servers' often are 'back-end servers'. In the X world the server is better thought of as a *front-end* server, mediating between the user and the rest of the application. The two communicate using a high-level protocol (the X protocol) which can be realized by a variety of mechanisms:

- If the two processes are running on the same (Unix) machine, they may use Unix streams or sockets.
- If the application is running on one Unix machine and the server is running on another, they may communicate over ethernet or optical cable using the TCP/IP protocol.
- An application on a Unix machine and an MS–DOS machine running as an X server can communicate over ethernet using TCP/IP. (Note that standard MS–DOS does not easily multiprocess and you will not find both the application and the server on the same MS–DOS machine, except through the help of a system like QuarterDeck.)

- Systems running VMS may use DECNet instead of TCP/IP.

The X protocol is being made into an IEEE standard.

The server and any application communicate by sending messages to one another. The messages are of three kinds:

- A *one-way request* from the application to the server. Such a request is not acknowledged. Typical requests are to open a window, change a background color or move a window. Such requests allow the application to continue processing without delay (Figure 1).

- A *round-trip request* may be sent from the application to the server. This requires information to be returned from the server. A typical request is a query by the application of the mouse position, or a query as to the number of color planes supported by the server. These requests may be slow in a heavily loaded network and should be avoided (Figure 2).

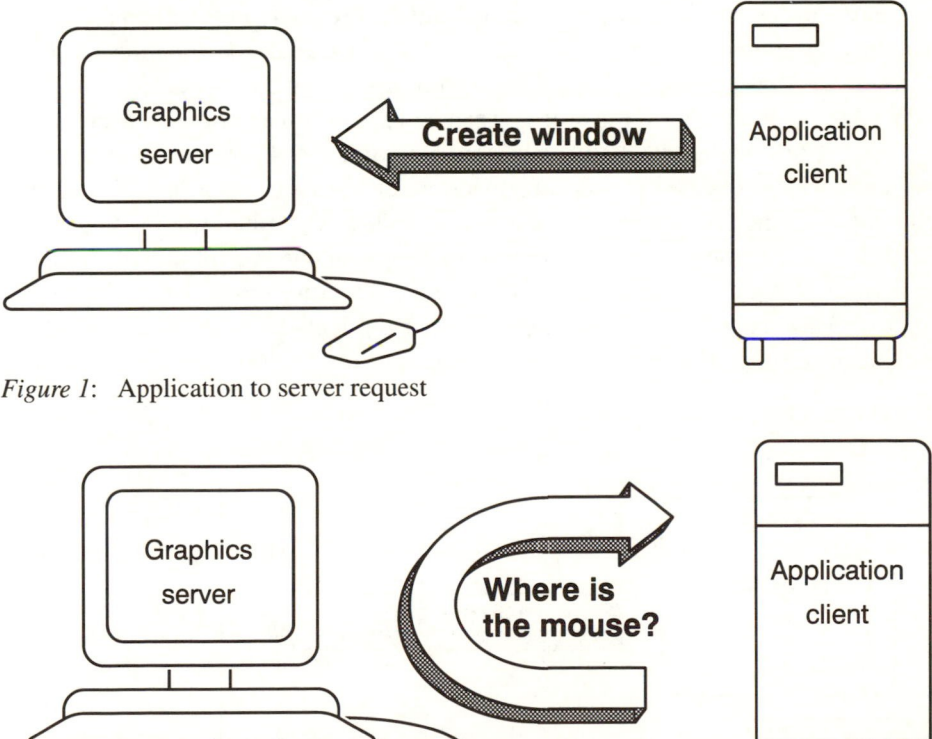

Figure 1: Application to server request

Figure 2: Round-trip request

- *Events* are sent from the server to the application, conveying information (Figure 3). Typical events are when the mouse crosses the boundary of a window, when a key is pressed or when part of a window is exposed. Users are usually responsible for the generation of these events as they move the mouse and handle the keyboard. Each window of an application states what type of events it wishes to receive. For example, a window that is not interested in mouse movements does not ask for them to be sent to it. From then on, any occurrence of a wanted event is sent to the window whenever it occurs, and unwanted events are not sent. This selective sending of events minimizes the network traffic. The events may be buffered and sent out in bursts to further minimize traffic. This may result in a mismatch between the state shown on a display and the state expected by the application. If needed, events may be 'flushed' out of any buffers, but this results in round-trip messages.

This model leads to a style of programming different to that of batch or simple interactive programs. The user is in control and the program must follow this, rather than the user obeying the program's idea of what to do. The program must be able to respond to any user request. This means that programs must be written in a *modeless* style, where components of the program can be activated at any time by user actions.

The X protocol controls the actual information sent between a server and an application. Whatever the physical connection, the two processes use this common protocol. This means that an application need only be compiled for the machine on which it is to run: any graphics server anywhere else can communicate with this application using the standard protocol. In the older computing environments of a single processor and many dumb terminals, the application would be compiled for, and run, on the central processor. Communication with the dumb terminals would be

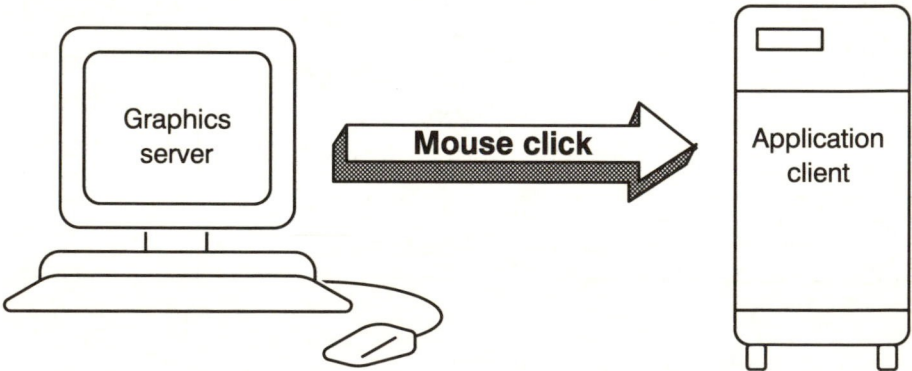

Figure 3:   Server event to application

via serial lines using a simple byte encoding. With the advent of graphics worksta-tions, each application would run and display on the workstation itself. To display on different types of workstations, the application would have to be run on it, meaning that each of them would have to be recompiled for each type of workstation. X re-stores the separation of application running and application display so that they can run on the same or on separate machines where the communication is by the X proto-col.

The X server needs to perform all graphics operations. It also maintains the windows, including their size and hierarchy. In addition, much of the graphics infor-mation is kept in the server (such as the size and color of windows and the width of lines). This helps to further separate the graphics functions from any other func-tions that an application must perform.

For the user and for the programmer much of the low-level nature of the X pro-tocol and its implementation is hidden by higher-level mechanisms. The result is im-portant though: graphics and windowing has become a network resource, running on the machines of a large number of vendors.

Chapter 2

X programs

This chapter examines some of the X applications that come with the standard X distribution, including a window manager. It also describes the Motif window manager mwm *because it comes as part of the Motif system. The emphasis is on the basics—what these applications are and what they look like.*

2.1 Keyboard and mouse

Programs in the X Window system may be driven by use of the mouse and by the keyboard. X assumes use of a three-button mouse. The left button is button number *one*, the middle button *two* and the right button *three*. Documentation and many configuration files use a standard notation to describe actions that may be performed using the mouse. Pressing the left button down, for example, is `Btn1Down`. Releasing the right button is `Btn3Up`.

In a similar way, keys on the keyboard may be described. However, there is a great variation in keyboards and apart from the basic alphanumeric and punctuation keys there is little commonality. There is even less if foreign-language keyboards are used. To get around this, X has adopted keysyms, which forms an abstraction above actual keyboards. The actual keys then have to be mapped to keysyms. Simple cases are things like a single character (e.g. `<Key>A` means the letter A by itself). In addition, there are the common modifier keys such as the Shift and Control keys. Modifiers may be attached to each key by prefixing it with the modifier (e.g. `Ctrl<Key>A` means the control key pressed simultaneously with A). To enforce case sensitivity the prefix ':' is used (for example, `:Ctrl<Key>A` means control–capital–A rather than control–any–A). A problem that faced the designers of X was the requirement for a special modifier key. Many keyboards have keys such as an Alt key, a function key, or some other key which is used as a modifier. Because of the lack of commonality, the X abstraction calls such a key the Meta key.

Most keys on the keyboard are straightforward. Some may not have such a clear meaning, such as Pop on an Apollo keyboard, or Again on a Sun keyboard. On the other hand, when the X documentation uses the Meta key it may not be obvious what this is. If there is no local documentation telling what is what, you just have to experiment. One way of finding out what each key does is to use the program `xev`. This sets up a couple of windows and places the mouse cursor within them. Each time something happens within these windows, such as a button press or key press, `xev` reports in great detail what is going on. To find out what any obscure keys do, press them and look at what X thinks they are; to find the Meta key, press every key on the keyboard until `xev` tells you that you have found it. For example, here is the output from `xev` when the left 'diamond' key on a Sun keyboard—which is the left-Meta key—is pressed:

```
KeyPress event, serial 13, synthetic NO,
    window 0x800001,root 0x80067, subw 0x0,
    time 2404252262, (21,90), root:(161,202),
    state 0x0, keycode 127 (keysym 0xffe7, Meta_L),
    same_screen YES,
    XLookupString gives 0 characters:  ""
```

It shows it is the Meta key in the bracketed part following the keycode.

2.2   Standard tools

The standard X environment supplies a *small* number of tools. None of them are inspiring. More substantial applications are appearing from the software vendors and from UseNet contributions.

2.2.1   xterm

`xterm` is a VT100/Tektronix emulator. It gives a 'terminal window' running a Unix shell. Within this terminal window, any standard Unix commands can be used, such as `ls` and the editor `vi`. Figure 4 shows an `xterm` running the Bourne shell, with a couple of Unix commands and their output (an X application `xwd`, `ls` and `ps`). As the figure shows, it is no different to Unix on an ordinary terminal. Any number of these terminal windows can be open, giving the user easy access to multitasking. The multitasking mechanisms of the Unix shells (such as the C shell's use of ctrl–Z to place a process into the background) can be largely avoided: simply open up another `xterm` and leave the first one running. New `xterm`s can often be started from a system menu, depending on how the window manager is set up, but can also be started from a Unix shell prompt by typing:

```
xterm &
```

Each one can be exited by giving the appropriate Unix command to the prompt——in the case of the Bourne shell this is the end-of-file ctrl–D. (A criticism

```
$ ls *.doc
Basic_concepts.doc        Part_summary.doc
Configuration.doc         X_programs.doc
Part_start.doc
$ ps
  PID TT STAT    TIME COMMAND
 5566 co IW      0:00 sh startx
 5567 co IW      0:00 xinit -- /usr/bin/X11/X -ar1 500
 5568 co S    1012:47 /usr/bin/X11/X :0 -ar1 500
 5569 co IW      0:00 sh /shome/jan/.xinitrc
 5570 co S       0:14 /shome/jan/motif1.1/clients/mwm/mwm
 5571 co IW      0:20 xclock -geometry 100x100-1+1
 5573 p0 IW      0:02 zsh
 5574 p0 IWN     0:00 sh /shome/jan/bin/ileaf
 5575 p0 S N     5:24 /interleaf/ileaf5/sun4/bin/ileaf
 5681 p1 S N     0:00 zsh
 5682 p1 S N     0:00 sh
 5685 p1 R N     0:00 ps
$ xwd > xterm.xwd
```

Figure 4:   An `xterm` window

of X is that it often results in screens showing a large number of the `xterm`s each giving a command line interface, rather than a 'proper' graphical user interface.)

`xterm` allows you to *select* text in a window and paste it into another. You can select text from an `xterm` window by pressing the left button once, dragging the mouse and releasing it, or by clicking twice to select a word, or three times to select a line. Selected text may be pasted into any suitable window at the text cursor position by clicking the middle button. A variety of options can control aspects of its behavior, some of which will be mentioned in Section 3.2 on 'Configuring the environment.'

The program has often been used as a test vehicle for various versions of X and leaves a lot to be desired. For example, it can only emulate a small number of terminals, rather than the full range that Unix supports.

2.2.2 xclock

A simple clock is given by this command. It can be a digital or analog clock.

2.2.3 xedit

This provides an editor with reasonable but rudimentary capabilities. Figure 5 shows the X11R4 version of `xedit`. It shows a bar along the top with some commands and an area for entry of a file name. Below this are a number of information areas and below them the editing area itself. This shows the text of a C program and as this is too long to fit in the window, a scrollbar is along the left to allow quick motion through the file. The scrollbar allows rapid movement through the file: click button one in the scrollbar to move down through the file, button three to move up, and button two to skip to locations within the file.

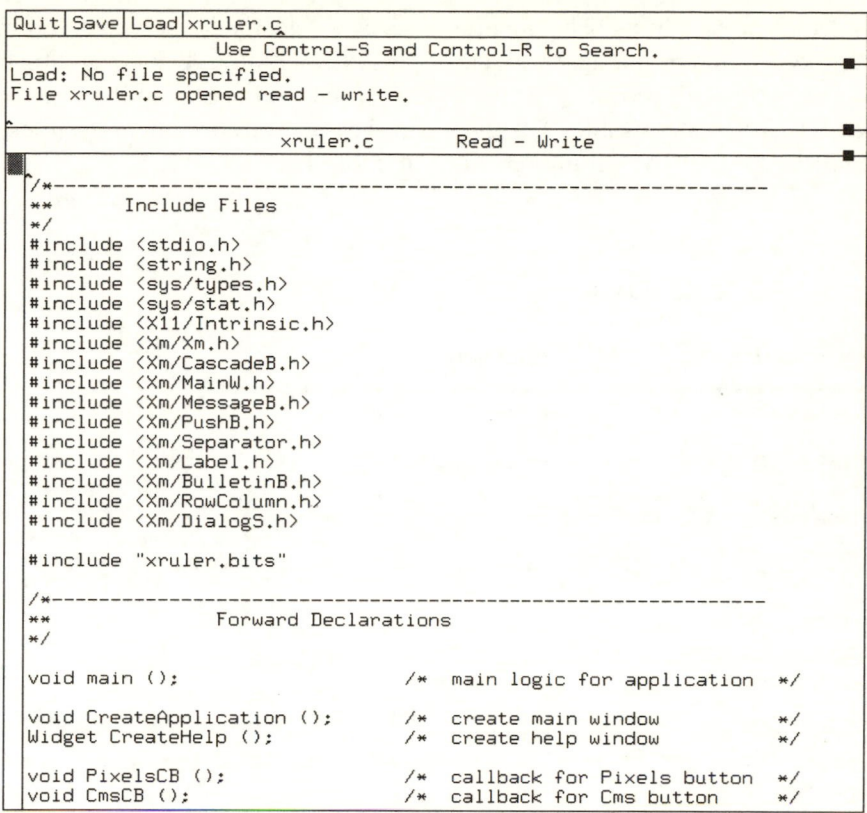

```
Quit Save Load xruler.c
               Use Control-S and Control-R to Search.
Load: No file specified.
File xruler.c opened read - write.


                   xruler.c        Read - Write

/*--------------------------------------------------------------
**         Include Files
*/
#include <stdio.h>
#include <string.h>
#include <sys/types.h>
#include <sys/stat.h>
#include <X11/Intrinsic.h>
#include <Xm/Xm.h>
#include <Xm/CascadeB.h>
#include <Xm/MainW.h>
#include <Xm/MessageB.h>
#include <Xm/PushB.h>
#include <Xm/Separator.h>
#include <Xm/Label.h>
#include <Xm/BulletinB.h>
#include <Xm/RowColumn.h>
#include <Xm/DialogS.h>

#include "xruler.bits"


/*--------------------------------------------------------------
**                 Forward Declarations
*/

void main ();                    /*  main logic for application  */

void CreateApplication ();       /*  create main window          */
Widget CreateHelp ();            /*  create help window          */

void PixelsCB ();                /*  callback for Pixels button  */
void CmsCB ();                   /*  callback for Cms button     */
```

Figure 5: An xedit window

xedit is a *text* editor and does not have the power of a word-processor. It is a modeless editor, as most are nowadays. To those familiar with Unix editors it is closer to emacs than to vi. emacs also is modeless where a key always does the same thing (an 'a' is always 'append an a'), whereas vi is modal ('a' can mean 'enter append mode' or 'append an a' if you are already in append mode). What you type in the main xedit window is entered as text unless it happens to be an xedit command sequence. You can move around the displayed text by using the up, down, left and right arrow keys. The location for text entry may also be selected by clicking the left mouse button at the point desired. It may be changed by the mouse again, or by keyboard commands.

To load a file, the mouse pointer must be placed in the window to the right of the Load window. Enter a file name, but do *not* press Return. Instead, click on the Load window. I find this extremely hard to do as I can never resist pressing the Return key and consequently never use this editor as I can never succeed in loading a file!

Much of the editing behavior of `xedit` is not clearly documented. It is hidden in the description of the 'text widget' of the Athena toolkit. Understanding of this documentation will probably not become clear until some time in Part Three (Section 11.1, 'Translation Tables'). Although the keys can be configured by the user, the default setup gives the editing functions of Table 1.

Table 1:   Editing functions for `xedit`

Key or button	Function
Ctrl<Key>F	forward character
Ctrl<Key>B	backward character
Ctrl<Key>A	start of line
Ctrl<Key>E	end of line
Ctrl<Key>N	next line
Ctrl<Key>P	previous line
Ctrl<Key>V	next page
Meta<Key>V	previous page
Meta<Key> >	end of file
Meta<Key> <	beginning of file
Meta<Key>F	forward word
Meta<Key>B	backward word
Ctrl<Key>D	delete next character
Ctrl<Key>H	delete previous character
:Meta<Key>d	delete next word
:Meta<Key>h	delete previous word
Ctrl<Key>W	delete selection
<Btn1Down>	begin selection
<Btn3Down>	extend selection
<Btn2Down>	insert selection

2.2.4   Other tools

A number of other tools may be available on your system. They will probably be in
`/usr/bin/X11`. The more useful general purpose ones are `xcalc` (a calculator),
and some games and miscellaneous demos such as the 16-puzzle and solitaire. More
specialized software will be in this directory to allow screen dumps (`xwd`), get font
lists (`xlsfonts`), etc. There is a large amount of publicly available software. It may
be found in two major sources: as contributed software on the MIT release or posted
to one of the networks such as UseNet. Software available includes calendars,
screen lockers, drawing tools, file managers and plenty more games. Non-X Window software such as mailers and debuggers may be found wrapped up in X Window frames to bring them into the X environment. Figure 6 shows a screen with a

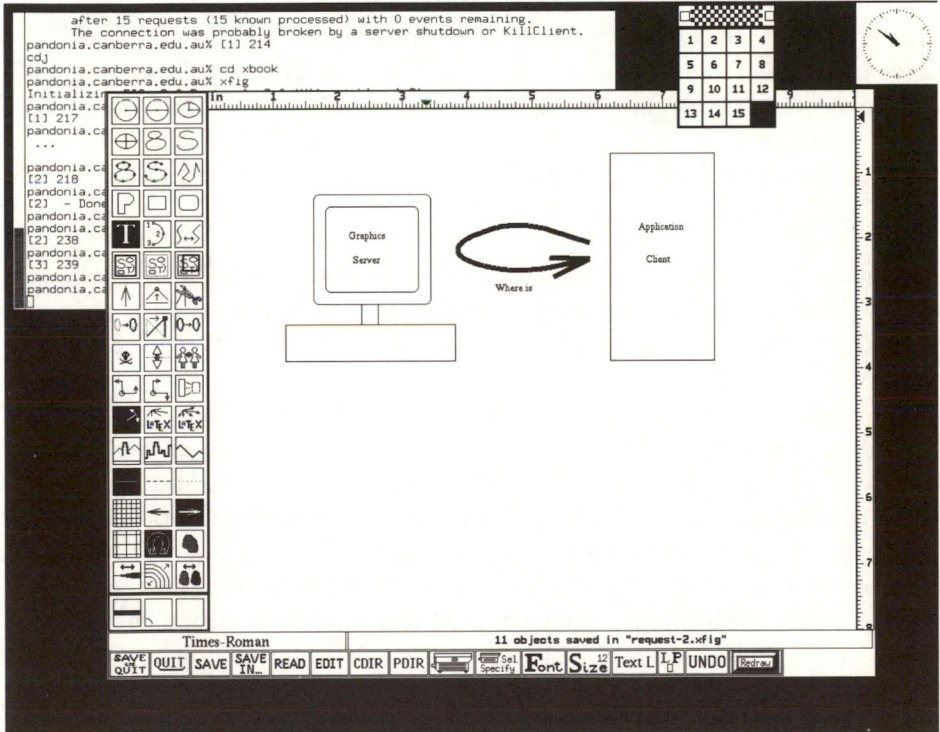

Figure 6:   A typical X screen

number of applications displaying concurrently: an `xclock` is in the top right corner, a 16-puzzle is next to it, partially covering the drawing program `xfig`, which in
turn is covering an `xterm` with a scrollbar along the left. This is all against a black
background, as set by the program `xsetroot -solid black`. The windows are

often overlapped. How does the user choose a window, or bring a window up above others? This is done by using window managers, which are described next.

2.3 Window managers

A window manager is chosen by the user to handle 'real-estate' issues such as the placement and movement of windows on the screen, iconification of windows, and mechanisms for starting and manipulating applications and their associated windows. Window managers may come from a variety of sources: the X Window System release from MIT has a window manager; others may be found in the contributed software; proprietary manufacturers or other software vendors sell/include window managers. The MIT X11 release 3 used the window manager uwm as the standard window manager, with twm as an option in the contributed software. The MIT X11 release 4 has reversed these. olwm is the OpenLook window manager of choice from AT&T and Sun. mwm is the Motif window manager of the Open Software Foundation (OSF), and gives a real-estate management similar to that of Microsoft Windows 3.

This section deals with twm and mwm.

2.3.1   twm

The window manager twm[1] has been adopted as standard window manager for X11 R4 onwards. Like all window managers, the way it manages real estate can be configured by the user. The default configuration for an xterm window managed by twm is shown in Figure 7.

Every application has at least one toplevel window. All window components of applications are contained within toplevel windows. twm decorates each toplevel window of an application with a title bar containing the name of the application. This bar also contains an iconify button on the left and a resize button on the extreme right. To resize a window vertically, drag the mouse in the resize button, first *upward* and then either up or down. Similarly, to resize it horizontally, drag the mouse in the resize button first to the right and then in the desired direction. You can move a window by placing the mouse in the title bar and dragging it by holding down the right button. To iconify a window, click the left mouse button on the iconify button. To restore the icon, double click the left mouse button on the icon. The default keyboard select model is the 'implicit focus' model, in that keyboard input will be directed to the window containing the mouse, even if that window is partially obscured. A system menu is available by clicking the left mouse button outside any application window. This system menu allows the user to manipulate applications windows in various ways. The default system menu is shown in Figure 8. To use the system menu,

---

[1] Once known as Tom's window manager after its first author, Tom LaStrange.

Iconify
button

Title
bar

Resize
button

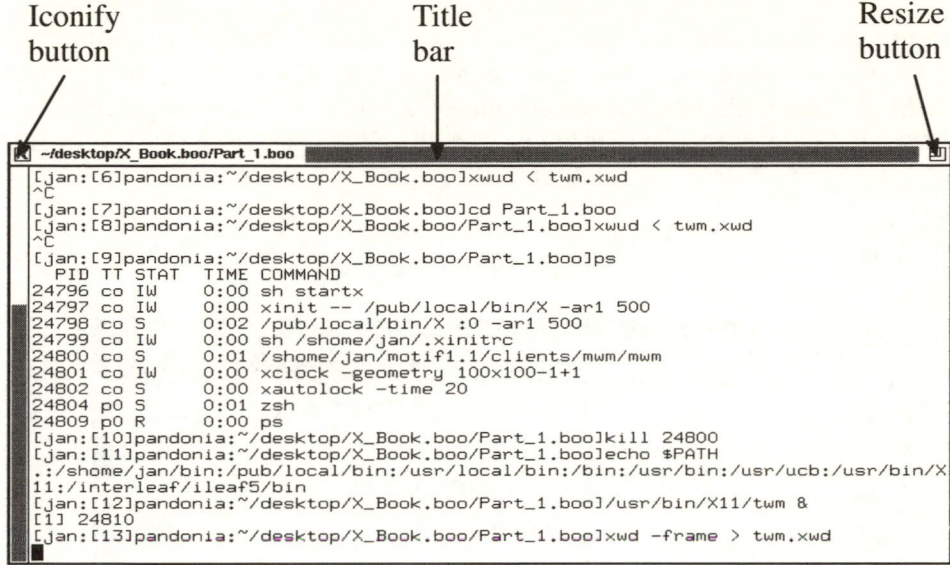

```
 ~/desktop/X_Book.boo/Part_1.boo
[jan:[6]pandonia:~/desktop/X_Book.boo]xwud < twm.xwd
^C
[jan:[7]pandonia:~/desktop/X_Book.boo]cd Part_1.boo
[jan:[8]pandonia:~/desktop/X_Book.boo/Part_1.boo]xwud < twm.xwd
^C
[jan:[9]pandonia:~/desktop/X_Book.boo/Part_1.boo]ps
  PID TT STAT   TIME COMMAND
24796 co IW     0:00 sh startx
24797 co IW     0:00 xinit -- /pub/local/bin/X -ar1 500
24798 co S      0:02 /pub/local/bin/X :0 -ar1 500
24799 co IW     0:00 sh /shome/jan/.xinitrc
24800 co S      0:01 /shome/jan/motif1.1/clients/mwm/mwm
24801 co IW     0:00 xclock -geometry 100x100-1+1
24802 co S      0:00 xautolock -time 20
24804 p0 S      0:01 zsh
24809 p0 R      0:00 ps
[jan:[10]pandonia:~/desktop/X_Book.boo/Part_1.boo]kill 24800
[jan:[11]pandonia:~/desktop/X_Book.boo/Part_1.boo]echo $PATH
.:/shome/jan/bin:/pub/local/bin:/usr/local/bin:/bin:/usr/bin:/usr/ucb:/usr/bin/X
11:/interleaf/ileaf5/bin
[jan:[12]pandonia:~/desktop/X_Book.boo/Part_1.boo]/usr/bin/X11/twm &
[1] 24810
[jan:[13]pandonia:~/desktop/X_Book.boo/Part_1.boo]xwd -frame > twm.xwd
```

Figure 7: twm managing an xterm

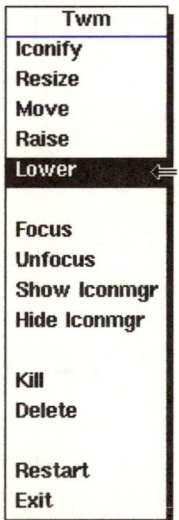

Figure 8: twm system menu

first select an action from it and then perform the action on a window by clicking the
mouse in the window.

2.3.2   The Motif window manager

The principal attraction of Motif is that it offers an environment compatible with Presentation Manager and Microsoft Windows and allows you to design CUA (IBM's Common User Access) compliant applications. A major component of this is the window manager mwm. See Figure 9 for an xterm managed by mwm, where the

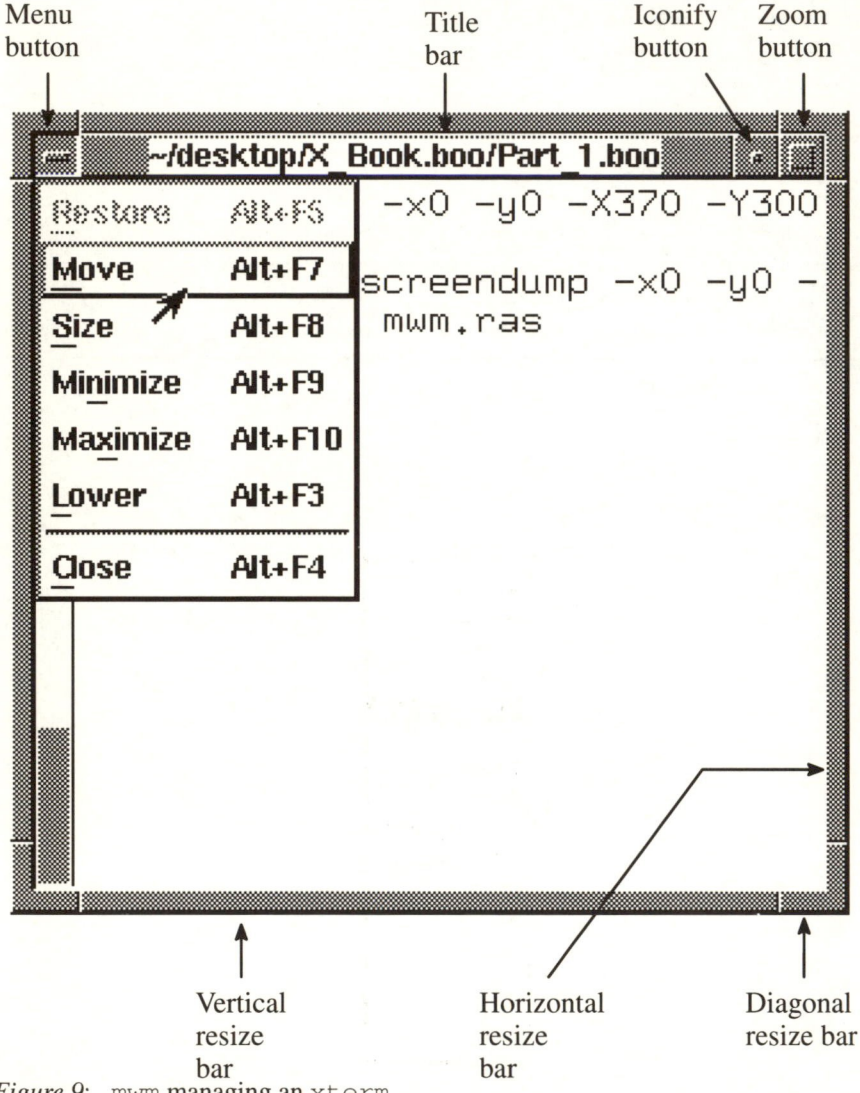

Figure 9:   mwm managing an xterm

Menu button has been pressed to show a pulldown menu of commands appropriate to the application.

The default behavior places bars around all sides of an application. Each side contains a resize bar in that direction. Each corner contains a diagonal resize bar. By dragging the left mouse button in these bars the application window will be forced to change size. By dragging the top title bar, the entire window can be moved. The default keyboard focus policy is the 'explicit' policy: to focus attention on a window, the mouse pointer must be clicked within that window. This causes the window to rise to the top and accept keyboard input. The mouse can be moved anywhere and not affect the focus until it is clicked again.

Chapter 3

Configuration

This chapter describes the controls that X users have over their environment. It shows how individual applications can have their appearance and behavior controlled in a variety of ways, and also how the window managers can be configured.

3.1 Policy versus mechanism

The user of any system or application will build a model of how to interact with it. This will contain the knowledge of how to do things with the system, the shortcuts available, and the conventions followed. For example, a common Unix convention for commands is that options must precede all filenames, and all options are prefixed with a minus '–' sign (as in `ls -l`). So prevalent is this convention that people make special note of the exceptions: for example, neither `tar` nor `ps` require the minus sign. This collection of conventions and styles is known as the *policy* of the system. Most of the Unix programs are in fact written in the language C, and nowhere in C is there any requirement to prefix options with a minus. C supplies *mechanisms* with which you can build any interaction style. Obviously it can be used to build applications following the standard Unix policy.

Over the years, character-based interfaces have evolved remarkably: under Unix the shells such as the C shell and Korn shell offer command histories, the ability to switch between foreground and background tasks and aids such as aliasing to customize the environment. Windows-based environments generally offer immediate improvements on these character-based environments, but it is far from clear that the answers are all known for window systems. For experiments to be performed, and for *other* software developers to design their own user interfaces, X provides mechanisms instead.

A central feature of X is that it does *not* mandate policy. X concentrates on providing *mechanisms*, and the application designer and the user can employ them in any manner they wish. In this it differs from IBM's SAA or Common User Access (CUA), Microsoft's Presentation Manager, and the Apple interface, which require applications designers to follow a particular policy.

For the application developer, it is important to fully realize the consequences of this decision. The intention of those who mandate policy is that it should provide a common interface for different applications, and that this interface will not change for any user. The user who has learnt this interface can thus move between applications without the expensive learning curve caused by inconsistent or different mechanisms.

Many different user interfaces can be built using X. The users of the software should be able to choose the interface they like best. For example:

- Users who mainly perform word-processing tasks will find only a limited amount of use for a mouse. They may wish to be able to 'park' the mouse out of the way of their document window to avoid obscuring it. For this user, the 'focus' of attention and the position of the mouse need not be correlated. This is the 'explicit focus' or 'click to type' focusing policy. The user must explicitly select a window for the keyboard focus by clicking the mouse in it and the focus will stay there until the user selects another window.

- A user of CAD programs will use the mouse heavily in selecting items out of menus and tables, moving them around designs, and performing cut and paste operations. For this user the attention focus will almost always be the same as the mouse position, to the extent that the user may wish windows to rise above any others, merely because the mouse is within its boundaries. This is the 'implicit focus' policy.

- Some users dislike typing into any window of which a portion is obscured, whereas others do not mind if, say, a clock covers an insignificant part of the window.

The upshot of this is that the user should be allowed to choose the style of interface desired and that any application should enforce its own style only with caution. Of course an expectation of this is that there will be certain 'standard' interfaces which can be used for the non-fussy users, for those with intermittent contact with the system, or for those who simply like a consistent policy. This places a burden on the application developer to remain as policy-free as possible, allowing the user to set policy.

This is clearly impossible, as any application of complexity must adopt a consistent internal policy in order to be usable. For example, if pressing the function key F1 somewhere in an application brings up a help menu, then pressing F1 elsewhere should also bring up a help menu. Various compromises must be adopted. One thing that should be under user control is the 'geometry' of windows, i.e. their size and their position on the screen. Any application should make an attempt to work in any size that the user has set it. There are a variety of ways of changing the geometry: a common way is to decorate windows with bars containing movement and iconification symbols. 'Hot' keys are another favorite. Again, the user should have control over this. It should not matter to an application where its main windows are. Users like various foreground and background colors, and stipple patterns for backgrounds. An application should be able to handle such user requests.

Part of the burden is placed on a program called a window manager. The user chooses a window manager and the window manager handles geometry ('real estate' management). This includes both the size and position of windows and the mechanisms for changing them. Focus policy is a matter for the window manager since it is a global matter. The application is responsible for obeying user requests for other components such as colors.

3.2   Configuring the environment

X applications generally allow the user to configure them to suit their own preferences. Some of the options concern:

- Starting X
- Server
- Geometry
- Fonts
- Window management
- Resource management

3.2.1   Startup using `xinit`

How the user begins an X Window session can vary quite dramatically from one system to another. The system may be set so that it runs under X all the time, and logins are performed by X, or it may be that you can invoke both an X server and applications like `xterm` from your `.profile` or `.login` (under Unix Bourne and C shells respectively), or you may have to invoke a special startup command. You will have to find out what procedure is used from your systems supervisor. However, you should have the power to control what comes up as your initial configuration.

A common mechanism for starting an X session (particularly in mixed windows/character mode systems) is for the user to start the X server and some initial programs by executing the command `xinit` (often through a program with a name such as `startx` or `xstart`). This can be done from a command-line prompt or from the `.login` or `.profile` files. `xinit` looks in the file `$HOME/.xinitrc` for X programs to execute. To start off with a clock, a terminal emulator window, an editor and a window manager (say `twm`), place these lines in your `.xinitrc`:

```
xedit &
xclock &
xterm &
twm
```

This starts the first three programs as asynchronous processes, using the normal Unix method of following the command with an ampersand &. The last process is `twm` running synchronously, so that when you exit `twm` you exit from the X Window system. Note that you must follow the first three commands with the &—you are running the four processes concurrently, with Unix and X supplying the mechanism to switch between them.

3.2.2 Startup using `xdm`

Where X is the only system used, it is common for the X Window system to be started at boot time using the program `xdm` and for each user to start a new session by logging into `xdm`. The same principles hold, though, that the user can configure the startup environment. In this case, the file `$HOME/.xsession` is used instead of `.xinitrc`.

3.2.3 Server

Much of the behavior of any X application can be controlled by command-line options. In the next sections we will mainly consider this mechanism. A more general one (resources) will be dealt with in Section 3.4 on 'Resource management.'

An application running can deliver graphics to, and receive input from, any suitable server. The server can be set on a per-application basis, so that different applications running on the same machine can direct the graphics output to different servers, or it can default to a server value set by the user or by the system supervisor.

The default server name is found in the Unix environment variable `DISPLAY`. You can test if this variable is set by the Unix command:

```
echo $DISPLAY
```

If this gives a blank line only, then the variable has not been set. If the system supervisor has not set it, you can do so in your `.profile` or `.login` files.

There are conventions for the value of the `DISPLAY` variable. First, it is made up of the server name as a machine on the network. My machine is named 'jan', so this forms the first part of the `DISPLAY` value. If X is running over TCP/IP the next component is a single colon ':', whereas if it is DECNet it is a double colon '::'. Following this is typically '0' (for the zero'th display on this server[2]). Thus if `jan` is a Unix machine I would set the `DISPLAY` environment variable as:

```
setenv DISPLAY jan:0
```

under the C shell, and

```
DISPLAY=jan:0
export DISPLAY
```

under the Bourne or Korn shells. If the `DISPLAY` has the special value `unix:0` it stands for the same machine as the application is running on.

A command-line option can override this default server:

```
command -display server-name
```

as in

```
xclock -display hotel:0
```

which starts up a clock showing on machine `hotel`.

Is this sort of thing worth doing? Well, of course it is as soon as you want to turn graphics into a network resource. For example, at one stage I had the drawing tool `xfig` running on a Sun SparcStation (called `longinus`) with an `xterm` and an `xclock` running on an Apollo 3500, both delivering graphics to a 386 PC server running MS–DOS (with `DISPLAY` value `jan:0`). I would log onto the Apollo using Telnet and execute:

```
DISPLAY=jan:0
export DISPLAY
xclock &
rsh longinus "xfig -display jan:0" &
xterm
```

to give me a terminal emulator and a clock running on the Apollo, and a drawing tool running on the Sun, all communicating with me sitting in front of the PC. This is shown in Figure 10.

3.2.4   Access permissions

Just to muddy the waters a little: there may be access problems. The *server* must grant permission to other machines to display their graphics on it. On Unix this will be done by entering machine names into `/etc/X0.hosts`, which only a system supervisor can do. That is, to run the clock application on machine `longinus`, displaying on the server `hotel`, the name `longinus` must appear in `/etc/X0.hosts` of `hotel`. Placing names in this file means that at any time X is run, applications from the other machine can display on the server. An alternative is to use the command:

```
xhost +longinus
```

---

[2] A server can have many displays. In turn, a display may have many screens (but usually does not). If this is the case, you should add the screen number as well, after a decimal point, as in jan:0.0.

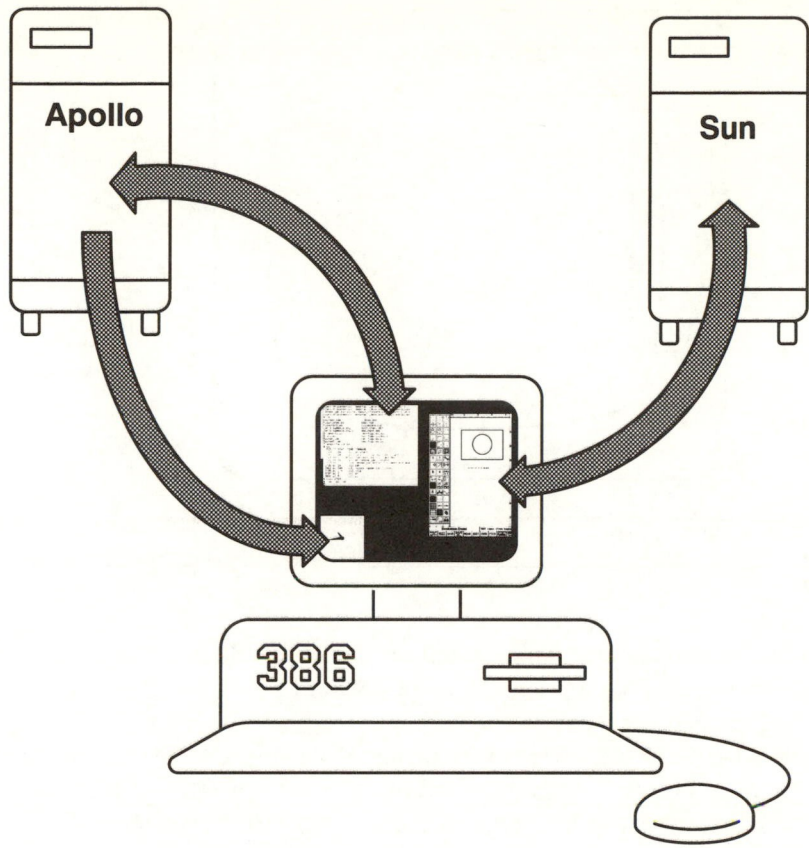

Figure 10:   Networking X applications

on the server `hotel` to add the client `longinus` for the duration of an X session. Alternatively, you can add *all* hosts by `xhost +`.

3.2.5 Geometry

When a window application commences, it may specify the initial screen coordinates and the horizontal and vertical extents of its toplevel windows. The coordinate system runs from left-to-right, top-to-bottom, as in Figure 11. There are often default values for this, to which the window manager may or may not pay attention. (For example, the manager `uwm` normally ignores default values of the initial screen coordinates.) The user may specify the geometry of a toplevel window by including a geometry option on the command line. Using EBNF, the syntax is:

```
command -geometry <width>x<height>{+-}<x>{+-}<y>
```

where the x and y coordinates are optional. The width and the height are usually in pixels. The offsets are in pixels. For example, to create a 50×30 pixel clock you would give the command:

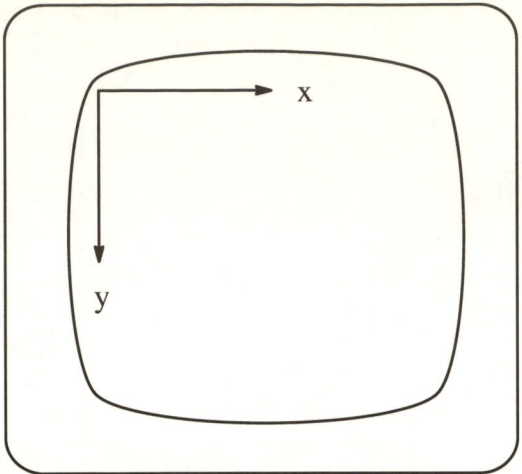

Figure 11:   Coordinate system

```
xclock -geometry 50x30
```
If you also wanted to place the top-left corner of the clock ten pixels in and twenty pixels down from the top-left corner you would give the command:
```
xclock -geometry 50x30+10+20
```
The width and height may be in units meaningful to the application: for example, to `xterm`, the width is in characters and the height in lines. To specify an 80 column by 24 line `xterm` window at (x, y) coordinates (10, 10), enter:
```
xterm -geometry 80x24+10+10
```
The meaning of negative coordinates is less standardized. Frequently a negative x coordinate is measured from the right, while a negative y coordinate is measured from the bottom. Thus a twenty by thirty pixel clock in the top-right-hand corner is given by:
```
xclock -geometry 20x30-0+0
```

3.2.6 Fonts

X allows an unlimited number of fonts. The typical X system will have over five hundred fonts, many donated by companies such as Adobe and Bitstream. The fonts are typically stored in `/usr/lib/X11/fonts`. Typically a person would only want a small number of fonts out of the range available. To find out what fonts exist is a multistage process. The command `xlsfonts` will list the full font *names* available (see Figure 12). These names are rather long——they contain an organization identifier, the font style, whether it is in bold, in italics, its point size, and other size information, often concluding with an ISO standards number! For example:
```
-adobe-courier-bold-o-normal--10-100-75-75-m-60-iso8859-1
```

This is not the kind of thing that the user will want to type frequently! You can use the asterix * as a wild card to match the pattern as in `-adobe*normal*10*`.

The command:

```
xfontsel
```

under X11R4 will display a window showing all the fields with a pulldown menu on each choice, so that you can see what each font looks like. Under X11R3 this command is not available and you have to use:

```
xfd -font font-name
```

This will display the fonts in a special window on the screen so that you can see what they look like (see Figure 12). To avoid typing mistakes in these names, combine some of the information already presented: use `xlsfonts` in an `xterm` window. This will display all of the names in the window. If you have set the scrollbar option on for the `xterm`, you will be able to browse through the names, but otherwise you will be limited to those showing on the screen. Find a font with an interesting name. Select the name by clicking on the leftmost character and dragging to the end of line. In another `xterm`, type the command:

```
xfd -font
```

leaving a space after the word 'font'. Then paste the rather long font names from the first `xterm` into this new one, and run the `xfd` command.

Servers vary vastly in display capability. An EGA monitor for a PC has 640 by 360 pixels on a screen about 10.5 inches by 8 inches. The VGA monitor has 640 by 480 pixels and the same physical size (the VGA pixels are 'square'). Both monitors are color. A Sun has 1152 by 900 pixels on a larger screen in either mono or color. Apollo workstations may have 1024 by 800 or 1200 by 1024 screens. A font that is crisp and clear on one screen may be close to unreadable on another. I use a different font on each display that I meet.

Once you have selected a preferred font you can use it for any particular program which allows font choice by including the font on the command line:

```
command -fn font-name
```

For example, to use `xterm` with the 9x15 font:

```
xterm -fn 9x15
```

Figure 12 shows two `xterm` windows, one with a twelve-point font showing some of the output from `xlsfonts` (with one font selected), the other with a larger twenty-four-point font invoking an `xfd` with an eighteen-point italic font. This particular screen dump was from a 1024 by 800 Apollo 2500 screen.

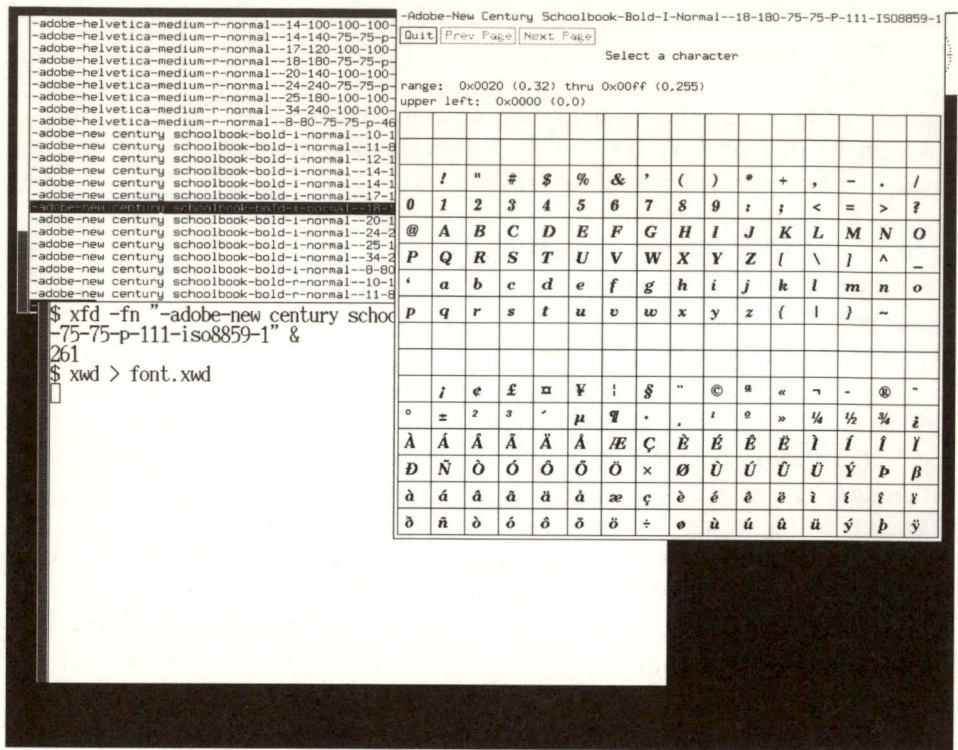

Figure 12:   Some different fonts in X

3.3   Further command-line options

There is a standard set of command-line options in addition to `display`, `font` and `geometry`. They are supported by most, but not all, applications. These options include:

- Foreground color by, e.g. `-fg blue` or `-foreground   red`. (A list of color names is often found in `/usr/lib/X11/rgb.txt`.)

- Background color by, e.g. `-bg blue` or `-background red`.

- Name of application by, e.g. `-name my_application`.

- Title of application by, e.g. `-title my_application`.

- Border width of window by, e.g. `-bw 5`.

- Start off as an icon by `-iconic`.

The default name of an application is usually the program name (such as `xterm`). Under some circumstances (see the next section) it may be useful to choose a different one. The `name` option can be used to select this. A window manager (such as `twm` and `mwm`) may place a title bar along the top of an application. This defaults to the application name (i.e. the program name or the command-line name option). It may be useful to have a different title. The option `title` can set this. An X command will often say in the documentation: 'understands all standard X command-line options.' This cryptic phrase includes the above options.

In addition, there may be a number of other options specific to the command. For example, to have scroll bars on an `xterm`, use the option `-sb`. The command `xterm` is an example of a command with a large set of command-line options.

3.4 Resource management

X Window applications exist in a windowed environment. An application will have at least one toplevel window, around which the window manager may place various bars and buttons. Within this window though, there may be many others. Each 'area' of an application may consist of a separate window and these may be nested to any depth. There must be methods to control the appearance, size and behavior of all these windows.

A *resource* is any feature of an application with a value, such as the color of the background to a window, the name of a font, or the geometry of a window. Resources belong to windows of applications, so there may be many resources in a running system. We have already seen one way of controlling some resources on a per application basis via command line options such as `xterm -fn 9x15`. X offers a number of other ways with more generality.

A particular application may make use of a file *.command*`rc` (as does `twm` with `$HOME/.twmrc`—see the next section). This follows a common Unix convention of files beginning with '.' and ending in 'rc'. These files are hidden from the Unix directory lister `ls` unless used with the '–a' option. Such a file is used when 'non-standard' resources such as menu definitions are required. This practice should not be too common with X applications.

The major X mechanism for resource control is to store name/value pairs in a 'resource database'. This database is constructed in a complex way from a number of files and programs. The most common method from the user viewpoint for this is to use a special file. The file used, and how it is used, depends on whether or not the program `xrdb` has been run as you start your X session. If it has, then you usually set resources in `$HOME/.Xresources`, and each time you change this file, rerun `xrdb` by `xrdb .Xresources`. This places resources in a database attached to the server and each time an application starts up it gets resources from the server. If `xrdb` has not been run, set resources in `$HOME/.Xdefaults`. Applications will look in this file when they startup. Generally, if `xdm` is used to start a session `xrdb` will have been run, whereas if `xinit` has been used it will not.

Before looking at more complex ways that resources may be specified, it is better to look at the format of name/value specifications. Since the mechanism has to deal with a number of applications, a standard format has to be used for resource specification files.

The simplest form is that lines in a resource file consist of:

```
application*resource: value
```

For example:

```
xterm*foreground: black
xterm*background: white
xterm*scrollBar:   true
xclock*geometry:   40x40+300+100
```

which will set the foreground of *all* windows in an `xterm` to black, the background of all windows to white, place a scrollbar along the edge and attempt to give any clock the geometry stated. This resource will apply to all *new* `xterm`s and `xclock`s—the ones already running are not affected.

A more complex resource specification consists of a number of dot-separated fields comprising a full resource name (much like the full path name of a file, with the dot '.' in X replacing the slash '/' of Unix). The application can use any number of fields, such as:

```
mydraw.menu_win.titlebar.background: blue
```

The first form uses an * as a wild card which can match any number of fields, including no fields. So patterns for `mydraw.menu_win.titlebar.background` include:

```
*background
mydraw*background
mydraw.menu_win*background
mydraw*menu_win*titlebar*background
```

There are rules governing the generality of patterns and when one overrides another. The formal expression of these rules is quite complex. They cover cases such as whether or not `mydraw.menu_win*background` is more specific than `mydraw*menu_win.background`. Normally the user would not need to know the full details of this, but only that a more specific pattern overrides a more general one.

The use of wildcard patterns also means that a pattern may refer to a number of resources at once. Thus `*background` refers to the background color of all windows in all applications. This may cause a problem if the pattern includes more resources than intended. For example, in a measurement program I once wrote, a resource controlled the orientation of the ruler between vertical and horizontal. Unfortunately the orientation of the menus was also controlled by a resource with the same name, but with a different path to it. By using the pattern:

```
ruler*orientation:   vertical
```

not only did the ruler point vertically, but so did the menus! Horizontal menus with dropdowns look fine, but vertical ones with the same dropdowns look decidedly odd. This was fixed by using a more specific resource pattern.

Individual fields can also be given 'pattern-matching' names, to stand for any value of the field name. The origin of this is object oriented: they are called class names, versus instance names. Conventions are that class names are the same as instance names but with some letters capitalized:

```
mydraw.AnyWin*background: blue
```

The application writer should properly document these resource names, class names and possible values if they are to be under user control, and obey the conventions. If they are not documented, some users will stumble across them and be confused, while others will become annoyed when they cannot find them. Standard resource names include:

- background (class Background),

- foreground (class Foreground),

- borderWidth (class BorderWidth),

- font (class Font),

- height (class Height),

- width (class Width).

Application writers should use these standard names whenever applicable. A larger list is in `/usr/include/X11/StringDefs.h`.

Finally, each application has an instance name (generally the name of the executable file) and a class name. For example, every `xterm` has a class name of `XTerm`, and every `xclock` has a class name `XClock`. This difference between instance and class names may be used as follows: suppose we want most `xterms` to have a white background, but some to have a red background and some a blue one. We can make copies of `xterm` called 'bluexterm' and 'redxterm' (or in Unix make symbolic links to it using ln). Then we control the behavior of both types together and individually by:

```
XTerm*background:       white
bluexterm*background:   blue
redxterm*background:    red
```

The class name matches all instances that are not matched by the instance patterns `bluexterm` and `redxterm`.

Now we can turn to the problem of how to let X know of these resource values. This is a complex matter, in part due to the nature of X, but also due to the evolution of the system. First, let us look at it for a single application. A large part of the appearance of an application should be set using the resource database. The developer of the application will need to set some resources. These resources are stored in a standard place in the directory `/usr/lib/X11/app-defaults`. In this directory are files with the class names of applications such as `/usr/lib/X11/app-defaults/XTerm`. This set of resources is read first. The user can also have application-specific resource files. The default is that these are files with the class name in the user's home directory. (If the environment variable XAPPLRESDIR is set to a directory, it is used instead of the home directory.)

The next set of resources may be used to control any applications. It may contain server-specific resources (such as the font used), or server-independent resources (such as the title of an application). These resources are often found in the file .Xdefaults. There is a problem with this in that it is not a good means of storing server-specific resources in a networked environment where any server may be used. To get around this, resources can be 'attached' to the server by the program xrdb. If xrdb has been run, resources are picked up from the server, but otherwise from .Xdefaults.

The final set of resources relates to the machine on which the application is running (which may be different from the server, and may be different to where the file system is stored). For example, you may be paying money to run programs on one particular machine. Giving it a red foreground could give you a visual signal that this is an expensive program to run. These resources are stored in files .Xdefaults-<*hostname*>.

Any command-line options override any of these preferences. The least desirable method is to use values hard-coded into the program.

3.5 Configuring window managers

3.5.1 twm

The behavior of twm is controlled by a number of files. The system administrator or installation process may have set a system-wide configuration file (typically /usr/lib/X11/app-defaults/Twm). The most common file that a user would use to configure twm is $HOME/.twmrc. Text on a line after a hash symbol '#' is a comment in the file.

The first way to configure twm is by a number of variables. Some of these act rather like Boolean variables: if they are present in the configuration file then the value is True, but if they are not in the file then their value is taken as False. Some have string or integer values, and others have list values of some kind. Typical Boolean type variables are:

```
DecorateTransients
DontMoveoff
```

which mean that short-lived (transient) windows such as pop-up dialogs will be given title bars, etc. and that windows are not able to be moved off the screen. If these variables do not appear, transient windows are not decorated and windows may be moved off the screen.

A simple example of a variable with a list value is NoTitle which takes an optional list of windows that will not be decorated with a title bar:

```
NoTitle {"xterm" "xclock"}
```
will not put title bars on an xterm application or on an xclock. (The syntax is relatively flexible as regards white space, so the listed items could appear on separate lines for clarity.)

The other major configuration component is the ability of users to set up their own menus and functions, tied to their choice of button and key combinations. To trigger a menu requires a number of components: first there is the key or button. Next follows any modifier keys such as the Shift or Control keys. After this is the context in which the key/button occurs—either in the root window (outside any application windows), in a window, a titlebar, an icon, etc. Finally the menu name or function follows. For example, to invoke a menu called 'MyMenu' when button 2 is pressed in a titlebar or when Control F1 is pressed when the cursor is in a window:

```
# Button  Modifiers   Context    Function
Button2 =            : titlebar : f.menu "MyMenu"
"F1"    = control    : window   : f.menu "MyMenu"
```

A number of functions are built-in to `twm`. They include `f.move` to move a window, `f.iconify` to iconify a window, `f.raise` to bring a window to the top, `f.kill` to kill an application and `f.exec` to execute a string as a Unix command. Such functions may be attached direct to key/buttons as above, but are often found attached to items in menus. A menu definition consists of the menu name, then a list of menu items as strings and the corresponding functions that will be invoked when the item is selected. For example, `MyMenu` may contain items to move a window, or to start another `xterm`:

```
Menu "MyMenu"
{   "Move window"   f.move
    "New xterm"     f.exec xterm &
}
```
Thus a complete `.twmrc` could look like:

```
DecorateTransients
DontMoveoff
NoTitle {"xterm1" "XClock"}
# Button  Modifiers   Context    Function
Button2 =            : titlebar : f.menu "MyMenu"
"F1"    = control    : window   : f.menu "MyMenu"
Menu "MyMenu"
{   "Move window"   f.move
    "New xterm"     f.exec xterm &
}
```
There are many other possibilities for managing the real estate. For example, other options include:

- Menus can have their individual components colored.

- Borders and title bars can have their individual components colored.

- Windows can be made to rise automatically to the top whenever the mouse enters the window.

- An icon window can show the applications currently running and whether or not they are iconified. The state can be changed by clicking on names in this icon window.

3.5.2   mwm

There is a vast range of resources that can be set for mwm. It includes the width of surrounding bars, their colors, etc., but also more complex items: the focus policy is a resource, as well as the number of bars around application windows. Unlike twm, mwm uses the standard resource database for as many of the resources as possible. For those that do not fit into the resource syntax such as key/button bindings and menu entries, mwm uses specialized files much as twm does.

The manual page contains most of the details of configuring mwm. The Motif Programmer's Guide contains more. I will give a very brief overview. A number of resources refer only to the behavior of mwm. Examples include the coloring of the decorations of the active window (the one that has the focus) and whether or not an attempt is made to position a window on the screen, even if it has requested to be off the screen. These are resources directly of mwm:

```
mwm.activeForeground:    blue
mwm.positionOnScreen:    False
```

Other resources control the interaction of mwm with specific applications such as the client decorations. These are specified by mwm.client-name.resource. For example, mwm can set decoration bars and buttons on a per client basis. Some of the decoration options are *none*, *all*, *border*, *maximize* (zoom button), *minimize* (minimize button), *title* (titlebar). To have no decoration on the clock:

```
mwm.xclock.clientDecoration:    none
```

To have a border and a minimize button:

```
mwm.xclock.clientDecoration:    border minimize
```

Further control of mwm using functions and key/button bindings is done using $HOME/.mwmrc rather than the resource database. The functions handled by mwm are similar to those of twm. For example, f.move to move a window, f.raise to raise a window to the top, f.exec to execute a string as a Unix command and f.menu to label a menu. Button and key bindings are performed separately using lists attached to the variables Buttons and Keys respectively. Each element of the list consists of a key or button (using the resource database syntax) followed by a context and a function. Each set of bindings is given a name. For example, this could be given in .mwmrc:

```
Buttons MyButtonBindings
{    Btn1Down        root   f.menu MyMenu
     Ctrl Btn2Down  window f.move
}
```

```
Keys MyKeyBindings
{   <Key> F1        window f.menu MyMenu
    Ctrl <Key> a    window f.move
}
```

Here things become a little complex: what is the purpose of the key and button binding names (here `MyKeyBindings` and `MyButtonBindings`)? Before these bindings can be used, mwm has to be informed of them. It is not sufficient simply to place them in `$HOME/.mwmrc`. The names have to be set using the resource database, under the resource names `buttonBindings` and `keyBindings`. Thus these lines would be needed in, say, `.Xdefaults`:

```
mwm.buttonBindings:     MyButtonBindings
mwm.keyBindings:        MyKeyBindings
```

The items in a menu list and attached functions are set as in twm. For example:

```
Menu MyMenu
{   "Move window"   f.move
    "New xterm"     f.exec xterm &
}
```

To summarize, here is what could be placed in the `.Xdefaults` file:

```
mwm.activeForeground:    blue
mwm.positionOnScreen:    False

mwm.xclock.clientDecoration:    none

mwm.buttonBindings:     MyButtonBindings
mwm.keyBindings:        MyKeyBindings
```

and here is what would be in the `.mwmrc` file:

```
Buttons MyButtonBindings
{   Btn1Down        root    f.menu MyMenu
    Ctrl Btn2Down   window f.move
}
Keys MyKeyBindings
{   <Key> F1        window f.menu MyMenu
    Ctrl <Key> a    window f.move
}

Menu MyMenu
{   "Move window"   f.move
    "New xterm"     f.exec xterm &
}
```

Exercises

1. Set resources in `.Xdefaults` so that all new `xterms` have a scroll bar on the left. How do you then create an individual `xterm` without a scroll bar?

2. Set resources in `.Xdefaults` so that `blackxterms` have a white foreground and a black background. What command-line option will make an `xterm` use these `blackxterm` resources?

3. Modify `.mwmrc` (or `.twmrc` if you are using `twm`) so that a variety of differently colored `xterms` can be called from the system menu.

4. Configure your X environment so that appropriate applications start up when you log in, and others are accessible from system menus.

5. When the `-e` option is used on an `xterm`, everything from the option to the end of the line is run as a Unix command within its own `xterm` window. Use this to run an ordinary Unix editor (such as `vi`) within its own `xterm` window.

Summary of Part I

> This part has demonstrated the basic tools available in the X Window System. It has discussed the principal means of controlling and configuring them. There is no exercise for this part, because what you need to do with the knowledge gained in this part is simply to set your X environment so that it looks and behaves as you want it. The better you do this, the more productive you will be. This means controlling the applications that start each X session, how they appear, and how to invoke new ones from window-manager menus.

PART II

Xlib programming

This part covers the main techniques for building windows applications using the Xlib library. Chapter 4 deals with the fundamental techniques that you need for any Xlib application and then Chapter 5 considers some of the ways in which you can further control the appearance and behavior of the application.

Chapter 4

Fundamental Xlib

This chapter covers the basic techniques that you need to build multi-window applications running in the X environment. It uses the library of C routines called Xlib.

4.1 Introduction

X is a large system. It contains a full set of windowing facilities, the ability to handle color, 2-D graphics drawing capability, network access mechanisms, and the ability to respond to user preferences. A basic introduction to X must deal with:

- Network connection between an application and a server
- Displaying windows on the server
- Drawing graphics and displaying text
- Receiving and responding to events
- Multiple window systems
- Handling user preferences
- Color

In addition to all of this, X is a *layered* system (see Figure 13). The bottom layer consists of Xlib, the set of library routines that implement the basic X calls. Xlib is at a relatively low level as it includes the 'building blocks' for any type of windowed application (although this is quite substantially higher than, say, the Unix windowing system 'curses', and far above the raw termcap/terminfo system). Above this are *toolkits* which give a structure and organization to Xlib. Toolkits are often divided into two layers: the upper layer conforms to the latest fad and deals with *objects*. An

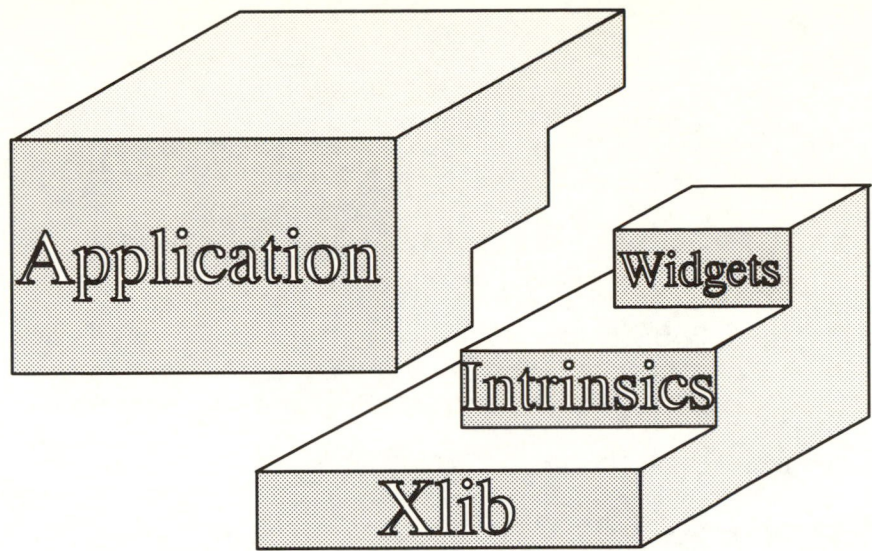

Figure 13:   Layers of X

object in a window system is a collection of windows, together with a set of semantic actions, such as a pull-down menu. Objects within X are called *widgets*. Beneath this is the 'glue' to hold object interaction together. This glue layer is called the *Intrinsics*. An application should be built above all of these. It may use any mixture of Xlib, the Intrinsics and Widgets. All three layers may be used in an application. This part deals with Xlib and the next with the set of Motif widgets. Widget sets usually define a particular 'look and feel' so that applications conform to the same interaction style. I have chosen to treat Xlib as a standalone layer so that the reader can see exactly what can be done at this level and can get a working experience of the Xlib calls.

4.2 Network connection

We can try our first Xlib program, `info.c`. It is not very adventurous and does not even draw any windows. It simply establishes a connection to the server, prints some information about it and exits.

Program 1: info.c

```
/*
** File: info.c
** Purpose: give general information about the server
*/
```

```
/*
** Needed for NULL pointer, as well as
** any IO to an xterm window
*/
#include <stdio.h>

/*
** General X include files
*/
#include <X11/Xlib.h>
#include <X11/Xutil.h>

/*
** Global variables
*/
Display *display;    /* the display device */
int      screen;     /* the screen on the display */

/*
** Connect to the server and get the display
** device and the screen number
*/
void
initX ()
{
    /* set the display name from
        the environment vbl DISPLAY */
    display = XOpenDisplay (NULL);
    if (display == NULL)
    {   fprintf (stderr,
                "Unable to open display %s\n",
                XDisplayName (NULL));
        exit (1);
    }
    screen = DefaultScreen (display);
}

/*
** Give general info about the server
** characteristics
*/
void
report_info ()
{
    printf ("There are %d color planes\n",
```

```
                    DefaultDepth (display, screen));
        printf ("The display width in pixels is %d\n",
                    DisplayWidth (display, screen));
        printf ("The display depth in pixels is %d\n",
                    DisplayHeight (display, screen));
        printf ("The display name is %s\n",
                    XDisplayName (display));
}
/*
** Terminate the program gracefully
*/
void
quitX ()
{
    XCloseDisplay (display);
    exit (0);
}

int
main (argc, argv)
    int argc;
    char **argv;
{
    initX ();
    report_info ();
    quitX ();
}
```

Compilation depends on the location of the libraries involved. The library required is usually `/usr/lib/libX11.a` (on Unix systems) giving:

```
cc -o info info.c -lX11
```

but this may be different in your environment.

Let us step through this program. The main routine calls three functions: `initX()` to establish contact with the server; `report_info()` to give some simple information about the server; and `quitX()` to finish up tidily.

The first step of the program is to establish a connection to the server itself using whatever mechanism is appropriate. The call:

```
display = XOpenDisplay (NULL)
```

attempts to connect to the server using whatever network or streams protocol is needed. If you look at the Xlib documentation for this call, it takes a string as argument. If this is given as a non-null string it will be the network name of the server, with extra values to give network-type connection (e.g. `jan:0`) as discussed earlier on connecting applications to servers. Here the argument is NULL, so it uses the default-server name, as given in the environment variable DISPLAY. A pointer to a structure of type `Display` is returned from the call. It is not necessary to know what is in this structure as you only ever pass around the pointer to it.

X has one aspect unusual to normal C programs: it is not usually necessary to check for error conditions (they are not even returned by most functions). A default error handler will take care of most error conditions. `XOpenDisplay()` is an exception to this, in that the user should check the return code and this check follows the `XOpenDisplay()` statement.

A server may have a number of screens. The `DefaultScreen()` gives connection to the default one. It takes the pointer to the display as argument (as do most Xlib calls). It is actually a macro and all that it does is to access a particular field of the display structure. You could do this yourself but only at the risk of making your application non-portable across different releases and versions of Xlib. You should use the macros supplied to avoid having to look into data structures that are meant to remain opaque.

Having established both the server and the screen to be used, the functions or macros in the rest of the program generally require both as parameters. They are: `DisplayHeight()` and `DisplayWidth()` which return the height and width respectively of the screen in pixels; `XDisplayName()` which gives the name of the server and `DefaultDepth()` which gives the number of color planes by default on the server. This gives the number of possible colors that can be shown at any one time as two to the power of the depth. (In fact, the server may support a different number of color planes, as some color hardware is quite complex. However, we will only consider the simple cases in this book.) The information is given to the user by ordinary C `printf()` statements. The program will typically be invoked by typing the program name `info` to an ordinary shell prompt in an `xterm` window. Standard output from the program will still be directed to this `xterm` window so that we get ordinary character-based output to this window. More sophisticated output that draws in its own window will be demonstrated later.

A number of other macros give further information. The Xlib documentation lists them under AllPlanes(3X11) and ImageByteOrder(3X11). This documentation fails to give the type of each macro and although most of them are obvious, some may need experimentation. The O'Reilly 'Xlib Reference Manual' breaks the macros out separately in the macro section and gives a better idea of macro types.

The program finally exits by calling `XCloseDisplay()`. This call is not necessary since the connection will be closed in any case upon exit, but it is neater to do so.

Why is the information given here important? There is a vast range of display hardware that can run X. Character-based programs make use of the termcap/terminfo databases to get information about terminals. Xlib instead uses calls such as these to find out about the server. Programs can then make use of the server characteristics to ensure, for example, that the windows displayed are large enough to be seen, but not so large that they cannot all fit onto the screen at once.

This program does not recognize any user preferences or command-line options. The only parameter which can be changed that the program will recognize is the environment variable `DISPLAY` which can be set by the user to different servers. Resource management will be dealt with at the end of the next chapter. Until then most programs will not be able to handle user preferences, either from the command line or from resource files.

4.2.1 Summary

This section has shown how to initiate and terminate an X application using:
```
XOpenDisplay ()
XCloseDisplay ()
```
Information about the display may be obtained from a number of macros including:
```
XDisplayName ()
DefaultScreen ()
DefaultDepth ()
DisplayWidth ()
DisplayHeight ()
```

Exercises

1. Use the macros documented in AllPlanes(3X11) and ImageByteOrder(3X11) to get more information on the server such as the width in millimeters.

2. Are the pixels on your display square? That is, is there the same number of pixels per vertical inch as per horizontal inch? If not, you will have to make allowances for this when drawing circles, etc.

4.3 Displaying windows

Xlib allows the programmer to create applications with large numbers of windows. The windows form a tree structure: the 'root' window is the full screen, and all windows are descendants from this. An application has as its toplevel window an immediate child of the root window (some window managers will re-parent them, but the application need not worry about this). Generally all other windows will be descendants of the toplevel window. Windows are always 'clipped' to their parent so that no part of them will show outside the parent. Some windows, such as those of pop-up dialogs, may need to appear outside their parent—such windows may also be parented off the root window.

To display windows with things inside them, a number of steps have to be performed. In summary:

- *A window must be created.* A window must be created with a number of characteristics such as parent window, width, height, x- and y-coordinates, background and foreground colors, width of border, cursor appearance within the window, etc.

- *Properties must be set.* A window will be merely part of the user's display, and so an application should attempt to make sure that it cooperates with any other applications running. One way of to do this is to inform the rest of the system of some of the properties of the window. A window manager, for example, can then make informed decisions about the geometry of the window and give it an actual position and size on the screen. Other properties must be set explicitly and still others may be left to 'default' values. A window always has a parent window within which it must appear and default values are usually picked up from the parent window. A number of Xlib functions are available to do all this: one relatively painless method is to use `XCreate-SimpleWindow()` to create the window and `XSetStandardProperties()` for property information.

- *A graphics context must be created.* An application does not create windows just for the fun of it: we would want to put something inside them. Before any graphics or text can be drawn in the window, various parameters such as the background and foreground colors, the font, the width of lines, etc. must be set. As an efficiency measure, these properties are maintained in a *graphics context* which is kept on the server. A program must create one or more graphics contexts using `XCreateGC()`.

- *The windows must be mapped.* Windows are not shown until they are mapped.

- *Drawing is then done.* Any graphics or text drawing is done using one of these graphics contexts.

The following program (`hello.c`) creates a window, draws a circle, displays some text, and exits after a short period.

Program 2:   hello.c

```
#include <stdio.h>
#include <X11/Xlib.h>
#include <X11/Xutil.h>

/*
** Constants
*/
char WINDOW_NAME[] = "Window";
```

```
char ICON_NAME[] = "Icon";

/*
** Globals
*/
Display *display;  /* the display device */
int     screen;  /* the screen on the display */
Window  main_window;
GC      gc;
unsigned long  foreground, background;

void
initX ()
{
    /* set the display name from the environment
       vbl DISPLAY */
    display = XOpenDisplay (NULL);
    if (display == NULL)
    {   fprintf (stderr, "Unable to open display %s\n",
                 XDisplayName (NULL));
        exit (1);
    }
    screen = DefaultScreen (display);

    /* use the default foreground
       and background colors */
    foreground = BlackPixel (display, screen);
    background = WhitePixel (display, screen);
}

/*
** Opens a window on the display device, and returns
** the window ID.
**
** It takes (x,y) coords, the width and height of the
** window, and the width of the border
*/
Window
openWindow (x, y, width, height,
            border_width, argc, argv)
    int x, y;              /* coords of the upper left
                              corner in pixels */
    int width, height;   /* size of the window
                            in pixels */
    int border_width;    /* the border width is not
                            included in the
```

```
                                    other dimensions */
        int argc;
        char **argv;
{

        Window  new_window;
        XSizeHints  size_hints;

        /* now create the window */
        new_window = XCreateSimpleWindow (display,
                         DefaultRootWindow (display),
                         x, y, width, height,
                         border_width,
                         foreground, background);

        /* set up the size hints for the window manager */
        size_hints.x = x;
        size_hints.y = y;
        size_hints.width = width;
        size_hints.height = height;
        /* and state what hints are included */
        size_hints.flags = PPosition | PSize;

        /* let the window manager know about the window */
        XSetStandardProperties (display, new_window,
                         WINDOW_NAME, ICON_NAME,
                         None,        /* no icon map */
                         argv, argc, &size_hints);

        /* Return the window ID */
        return (new_window);
}

/*
** Create a graphics context using default values, and
** return it in the pointer gc
*/
GC
getGC ()
{   GC gc;
    XGCValues gcValues;

    gc = XCreateGC (display, main_window,
                (unsigned long) 0, &gcValues);

    XSetBackground (display, gc, background);
    XSetForeground (display, gc, foreground);
```

```
        return (gc);
}


/*
** Terminate the program gracefully
*/
quitX ()
{
    XCloseDisplay (display);
    exit (0);
}


/*
** Write a string
** and draw a circle
*/
display_something ()
{   /* Ignore these three lines for now */
    XEvent event;
    XSelectInput (display, main_window, ExposureMask);
    XNextEvent (display, &event);
    /* end of ignore lines */

    /* the proverbial string */
    XDrawImageString (display, main_window, gc,
                    10, 10, "Hello world",
                    strlen ("Hello world"));

    /* and a world (circle) to go with it */
     XDrawArc (display, main_window, gc,
             30, 30,
             100, 100,
             0, 360*64);
    XFlush (display);
}


main (argc, argv)
    int argc;
    char **argv;
{
    initX ();

    main_window = openWindow (10, 20, 500, 400,
                                    5, argc, argv);

    gc = getGC ();
```

```
      /* Display the window on the screen */
      XMapWindow (display, main_window);

      display_something ();
      sleep (30);

      quitX ();
}
```

There is a lot of program here to say 'hello world,' but on reflection a lot is being done. This program will run on a large range of hardware, even across a network, in an environment with many other asynchronous windows-based programs, under the control of a window manager that can move the window around the screen.

Again let us step through this program. Large components of the program are unchanged and do not need to be discussed. Many parts are new. To enable the reader to distinguish between the parts, *revision bars* (as on the left of these lines) have been placed in the margin alongside the new or changed parts. The main routine calls initX() as before and then creates a window and a graphics context. Something is then drawn, the program displays it for 30 seconds and then exits.

The changes made in initX() are related to the drawing and text functions: we need some colors. Black and white are always available on any screen so we ask the server for their values by BlackPixel() and WhitePixel(). The revision bars show these changes in the calls to BlackPixel() and WhitePixel().

The function openWindow() is entirely new. It has a large number of tasks to perform. First it creates a window by means of the call XCreateSimpleWindow() with a large number of parameters.

```
      XCreateSimpleWindow (display,  parent_window,
                           x, y, width, height,
                           border_width, border_color,
                           background);
```

This does *not* display the window: it merely creates it with these values. Note that the (x, y) coordinates are relative to the parent window, measured with x running from zero from the left of the parent to the right, and y running from zero from the top of the parent to the bottom. X does not place any constraint on these values: you may create a window with part of it outside its parent. It just will not show anything outside its parent (it is 'clipped' to its parent). The parent window in the example is DefaultRootWindow(). This is the whole screen and makes our window a top-level window on the screen, around which the window manager can place title bars, etc. XCreateSimpleWindow() sets some parameters and defaults to others such as the cursor shape. If more control is needed, you can use `XCreateWindow()`. The remaining parameters should be self-explanatory.

Alas, this is not all that has to be done. The window has been created as a toplevel window, one that is under the control of a window manager. Window managers (as chosen by the user) are responsible for layout of toplevel windows on the screen. Even though we have created a window with a particular size and position, it is still necessary to inform the window manager of all these geometric properties to let it make its decisions about what geometry it will give the application. This is done by using the structure `size_hints` of type `XSizeHints`. Into this are placed the x, y, width and height values desired by the application. In addition, the window manager may want to know who is actually setting the size and location: is it the program setting these, or is the program merely passing on information supplied by the user, possibly through command-line options? User set information may be given more attention than program set information. The 'flags' field states not only what fields are set, but also their origin: `PPosition` means 'Program set Position' whereas `UPosition` would have meant 'User set Position.' As well as size and location, the window manager is responsible for annotating toplevel windows with names if the user desires. All this information is globally broadcast by `XSetStandardProperties()`. These hints may be ignored or acted upon; they are only hints to the window manager. (It may also be necessary to use `XSetWMHints()` to keep all window managers happy.) If this call is not made, the window manager is more likely to decide for itself the window size and location. Finally, the window ID (which is actually an integer) is returned from the function.

Does this show the window? Well, no. It *creates* the window but does not show it. It is left to the later call `XMapWindow()` in `main()` to show it.

The new function `getGC()` creates a graphics context by `XCreateGC()` and sets various parameters. The graphics context controls how text and lines are drawn. An application can have more than one of them and probably would if it used a variety of styles. A graphics context controls line thickness, dots-and-dashes, foreground and background colors, and fonts, among other properties. Many of these can be left to default values until you want to change them. The only ones explicitly set are the foreground and background colors by `XSetForeground()` and `XSetBackground()` (and even these could have been left to default values). Note that although we have already set the background of the window, the background of the graphics context is different——it controls the background of text and lines that are drawn. That is, the window could have a background, say, of green. The graphics context could have a background of red and a foreground of white. Parts of the window that have not been drawn on will show up green. If text is drawn on the window using its background and foreground it will show as white text in a red bar.

The `XCreateGC()` function has parameters:

```
XCreateGC (display, window, valuemask, values)
```

The last two parameters may be used to set various components of the graphics context such as its background and foreground colors. There are two parts to this: there is information about *which* components are being set and there are the values being set. The information about which components are being set is contained in the `value-mask`, which is an or-ed set of components such as:

```
GCForeground | GCBackground
```

The values are set using a structure of type `XGCValues` with the fields corresponding to the value mask filled in. In the example, the `valuemask` is set to zero, so no fields are being set. The `gcValues` variable is unused in the example. The values of the foreground and background are set using separate calls to `XSetBackground()` and `XSetForeground()`.

Finally we can turn to the drawing. Ignore the first few lines until the next section; these are there for reasons discussed in the next section. There are a number of text-drawing functions: `XDrawImageString()`, `XDrawString()`, `XDrawText()`, ... The simplest is the one we use. Text is drawn in X using bitmaps of characters from fonts. This call simply draws it, using the current foreground and background in the graphics context, using the default font.

```
XDrawImageString (display, window, gc,
                  x, y, string, string_length)
```

Similarly, the circle is drawn using the graphics context:

```
XDrawArc (display, window, x, y, width, height,
          start_angle, angle_extent)
```

where the x, y, height and width values are those of a bounding rectangle to the arc, and the starting angle is relative to 3 o'clock. The angle measurements are performed in one sixtieth of a degree increments so that 360×64 is a full circle.

These commands certainly draw the text and circle. But X is a network model and the drawing requests may be caught in a buffer somewhere. In most interactive applications these buffers would get flushed out fairly quickly. Ours does nothing else, so flush it explicitly by `XFlush()`. Do not flush things out as a matter of course: do it only when you need to get the requests out to the server without waiting for other things to happen.

4.3.1 Summary

This section has shown how to create an application consisting of a single window, inform the rest of the system of this, and show the application by:

```
XCreateSimpleWindow ()
XSetStandardProperties ()
XMapWindow ()
XFlush ()
```

To draw text or graphics, a graphics context must be created and set by:

```
XCreateGC ()
XSetBackground ()
XSetForeground ()
```

Drawing is done by:
```
XDrawImageString ()
XDrawArc ()
```

Exercises

---

1. Draw a triangle instead of a circle (see XDrawLine(3X11)).

2. Make the window occupy half the width and height of the screen.

3. Fill in the circle using `XFillArc()` (see XFillRectangle(3X11) and XSetFillStyle(3X11)).

4. Make the window move around the screen several times with `XMoveWindow()` (in XConfigureWindow(3X11)).

5. Draw a dashed line instead of a solid line using `XSetDashes()` (see **XSetLi-neAttribute**(3X11)).

6. Draw the string in the middle of the circle using `XQueryTextExtents()` (hard).

4.4 Events

The programs so far have been non-interactive. X is usually a modeless system in which the users have the freedom of choice in what to do. They can choose to use the mouse or the keyboard, to initiate a dialog with any component of any application or with a window manager. The program cannot be simply controlled in a deterministic manner but must rather take what the user gives it and react to that. Interaction to an Xlib application is driven by *events*. Events are changes in the *server* environment, such as mouse movement, key presses, window resizing. A non-exhaustive listing of X events is:

*   ButtonPress
*   ButtonRelease
*   CreateNotify (a window has been created)
*   DestroyNotify (a window is about to be destroyed)
*   EnterNotify (the boundary into a window has just been crossed by the mouse)

- LeaveNotify (the mouse has just left the window)

- Expose (a portion of the window has been uncovered)

- KeyPress

- KeyRelease

- MotionNotify (the mouse has been moved inside the window)

- ResizeRequest (the size of the window is being changed)

An individual window will typically want to know about a subset of events. It will be interested only in certain types of events and it will be interested only in those events which refer directly to it. For each window a 'mask' of interesting event types is sent to the server, informing it of these types using `XSelectInput()`, and from then on the server will send events to the window only when the event is one of those the window has asked for and the event refers to the window.

Nearly all windows will want to know about expose events because these are sent when a portion of the window becomes uncovered. X does not usually retain information about covered parts of windows, so if a window receives an expose event, it should redraw the contents of the exposed portion. In particular, when a window is drawn for the first time (mapped) it is sent an expose event as one of the first events it ever receives. No drawing should take place into a window until this first expose event has been received.

Windows that need to process keyboard input will need to know about key presses but are less likely to be interested in key releases.

Many windows will want to know about both mouse button presses and releases occurring within them. You should note that the user may press a mouse button within one window and may move the mouse out of the window into another before releasing the button. If the first window wants both press and release events, a special-case mechanism within X (mouse grab) arranges for the window to receive both, even though the second occurred in a different window. A practical use for this is in moving a window: this can allow the user to 'drag' a window to a new location by pressing the mouse in a window and then moving the mouse to the new location before releasing it. The window would need to know about the release in order to move to it. Motion notify events tell about the mouse movements. Many applications can quite happily ignore this unless they need to track the mouse.

In a hierarchy of windows, a subwindow may choose to ignore a type of event but a parent or other ancestor may have opted to receive it. When an event of this type occurs in the subwindow, it is not sent to the subwindow since it did not want it. Rather than being discarded, it is sent to the first ancestor that did want it. Only if no ancestor wants it is the event discarded. This allows a group of windows to be handled as one for some events by giving them all a common ancestor which selects that type of event. For example, a group of windows may not need keyboard input and so would not select for it. However, it is common practice that pressing a special key (such as the function keys F1 or F10) anywhere in an application's windows will invoke a help system. This can be done by letting a window high in the hierarchy receive the keypress events. The keypress events ignored by the lower level windows will then be received by this higher level one and *it* can invoke the help system.

Once windows have been created and the event mask sent to the server, *every* application enters a main loop of 'get the next event and process it.' The type XEvent is a union of many individual event types, but they all have a common field of type to distinguish them. The event loop therefore always contains a switch on the event type, branching to appropriate routines for each type.

A standard schema (with some minor additions) is in the program onewindow.c:

Program 3:   onewindow.c

```
/*
** File: onewindow.c
** Generic program schema for a one window program
*/

#include <stdio.h>
#include <X11/Xlib.h>
#include <X11/Xutil.h>

/*
** debug lists all events to an
** xterm window as they occur
*/
#define DEBUG

char WINDOW_NAME[] = "Window";
char ICON_NAME[] = "Icon";

Display *display;  /* the display device */
int     screen;    /* the screen on the display */
Window  main_window;
GC      gc;
unsigned long  foreground, background;

/*
**
*/

Window
openWindow (x, y, width, height, border_width,
```

```
                    argc, argv)
        int x, y;   /* coords of the upper left
                       corner in pixels */
        int width,
            height;   /* size of the window in pixels */
        int border_width;   /* the border width is
                               not included in the
                               other dimensions */
        int argc;
        char **argv;
{

        Window  new_window;
        XSizeHints  size_hints;

        /* now create the window */
        new_window = XCreateSimpleWindow (display,
                        DefaultRootWindow (display),
                        x, y, width, height,
                        border_width,
                        foreground, background);

        /* set up the size hints for the window manager */
        size_hints.x = x;
        size_hints.y = y;
        size_hints.width = width;
        size_hints.height = height;
        /* and state what hints are included */
        size_hints.flags = PPosition | PSize;

        /* let the window manager know about the window */
        XSetStandardProperties (display, new_window,
            WINDOW_NAME, ICON_NAME,
            None,       /* no icon map */
            argv, argc, &size_hints);

        /* Decide what events the window will receive */
        XSelectInput (display, new_window,
            (ButtonPressMask | KeyPressMask |
             ExposureMask));

        /* Return the window ID */
        return (new_window);
}

/*
**
```

```c
*/
GC
getGC ()
{   GC gc;
    XGCValues gcValues;

    gc = XCreateGC (display, main_window,
                (unsigned long) 0, &gcValues);

    XSetBackground (display, gc, background);
    XSetForeground (display, gc, foreground);
    return (gc);
}

/*
** Terminate the program gracefully
*/
quitX ()
{
    XCloseDisplay (display);
    exit (0);
}


/*
** An expose event occurs when the contents of
** a window are invalidated and at least some
** of it needs to be redrawn
*/
void
doExposeEvent (pEvent)
    XExposeEvent *pEvent;
{
    XDrawImageString (display, main_window, gc,
        10, 10, "Press q or any button to quit",
        strlen ("Press q or any button to quit"));
}

/*
** A button has been pressed within the window - quit
*/
void doButtonPressEvent (pEvent)
    XButtonEvent *pEvent;
{
    quitX ();
}
```

```
/*
** A key has been pressed.
** It needs to be decoded and acted on.
** Quit if it is a 'q'.
*/
void
doKeyPressEvent (pEvent)
    XKeyEvent *pEvent;
{   int key_buffer_size = 10;
    char key_buffer[9];
    XComposeStatus compose_status;
    KeySym key_sym;

    XLookupString (pEvent, key_buffer,
        key_buffer_size,
        &key_sym, &compose_status);
    if (key_buffer[0] == 'q')
        quitX ();
}


void
initX ()
{
    /* set the display name from the
    ** environment vbl DISPLAY */
    display = XOpenDisplay (NULL);
    if  (display == NULL)
    {       fprintf (stderr,
                "Unable to open display %s\n",
                XDisplayName (NULL));
            exit (1);
    }
    screen = DefaultScreen (display);
    /* use the default foreground and
    ** background colors
    */
    foreground = BlackPixel (display, screen);
    background = WhitePixel (display, screen);

}

main (argc, argv)
    int argc;
    char **argv;
{   XEvent event;
```

```
        initX ();

        main_window = openWindow (10, 20, 200, 100, 5,
                                    argc, argv);
        gc = getGC ();

        /* Display the window on the screen */
        XMapWindow (display, main_window);
        XFlush (display);
        while (True)
        {
                XNextEvent (display, &event);
#ifdef DEBUG
                printf ("Event number is %d\n", event.type);
#endif
                switch (event.type)
                {
                case Expose:
                        doExposeEvent (&event);
                        break;

                case ButtonPress:
                        doButtonPressEvent (&event);
                        break;

                case KeyPress:
                        doKeyPressEvent (&event);
                        break;

                case MappingNotify:
                        XRefreshKeyboardMapping (&event);
                        break;
                }
        }
}
```

Some further explanation of what is going on is needed since the program has grown in complexity even more from a simple display with no interaction. First, in main() the program enters an infinite loop which gets an event each time by XNextEvent(). The events we get are those asked for at the end of openWindow() where we used XSelectEvent() to select button presses, key presses and expose events. The main program does a switch on the event type each time round the loop. For expose, button-press and key-press events, the appropriate branch calls a function to process the event. The code for each could have been placed in line as the routines in this case are all quite short, but it looks cleaner and in a real application would probably be preferred.

However, an extra branch has crept into the switch statement, apart from the three specified: `MappingNotify`. This is because other applications may be playing games with the keyboard, such as changing the key mappings from QWERTY to, say, DVORAK. Any application has to take this into account or all key presses will be decoded incorrectly. Just copy the statements in that branch for all your programs: `XRefreshKeyboardMapping()` sets everything right for the program.

Let us take each of the other events in turn. When a button is pressed, our function `doButtonPressEvent()` is called with the (address of the) event as parameter. The type of the event in the call was declared as type `XEvent`. This type is a union of each of the individual types for each different event, and each of these has different component fields. To ensure that correct code is generated to select the correct fields, the argument has to be coerced somewhere into the right type. It is good enough to coerce the formal parameter, which is declared as type `XButtonEvent` for the button press event, and similarly for the other functions.

The body of the function here just does a `quitX()`. Much more could have been done, based upon information in the event argument. A button-press event contains a number of fields, including:

```
Window window;  /* event window that asked
                        for button press */
Time    time;   /* time in milliseconds of event */
int     x, y;   /* co-ords relative to window */
unsigned int button;   /* button that triggered event */
```

Some of this information is used in the exercises.

The earlier drawing routine has been moved into the function handling an expose event. There are a number of critical features of X here. First: when can you first draw into a window? After it shows on the screen, of course. But when does that happen? One would expect it to happen after mapping the window. That is what `XMapWindow()` is for——to show the window. But X is a network model, working in a multitasking environment, and the window may not show up until some time later. Any drawing done before the window is visible is simply discarded. What we need is a signal from the X server that the window is in fact now showing. The first event sent by the server is an expose event——precisely to show that we can now begin drawing into the window. On some servers you may be able to get away with drawing without waiting for the expose event. It can then be quite a shock to move to another server which never shows anything because it has already discarded your drawing before mapping the window! This is probably the most common error when beginning Xlib programming.

It goes much deeper than this, though. Our 'one-window' application may be obscured by some other application. After all, no user is going to place a 'hello world' message on top all the time. They may cover it with an editor, a mailer, etc.

This may well obscure part or all of our message. What happens when it is later *uncovered*? The part of the window that was obscured must be restored somehow. Most X servers will not do it——it is up to the individual application. That is, we have to redraw the message and the circle. To signify that a part of the window was uncovered, the X server sends an expose event.

The expose event contains information about the parts of the window that were uncovered so that the application can perform a minimal restoration of the window. Our application does it the brute force way: redraw everything. This is satisfactory here as we do not have a complex thing to redraw. Whether you draw a little or a lot, you have to remember: *anything drawn in a window may need to be redrawn on an expose event.*

Finally, we turn to the key-press handling. Keyboards are complex things. They generate hardware codes on press and release, keys may be 'composed' into more complex sequences, keys may be modified in complex ways, e.g. <Ctrl><Alt><Shift>x, and they may be remapped into other keys. A single key press may go through a number of changes and even end up as a sequence of characters. This needs to be translated from the original keystroke to its sequence of characters. This is performed by the `XLookupString()` call which stores the resultant characters in the key buffer. Then we can inspect the first character to see if it was a quit character.

The leap from a program which only displayed text, to one that can interact with the user, seems quite major. But from now on we reach something of a plateau: every interactive X window application has an event loop branching on the type of event and each branch may be handled separately. Anything drawn may need to be redrawn in response to an expose event. In particular: do not attempt to draw until you get your first expose event.

4.4.1 Summary

There are many event types to which windows can respond, such as:

```
ButtonPress
KeyPress
Expose
```

A window states the event types it wants by:

```
XSelectInput ()
```

The application sits in an event loop getting events by:

```
XNextEvent ()
```

The `type` field in each event states the type of event received, so that the application can switch on the type.

Exercises

1. When a button is pressed, write 'Ouch!' at the location of the mouse. (See the `XButtonEvent` structure in `/usr/include/X11/Xlib.h`.)

2. Print the actual geometry of the window after it has been mapped and the window manager has allowed it to be displayed using `XGetGeometry()` (see XGetWindowAttributes(3X11)).

3. Get `MotionNotify` events and track the position of the mouse within the window, writing the coordinates instead of the string.

4.5 Multiple windows

Windows are a cheap resource under X. An application could have several hundred windows running. All windows are subwindows of others, except for the root window which is an ancestor of all windows. An immediate child of the root window is a toplevel window. A window manager may interfere with the geometry of a toplevel window or place decorations around it. For each toplevel window that an application has, it is expected to publicize various resources such as its geometry. The application is responsible for all aspects of its non-toplevel windows and need not tell anyone else about them.

In a multiwindow system, the application will create all the windows one after another. It can map them as they are created, or leave it to the end and map them all together. A window will not be displayed until both it, and all of its ancestors, have been mapped.

Each window will need to select its own events. Windows can have individual graphics contexts, or share them. It depends on whether you want to control their apearance individually or *en masse*.

Each application will sit in a loop getting events. There are a number of options for controlling the sending of these events to windows:

*   Let the toplevel windows receive all events. They can then work out which windows they referred to by (say) examining the position of the mouse. They can then call appropriate routines. This loses all the information the server can give the application about the windows that events really occurred in and consequently is not a very good method.

*   By examining the window field of the event, determine which window owns the event and call an appropriate window routine. This window routine will

then do a switch according to the different types of event. This matches an object-oriented approach in which the window is the object, and the event is the message. The X world does not support this approach, as some events do not seem to belong properly to individual windows.

- Switch on the type of event and call a routine based on this type. Each of these routines will work out which window it refers to, and then perform an action. It leads to code in which the behavior of a window is scattered among a large number of routines based on event types. This is the preferred method in X.

(*Note*: Sometimes a window such as a menu will want to force the user to choose an option before doing anything else in a modal dialog. This may happen, for example, when the application cannot find a file and wants the user to take immediate action. It will pop up a warning window where the window will 'grab' the mouse and have a little event loop of its own. This is generally considered to be antisocial to other applications and should not be the norm.)

For a simple multiwindow application, consider a training program in using the mouse. A small box appears in a window. Using the mouse, you have to put the pointer in this box and then click any button. The box then moves to a random part of the window. The hit score and the miss score are kept at the top of the window and are updated on each mouse click. The windows involved in this are:

- The box to aim at can be a small window of its own which is moved around by the program.
- The hit scores would be displayed in their own window.
- The miss scores would be displayed in their own window.
- The box is moved around inside a window. This window (which we will call the pane) should be distinct from the hit window and the miss window. The box will be constrained to move within the pane, so it might as well be a subwindow of the pane.
- The hit, miss and pane windows will all be siblings. If they were all toplevel windows, the window manager could move them independently, making a very messy display. To avoid this, make them all children of a window which acts as a frame. Then whenever the frame is moved, all the subwindows will move with it.

The application will look like Figure 14, with the window tree given in Figure 15. The events that these windows will receive are:

- If the mouse is clicked in the small box, it must update the hit score. The box window will therefore want `ButtonPress` events.

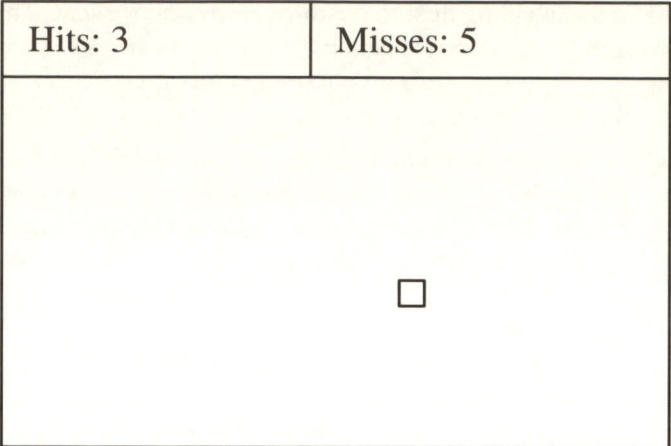

Figure 14:   The catch screen

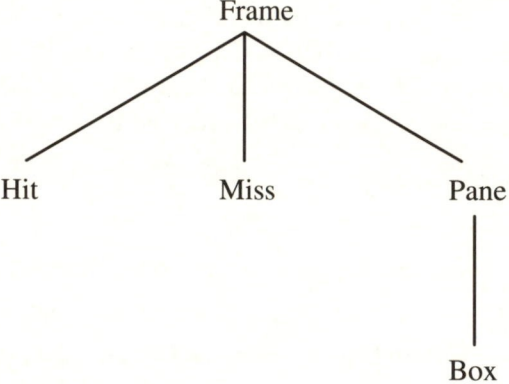

Figure 15:   Window tree for the catch program

- If the mouse is clicked in the pane, it must update the miss score. The pane will therefore want `ButtonPress` events too.

- Neither the hit nor miss window needs to respond to either key or mouse events. Because they contain text, they must be redrawn each time they are uncovered. They need `Expose` events. They need only display the scores and update them when they change. This could be done by polling the values continuously, but this would be cumbersome. A simpler method is to allow the box or pane windows to invalidate the contents of the hit or miss window when a value changes, so that the hit or miss window has to redraw itself. There is a mechanism to invalidate windows which involves clearing their contents and sending them `Expose` events. Thus these windows have to respond only to `Expose` events.

- We need a mechanism to exit the program. If we type 'q' anywhere, the program will exit. The hit, miss, pane and box windows have no need of `Key-Press` events themselves as they do nothing specific with them. If they do not select for `KeyPress` events, the events will be sent to a parent window if it wants them. We simply let the frame window respond to `KeyPress` events and look for the 'q' in its events.

This program is called `catch.c`.

Program 4: catch.c

```
/*
** Chase a box around the screen,
** attempting to click the
** mouse in the box.
** Scores are kept of your accuracy
*/

#include <stdio.h>
#include <X11/Xlib.h>
#include <X11/Xutil.h>

#define DEBUG

#define BOX_SIZE 4   /* in pixels */
#define TEXT_HT 20   /* in pixels - and a kludge */
char WINDOW_NAME[] = "catch";
char ICON_NAME[] = "catch";

Display *display;        /* the display device */
int     screen;          /* the screen on the display */
int     theDepth;        /* number of color planes */
GC      gc;              /* graphics context */

Window frame_window;     /* holds all the other windows */
Window hit_window;       /* the count of hits */
Window miss_window;      /* the count of misses */
Window pane_window;      /* the background window for
                            the box to move in */
Window box_window;       /* the box to hit with the
                            cursor */
unsigned long  foreground, background;
int hits = 0;            /* start off with zero score */
```

```
    int misses = 0;           /* start off with zero score */

    int frame_x, frame_y,
        frame_width, frame_ht;  /* size of frame window */

/*
** function openWindow
*/

Window
openWindow (x, y, width, height, border_width, parent,
           istoplevel, argc, argv)
    int x, y;   /* coords of the upper left
                   corner in pixels */
    int width,
            height;  /* size of the window in pixels */

    int border_width;  /* the border width is
                          not included in the
                          other dimensions */
    Window parent;
    int istoplevel;  /* a Boolean value */
    int argc;
    char **argv;
{
    Window  new_window;
    XSizeHints  size_hints;

    /* now create the window */
    new_window = XCreateSimpleWindow (display,
                parent,
                x, y, width, height,
                border_width,
                foreground, background);

    /* If the window is a toplevel window,
       set up the size hints for the window manager */

    if (istoplevel)
    {
        size_hints.x = x;
        size_hints.y = y;
        size_hints.width = width;
        size_hints.height = height;
        /* and state what hints are included */
        size_hints.flags = PPosition | PSize;
```

```
                    /* let the window manager know about
                       the window */
                    XSetStandardProperties (display, new_window,
                          WINDOW_NAME, ICON_NAME,
                          None,   /* no icon map */
                          argv, argc, &size_hints);
         }
         /* Display the window on the screen */
         XMapWindow (display, new_window);

         /* Return the window ID */
         return (new_window);
}


/*
** function getGC
**
** create a graphics context using default values, and
** return it in the pointer gc
*/
GC
getGC ()
{   GC gc;

    gc = XCreateGC (display, frame_window, 0, NULL);

    XSetBackground (display, gc, background);
    XSetForeground (display, gc, foreground);
    return (gc);
}


/*
** function quitX
**
** terminate the program gracefully
*/
quitX ()
{
    XCloseDisplay (display);
    exit (0);
}


void
doExposeEvent (pEvent)
    XExposeEvent *pEvent;
```

```
{
    if  (pEvent->window == hit_window)
    {       char hit_str[20];

            sprintf (hit_str, "Hits: %d", hits);
            XDrawImageString (display, hit_window, gc,
                5, 10, hit_str, strlen (hit_str));
    }
    if (pEvent-> window == miss_window)
    {       char miss_str[20];

            sprintf (miss_str, "Misses: %d", misses);
            XDrawImageString (display, miss_window, gc,
                5, 10, miss_str, strlen (miss_str));
    }
}

void
doButtonPressEvent (pEvent)
    XButtonEvent *pEvent;
{   int box_x, box_y;

    if (pEvent->window == pane_window)
    {
            misses++;
            XClearArea (display, miss_window, 0, 0,
                0, 0, True);
    }
    else /* pEvent->window == box_window */
    {
            hits++;
            XClearArea (display, hit_window, 0, 0,
                0, 0, True);
    }
    box_x = rand () % (frame_width - BOX_SIZE);
    box_y = rand () % (frame_ht - TEXT_HT - BOX_SIZE);
    XMoveWindow (display, box_window, box_x, box_y);
}

void
doKeyPressEvent (pEvent)
    XKeyEvent *pEvent;
{   int key_buffer_size = 10;
    char key_buffer[64];
    XComposeStatus compose_status;
    KeySym key_sym;
```

```
    XLookupString (pEvent, key_buffer, key_buffer_size,
        &key_sym, &compose_status);
    if (key_buffer[0] == 'q')
    {       printf ("Hits: %d; Misses: %d\n",
                    hits, misses);
            quitX ();
    }
}

initX ()
{
    display = XOpenDisplay (NULL);
    screen = DefaultScreen (display);
    /* use the default foreground and
       background colors */
    foreground = BlackPixel (display, screen);
    background = WhitePixel (display, screen);
}
main (argc, argv)
    int argc;
    char **argv;
{   XEvent event;
    int box_x, box_y;

    initX ();

    /* create the frame window to occupy a
       large area of the screen,
       in the middle */
    frame_width = DisplayWidth (display, screen) / 2;
    frame_ht = (DisplayHeight (display, screen)*2) / 3;
    frame_x = frame_width / 2;
    frame_y = frame_ht / 6;
    frame_window = openWindow (frame_x, frame_y,
                    frame_width, frame_ht, 5,
                    DefaultRootWindow (display),
                    True, argc, argv);
    hit_window = openWindow (0, 0, frame_width / 2,
                    TEXT_HT,
                    1, frame_window, False, 0, NULL);
    miss_window = openWindow (frame_width / 2, 0,
                    frame_width / 2, TEXT_HT,
                    1, frame_window, False, 0, NULL);
    pane_window = openWindow (0, TEXT_HT,
                    frame_width, frame_ht - TEXT_HT,
```

```
                                1, frame_window, False, 0, NULL);
        srand (1);
        box_x = rand () % (frame_width - BOX_SIZE);
        box_y = rand () % (frame_ht - TEXT_HT - BOX_SIZE);
        box_window = openWindow (box_x, box_y, BOX_SIZE,
                        BOX_SIZE, 1,
                        pane_window, False, 0,
                        NULL);
        gc = getGC ();
        XSelectInput (display, frame_window,
              KeyPressMask);
        XSelectInput (display, pane_window,
              ButtonPressMask);
        XSelectInput (display, hit_window,
              ExposureMask);
        XSelectInput (display, miss_window,
                         ExposureMask);
        XSelectInput (display, box_window,
                         ButtonPressMask);


        while (True)
        {
                XNextEvent (display, &event);
#ifdef DEBUG
                fprintf (stderr, "Event number is %d\n",
                        event.type);
#endif
                switch (event.type)
                {
                case Expose:doExposeEvent (&event);
                        break;
                case ButtonPress:
                        doButtonPressEvent (&event);
                        break;
                case KeyPress:
                        doKeyPressEvent (&event);
                        break;
                case MappingNotify:
                         XRefreshKeyboardMapping (&event);
                        break;
                }
        }
}
```

Much of the basic program remains unaltered. The transition at each stage has been to add functionality by adding code. Some minor changes to some functions have occurred: as some windows are children of the toplevel window frame, an extra field has been added to `openWindow()` to signify toplevel or otherwise. Only if it is a toplevel window will the size hints be passed to the window manager. `initX()`, `quitX()` and `getGC()` remain unchanged.

This program occupies the middle third of the screen by program preference. It gets the server geometry as we did in `info.c` and sets the x, y and size values of the frame to occupy this middle section. Each window is then created in turn as a child or descendant of the frame. The coordinates of each child are relative to the parent so they will always appear in correct relation within the parent. The position of the small box window is set using the C random number generator and it is always constrained to be within the frame. We have set a height of twenty pixels and a width one-third of the screen for each of the hit window and the miss window.

The program has a number of flaws. First, it assumes that it actually gets the size requested from the window manager. If it is given a different location, that does not matter. If it is given a different width, an immediate effect is that the hit window and miss window will not be properly aligned in the frame. Methods to find out how big it actually is are left to the exercises. A worse consequence of not getting the size requested is as follows. Suppose the frame is made narrower than requested. Then the right-hand side of the pane will be 'clipped' and will not show. The box movement is constrained to be within the pane, but part of this may be invisible! It is hard clicking the mouse on a box that is nowhere visible. There is another flaw in this geometry assignment: the hit window and miss window are built on the assumption that they will actually be big enough to contain the text strings. If the user happens to be using a font with a height greater than twenty pixels, some of this will be clipped too. We have not discussed fonts and at present have no way of knowing whether or not the text will actually fit in this space. This is discussed in the next chapter.

Each window requires different events. The event masks are set individually. The program then enters the event processing loop, branching on the type of event. Within each event branch an if-then-else may be used to determine which window actually owns the event. This conditional uses the window field common to a large number of event types, including the event types of this program.

New Xlib calls introduced in this program are `XClearArea()` and `XMove-Window()`. The parameters for `XClearArea()` are:

```
XClearArea (display, window, x, y ,
            width, height, expose)
```

where the `x`, `y`, `width` and `height` values determine the portion of the window to clear. As a special case, a width of zero and a height of zero cause the entire window to be cleared. In the way the call is used in this program, it wipes out the current hit or miss score. What redraws it with the new value? We already have code in the expose event section to redraw these strings in any case, and the last parameter (`expose`) of `XClearArea()` allows us to force an expose event to be generated when the area is cleared. Thus the expose-event section handles all the initial drawing when the hit window and miss window are first created and exposed, at any time that they are later uncovered, and also when they have to be redrawn because the score changes.

The other call introduced was `XMoveWindow()`. This simply moves a window relative to its parent. While this works well for non-toplevel windows, it may not seem to work correctly on moving toplevel windows around the screen under some window managers, as they may have inserted extra windows between themselves and the root window.

4.5.1 Summary

Windows are placed in a tree parented off the root window. The application's toplevel windows are children of the root window. Only toplevel windows need to set their properties. Windows are clipped to their parent. Individual windows select their own events. Events not selected by a window go to an ancestor if it has selected them. The event loop branches on the type of event and then branches on each window that has selected that type.

Exercises

1. Make the box invert colors when the mouse is within it. (Use `EnterNotify` and `LeaveNotify` events, window redrawing and see `XSetWindowBackground()`).

2. Make the mouse cursor change to a circle when the mouse is inside the box. (Create the cursor, XCreateFontCursor(3X11) and attach it to a window, XDefineCursor(3X11). The cursor shape is `XC_circle`).

3. Find the dimensions of the windows using `XGetGeometry()` and use this information to ensure the box moves correctly..

Chapter 5

Controlling Xlib

This chapter examines some of the ways in which you can exercise further control over the appearance of Xlib applications. It covers fonts, color, handling user preferences and setting application icons.

5.1 Fonts

Text is *drawn* in X, using font tables which are bitmaps of each character. Characters may be 8 or 16 bits. I have used the call `XDrawImageString()` for this. There is a large set of fonts. They have not been standardized by the MIT Consortium so there is no guarantee that they will remain, or even that they will be available. Many of them are in `/usr/lib/X11/fonts`. The set of fonts can be extended and often is— each application writer seems to think it needs 'special' fonts. Fonts exist on the *server*, so if you design a new font it must be done for every server the user wants to run it on, not just the machine the application runs on. The common font encoding is machine dependent[3].

Fonts that seem to be available on every system are `8x13`, `9x15`, `variable`. A set supplied by Adobe is usually available. Fonts are characterized by the number of pixels they use; pixel size varies between displays. A program that requires a particular font size will be too large on some displays and too small on others. The font must be a user-configurable option. The default can be whatever font is inherited in the graphics context.

At the user level the fonts on a server can be found by using `xlsfonts` and you can view them by `xfontsel` or `xfd`. At the program level there are a number of calls available to find and set fonts. The query:

```
char **
XListFonts (display, pattern, maxnames, count)
```

---

[3] This has been fixed in X11R5.

```
Display *display;
char *pattern;
int maxnames;
int *count;
```

returns an array of font names matching a given pattern. The `count` is the actual
number of font names found, whereas `maxnames` is the number of names asked for.
Space for this array of font names can be reclaimed afterwards by `XFreeFont-`
`Names()`. After a font has been chosen, it can be installed in the server by `XLoad-`
`Font()`. Once in the server it can be set in any graphics context by `XSetFont()`. At
the end of the session it should be removed by `XUnloadFont()`. This is for memory
management: it allows the server to reclaim space for the font if it is now unused.
Otherwise the server would grow in size with each font loaded and possibly use up
all available space.

A program that uses a different font is `font.c`. Here are some extracts from
it—the bits that would need to be changed in any of `catch.c`, `onewindow.c`, etc.

Program 5: font.c

```
char FONT[] = "9x15";

Font     font;

initX ()
{   char **font_list;
    int count;

    /* set the display name from the environment
       vbl DISPLAY */
    display = XOpenDisplay (NULL);
    ....
    font_list = XListFonts (display, FONT, 1, &count);
    if (count > 0)
    {   /* found the font we want,
           use the first match */
        font = XLoadFont (display, font_list[0]);
        XFreeFontNames (font_list);
    }
    else
    {   /* this font not on the server. set it to
        ** a non-existent value
         */
        font = (Font) 0;
        fprintf (stderr, "couldn't find font %s\n",
                 FONT);
```

```
        }
}
GC
getGC ()
{
    GC gc;
    XGCValues gcValues;

    gc = XCreateGC (display, main_window,
                (unsigned long) 0, &gcValues);
      ....

    if (font != 0)
        XSetFont (display, gc, font);

    return (gc);
}

/*
** Terminate the program gracefully
*/
quitX ()
{
    if (font != 0)
        XUnloadFont (display, font);
    XCloseDisplay (display);
    exit (0);
}
```

We start with the pattern for fonts to be found. Here the pattern is exact as
'9x15'. In `initX()` we ask for one font matching this pattern by `XListFonts()`. If
it exists, `count` is returned as non-zero and we can load the font into the server.
Otherwise the font value is set to a non-font value (0). Attachment to a graphics context is trivially done by `XSetFont()` in `GetGC()`. Finally, space for the font is reclaimed at the end in `quitX()`.

A graphics context is created with a default font that can be reset to a new font
as shown above. If any text is drawn using the font in the graphics context, then the
size of the string drawn will depend on the font characteristics. In programs like
`hello.c` and `catch.c` mentioned above, the possible size variations were ignored. We now rectify that and show how to calculate the size of any string before it
is drawn. The simplest way is first to find the font being used. This is stored in a field
of the graphics context which is of type `GContext` and is used in various calls. The
field is accessed by the macro `XGContextFromGC()`. The call `XQueryTextExtents()` takes as parameters the display, a window, a `GContext`, a string (and its

length) and returns four values: the direction of the string (`FontLeftToRight` or `FontRightToLeft`), the ascent and descent of any string in this font (the height and depth about the bottom of the text) and a structure of type `XCharStruct`. This contains a field `width` that gives the horizontal extent of the string:

Program 6: fontinfo.c

```
char string[] = "hello world";
void
fontinfo ()
{
    int direction, ascent, descent;
    int height, width;
    XCharStruct overall;
    GContext font;

    font = XGContextFromGC(theGC);
    XQueryTextExtents (theDisplay, font,
            string, strlen (string),
            &direction, &ascent,
            &descent,
            &overall);
    height = ascent + descent;
    width = overall.width;

    fprintf (stderr, "height : %d, width: %d\n",
        height, width);
}
```

5.1.1   What has been left out

There is much more to fonts than we have discussed. Each character in a font has a number of dimensions attached to it. For example, each character requires a box of a certain size to draw it without overlapping other characters. However, it cannot completely fill this box, or characters would 'touch' each other. There are internal dimensions that control the placement of a character within its bounding box. For simple character drawing, what we have done is adequate, but for more exacting situations one would need to know more of the structure of each font and each character within it.

5.2 Color

Color in X is very complex as there is a vast range in the mechanisms used to implement it. Display devices may be monochrome, 4–8 planes (reasonable cost) to 24-plane high-cost devices. Some may have fixed colors; others may allow the user to set them. Some use red/green/blue pixel values; some have fixed lookup tables (color maps). Color programming in X *can* be simple but you can also make it as hard as you want to. For portable applications, remember these rules:

- Your application should be able to function even on monochrome displays.

- Some users may be color blind and be unable to distinguish shades of blue, or worse, green from red.

- Color only the 'black' bits.

- Use a small number of colors——say less than seven.

- Use the X defaults where possible.

The simplest of the X color mechanisms relies on a readable database of colors. This is typically stored in the file `/usr/lib/X11/rgb.txt`. This database contains a list of color names such as red, green, aquamarine, blue violet, cadet blue, and so on. It also contains the amount of red, green and blue that, when mixed together, will produce that color. For example, the color aquamarine uses 112 parts of red, 219 parts of green, and 147 parts of blue. (A vendor may have changed these values to suit server hardware.) Note that the entries in this table are *not* part of the X standard, but derive from X history. However, they are unlikely to change, so you should use these color names.

The hardware may not support the color chosen even though it is in the color database. The next step is to look up the closest color that the hardware supports by a call to:

```
XLookupColor(display, cmap, color, rgb, hardware)
    Display *display;
    Colormap cmap;
    char *color;
    XColor *rgb, *hardware
```

This returns both the mix of red, green and blue (as in the database) in the `rgb` parameter, while in the `hardware` parameter the closest equivalent that the hardware will support is returned. The `cmap` parameter is a color map, and is used here simply to identify the screen on which the colors are displayed.

There will always be a default color map for each display. Depending on the hardware, this may be fixed or it may be read/writeable. Programs using color in a simple way will just use this default color map. Although the call `XLookupCo-`

lor() returns a value that the hardware supports, it may or may not be available in the default color map. For example, the EGA screen can display sixteen colors at any time out of a total of sixty-four possible colors. Although the hardware may be able to show a color, sixteen colors may already be in use and the desired one may or may not be in them. On the other hand, less than sixteen may be in the color map, and the extra color can be added to it. This is done by a call to XAllocColor() which takes the display, the color map and the requested color as parameters. It returns in the requested color the closest or the actual pixel value for that color. This can be extracted from the XColor variable and used for, say, foreground and background colors.

Here is an extract from 'hello world' in red and blue (color.c):

Program 7: color.c

```
char RED[] = "Red";
char BLUE[] = "Blue";
XColor     RGB_color, hardware_color;
Colormap     color_map;

initX ()
{    int depth;
    /* set the display name from the environment
        vbl DISPLAY */
    display = XOpenDisplay (NULL);
    ....
    /* Find the depth of the color map */
    depth = DefaultDepth (display, screen);

    /* set the defaults in case we can't use color */
    foreground = BlackPixel (display, screen);
    background = WhitePixel (display, screen);

    if (depth > 1)
    {   /* not monochrome */
        color_map = DefaultColormap (display, screen);
        if (XLookupColor (display, color_map,
                RED, &RGB_color, &hardware_color) != 0
            &&
            XAllocColor (display, color_map,
                &hardware_color) != 0)
            background = hardware_color.pixel;

        if (XLookupColor (display, color_map,
                BLUE, &RGB_color, &hardware_color) != 0
            &&
            XAllocColor (display, color_map,
```

```
                    &hardware_color) != 0)
            foreground = hardware_color.pixel;
    }
}
```

All the changes made here are to `initX()` to set the background and foreground to the new colors. These are then used exactly as before for backgrounds to
windows and for drawing text and graphics. The only difference is that they may be
red and blue instead of black and white.

5.2.1 What has been left out

Some applications require the ability to set their own colors, not just using the ones
available at the time. Machines with many color planes can display millions of colors. X gives mechanisms for the fine control of color needed for such uses and machines.

5.2.2 Summary

This section has shown how to add colors to your application. It uses the default
color map by the calls:
```
DefaultColormap ()
XAllocColor ()
XLookupColor ()
```

5.3 User preferences

The user of an application should have the ability to configure a large number of the
program's resources, or leave them to default values if desired. Users express preferences   in a number of ways: through command-line arguments, in a file
`$HOME/.Xdefaults` or in a file pointed to by the environment variable `XENVI-`
`RONMENT`, among others. In addition the program may have system-wide defaults
set up in `/usr/lib/X11/app-defaults`, or may hard-code them into the program.

A program wishing to respond to user preferences may go through the rather
tedious process of parsing the command line and examining the contents of various
files. Xlib does not have a single mechanism for performing all of this, but does have
a number of tools to aid in the process. It remains a tedious task. The following program segment illustrates how they can be used to get two relatively complex options: the display device and the geometry. The program is called `catch_option-`
`s.c`. It is not a nice piece of code and is given more for completeness than with the
expectation of its use. All of this is done for you if you use the methods of the next
part of the book.

Program 8:   catch_options.c

```
#include <X11/Xresource.h>

int main_x = 10;    /* size of main window.
                         the default values hard */
int main_y = 10;   /* coded here should never
                         be used directly */
int main_width = 400;
int main_ht = 400;

/*
** Get the options from the user or from a data base
**
** Options may be set in a number of ways:
**          - on the command line
**          - as resources attached to the root window
**          - in the file $HOME/.Xdefaults or
**          - in the file pointed to by
**            environment vbl XENVIRONMENT
**          - in the file /usr/lib/X11/app-defaults/
**          - hard coded into the program
** Each mechanism overrides options set
** in later methods.
**
** Some standard options are:
**          - the display device
**          - the geometry of the top-level window
**          - the font used for writing
**          - the background and foreground colors
*/

char CLASS_NAME[] = "Catch";

static int opTableEntries = 2;  /* size of opTable
                                     array below */

static XrmOptionDescRec opTable[] =
{
{"-display",  ".display",  XrmoptionSepArg,
            (caddr_t) NULL},
{"-geometry", "*geometry",  XrmoptionSepArg,
            (caddr_t) NULL}
};
```

```
static XrmDatabase commandlineDB, rDB;

void
getUserOptions(argc, argv)
int *argc;
char **argv;
{       XrmDatabase applicationDB, serverDB, homeDB;
        char instance_str[50], class_str[50];
        char *str_type[20];
        char file_db[1024], *env;
        char Geostr[50];
        char theDisplayName[1024];
        XrmValue value;
        long flags;
        extern char *getenv();

        /* set up an empty resources data base */
        XrmInitialize();

        /* get the stuff off the command line.
           Not only does this give the most
          important options (the user set
          ones), but also may tell us
          which display device to use
        */
        XrmParseCommand(&commandlineDB, opTable,
                        opTableEntries,
              argv[0], argc, argv);

         /* make sure no illegal options are left over */

        if (*argc != 1)
                exit(1);

        /* get the display now, because we
           need it for the other
           data bases */
        strcpy(instance_str, argv[0]);
        strcat(instance_str, ".display");
        strcpy(class_str, CLASS_NAME);
        strcat(class_str, ".Display");
        if (XrmGetResource(commandlineDB, instance_str,
                      class_str, str_type, &value) ==
                                      True)
                strncpy(theDisplayName, value.addr,
                      (int) value.size);
```

```
else
        *theDisplayName = NULL;

/* open the display now - the next
   set of options is attached
   to the root window */
theDisplay = XOpenDisplay(theDisplayName);
if (theDisplay == NULL)
        exit(1);

/* now get the file databases,
   least important ones first */
/* first the default application ones */
   strcpy(file_db, "/usr/lib/X11/app-defaults/");

strcat(file_db, CLASS_NAME);
applicationDB = XrmGetFileDatabase(file_db);
XrmMergeDatabases(applicationDB, &rDB);

 /* then the ones attached to the root window */

if (theDisplay->xdefaults != NULL)
/* shouldn't access structure members */
{
        serverDB = XrmGetStringDatabase(
                        theDisplay->xdefaults);

        XrmMergeDatabases(serverDB, &rDB);
}

/* then the ones in .Xdefaults or
   in XENVIRONMENT */
if ((env = getenv("XENVIRONMENT")) ==
            (char *) NULL)
{
        strcpy(file_db, getenv("HOME"));
        strcat(file_db, "/.Xdefaults");
        homeDB = XrmGetFileDatabase(file_db);
}
else
        homeDB = XrmGetFileDatabase(env);
XrmMergeDatabases(homeDB, &rDB);

/* put the most important DB in */
XrmMergeDatabases(commandlineDB, &rDB);
```

```
        /* All the stuff should be in there now.
           We can start extracting it */

        /* extract the geometry */
        strcpy(instance_str, argv[0]);
        strcat(instance_str, ".geometry");
        strcat(class_str, CLASS_NAME);
        strcat(class_str, ".Geometry");
        if (XrmGetResource(rDB, instance_str, class_str,
                    str_type, &value) == True)
                strncpy(Geostr, value.addr,
                        (int) value.size);
        else
                Geostr[0] = NULL;

        /* parse and assign the geometry */
        if (Geostr[0] != NULL)
        {
                flags = XParseGeometry(Geostr, &main_x,
                                               &main_y,
                            &main_width, &main_ht);
                if ((XValue | YValue) & flags)
                      theSizeHints.flags |= USPosition;
                else        theSizeHints.flags |=
                                                PPosition
                if ((WidthValue | HeightValue) & flags)
                      theSizeHints.flags |= USSize;
                else        theSizeHints.flags |= PSize;
                /* should check for negative values,
                    minimum values etc,
                    but didn't */
        }
        else        theSizeHints.flags |=
                        (PPosition | PSize);
        theSizeHints.x = main_x;
        theSizeHints.y = main_y;
        theSizeHints.width = main_width;
        theSizeHints.height = main_ht;
}
```

5.3.1 Summary

This section has shown how to obtain application resources. It involves searching a number of databases, merging each one in turn. This is done by:

```
    XrmInitialize ()
    XrmGetFileDatabase ()
```

```
XrmGetStringDatabase ()
XrmMergeDatabases ()
```
Resources are extracted from the database by:
```
XrmGetResource ()
```
The special case of geometry can be found from the resource string by:
```
XParseGeometry ()
```

5.4 Icons

An application may be iconified by a window manager. The application is then represented by a window showing an icon. Ideally this should be some stylized representation of the application so that it may be easily identified. The icon is part of the application, so it must be designed and created by the application writer. The icon is displayed by the window manager so it must be informed of the icon.

The program `bitmap file` allows data to be created for an icon image. It shows a grid (16×16 default) corresponding to individual pixels which can be turned on or off. `bitmap` stores the resultant data in the file given as argument. The output data stored in this file consists of three variables: a rectangular array of bitmap information and the width and height of this array. The variable names are constructed from the file name in a simple way. For example, Figure 16 shows the bitmap editor used to draw a cat-like shape for the program `catch.c`, storing the output in file `catch_icon.h`. (This could be made more realistic by using a larger bitmap such as 64×64 or a better artist.) The contents of this file are:

```
#define catch_icon_width 16
#define catch_icon_height 16
static char catch_icon_bits[] = {
    0x00, 0x00, 0x00, 0x00, 0x10, 0x00, 0x18, 0x00, 0xa4,
    0x8f, 0x42, 0x50, 0x0a, 0x20, 0x14, 0x20, 0x30, 0x10,
    0xc8, 0x2f, 0x0c, 0x40, 0x02, 0x80, 0x00, 0x00, 0x00,
    0x00, 0x00, 0x00, 0x00, 0x00};
```

To install this as an icon, two steps are needed: create a `Pixmap` from the data using the call `CreateBitmapFromData()` and inform the window manager by a parameter in `XSetStandardProperties()`.

Program 9: catch_icon.c

```
#include "catch_icon.h"

Pixmap     icon_map;
icon_map = XCreateBitmapFromData (theDisplay,
                                  parent,
                                  catch_icon_bits,
```

```
                                   catch_icon_width,
                                   catch_icon_height);
    XSetStandardProperties(theDisplay, theNewWindow,
                    THE_WINDOW_NAME, THE_ICON_NAME,
                    icon_map,   /* the icon map */
                    argv, argc, &theSizeHints);
```

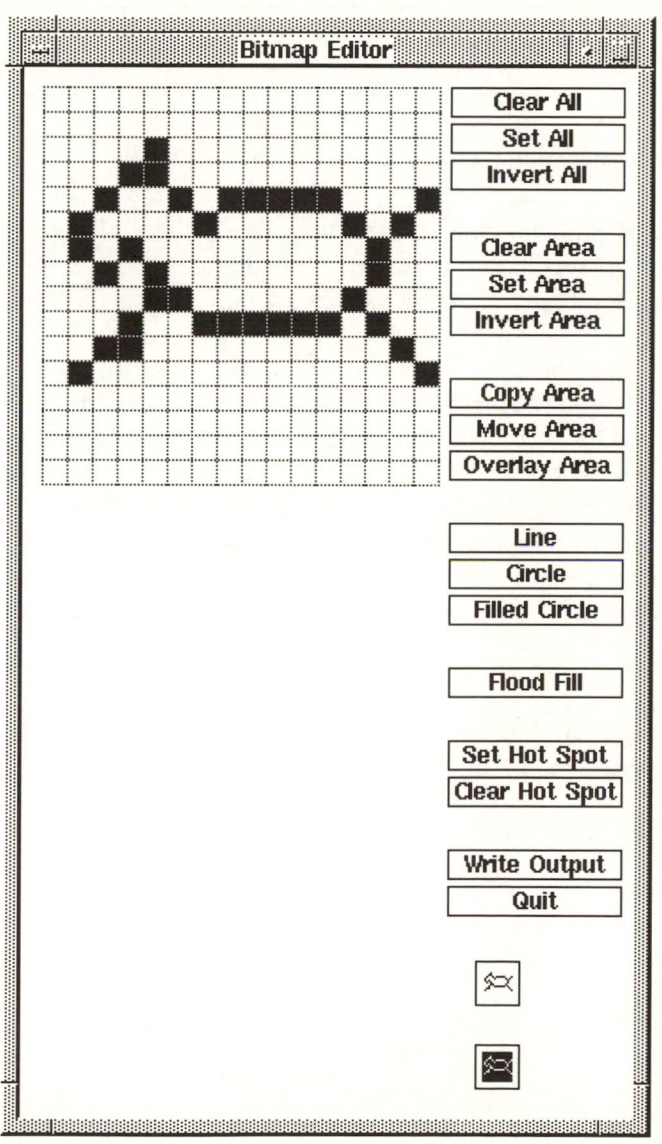

Figure 16:   Drawing the icon for `catch.c`

5.4.1 Summary

This section has shown that an icon may be drawn using the program:
```
bitmap
```
The resultant array of bits is added to an application as an icon by:
```
XCreateBitmapFromData ()
XSetStandardProperties ()
```

Exercises for Part II

This is a more substantial Xlib program that could be set as a major assignment in Xlib.

The game of noughts and crosses (tictactoe) is a two-player game played on a 3×3 grid. One player has the 'noughts', the other the 'crosses'. Players take turns entering their symbol into a vacant square. A player has won when he or she has three noughts or three crosses in a horizontal, diagonal or vertical line. Write a program to display the noughts and crosses board, allowing two players taking turns to use the mouse. When a player clicks the button in a square it draws a symbol in that square (if it was vacant before) and then the other player has a turn. In addition to the nine squares on the board, the program should also show a status bar at the top displaying whose turn it is. Further, pressing the letter 'q' anywhere should terminate the application, whereas pressing 'n' will start a new game.

A number of extensions are possible:

1. Make the mouse cursor change into a nought or cross as appropriate.

2. Allow options to control which of 'X' or 'O' starts.

3. Keep track of the game to determine if someone has won. Take suitable action when a win is found, such as inverting colors of the winning line.

4. Make the program play one side of the game.

Summary of Part II

This part has formed an introduction to the Xlib library, sufficient for the user to write reasonable-size applications. There are many complexities to Xlib which we have not gone into, but sufficient has been covered for you to be able to read the more specialized books. The following topics have been covered:

- Event processing
- Multiple windows
- Font control
- Color
- Icons
- Control of options

PART III

The Motif toolkit

This part of the book discusses the Motif toolkit. This is a set of functions that give an object-oriented view to X programming. The part discusses this object model and then shows how to build simple applications. It proceeds to build increasingly more complex applications, surveying the set of Motif objects along the way. It concludes with some techniques at the intermediate level.

Chapter 6

Overview

This chapter discusses the object-oriented model and how it is used in X and Motif programming.

6.1　Objects

Structured programming has the advantage of giving organization to the control mechanisms of a program, removing the 'spaghetti' code methods that were once prevalent. However, they do not in themselves give the same organization to the data types that are used and external standards often have to be imposed on programs to organize the data as well. Object-oriented programming has become popular recently as a means of avoiding 'spaghetti' *data types*. An object consists of a data type plus all the internal and external procedures that can act on it. An object has a public interface of data values and procedures that other parts of the application can access, and private parts that can only be dealt with by the object itself. For example, a stack is a simple object on which things can be 'pushed' and later 'popped'. This is the public interface to a stack. How it does this, and what data structures it internally uses, should be private and invisible to the external world.

Individual objects are *instances* that belong to a particular class. All cars have wheels, so any particular car has wheels. Instances may have values that the class does not have: for example, my car is colored yellow. All cars have *some* color, but the color cannot be specified at the class level. However, like all cars, mine responds in the same way to certain actions (like refusing to start when it is critical that I be on time).

The concept of data hiding can be performed in a number of languages which are not called 'object' languages. A further component of object-oriented programming is *inheritance*. An object may be a specialization of another, inheriting all of its behavior and characteristics and adding more of its own. Some typical examples are the hierarchies formed by the different types of motor vehicles: cars and trucks are different specializations of vehicles. Since they are vehicles, they inherit common properties such as having wheels and usually travelling on roads. In addition, each type has additional features: for example, cars generally have petrol engines, whereas trucks generally have diesel engines.They may be further specialized, for cars may be sedans or sports-cars. Sedans generally have four seats for passengers and driver, while sports-car only have two. Classes higher in the hierarchy (such as vehicles to sedans) are known as *superclasses* of the class.

The final major component of 'objects' in an inheritance hierarchy is that a subclass can override properties of its parent class. For example, cats are a subclass of mammals, a subclass which (among other things) has tails. Manx cats, on the other hand are a specialization of cats which do *not* have tails—the property has been overridden for this subclass. Similarly, behavior can be overridden for subclasses: whereas most humans are meat eaters, the subclass of vegetarians is not.

There is a large number of languages designed specifically for object-oriented programming, such as Simula, SmallTalk, Eiffel and Actor.

6.2   Toolkits

Visual systems, such as window systems, often abound in things that can be labelled as objects. For example, menus, buttons and labels are frequent objects in a window system. Menus form a class of objects that display choices and allow selection of one of them. Buttons are objects that can be pushed. Labels simply display a piece of text.

In Xlib, construction of one of these 'objects' can be quite complex. For example, to have a label object requires a window, a drawing function to draw the label, and a way of calling this function each time the window becomes exposed. A menu is a much more complex object. It will contain a set of windows, one for each menu entry. When the mouse is clicked on a menu entry, or when the arrow keys are used to traverse the menu, its appearance will often change to highlight selected items.

The name used for objects in X is *widgets*. The designers of the object-support system wanted to avoid the actual word *object* and settled instead on the word *widget* as representing a similar idea. (A widget is something generic made in US factories when you don't want to be too specific about it.)

To avoid the necessity of each application writer having to reinvent these objects/widgets for each program, it is *highly* desirable to have them supplied in a library for immediate use. There are many libraries of widgets: the Athena widgets from MIT, the Andrew widgets from Carnegie–Mellon, the OpenLook widgets from AT&T and Sun Microsystems, and the Motif widgets from OSF.

There is a problem in the implementation of objects/widgets in C: C is not an object-oriented language. Essentially an object interpreter is required and the objects must be C code written in a style corresponding to this object-oriented approach. In addition, the designers of this object-oriented layer, just like the designers of X, tried to be policy free so that any set of window-based objects could be implemented. This leads to two layers to the object-oriented system: a bottom layer acting as the interpretive support to widgets, and the widgets themselves. This bottom layer is called the *Intrinsics* and is defined in the Xt library, while the top layer forms a *widget set*. Together they form a *toolkit* (refer back to Figure 13 on page 37). In order to do this, there are a number of contortions in the usual C programming style and the typical structure of a C program is replaced with one that allows this object-oriented approach. This consists of an object initialization phase followed by a call to the object-interpreter loop.

Most widgets are built using an object-oriented approach. There is data hiding and public access. There is an inheritance hierarchy.

A widget set generally imposes some measure of policy although they should allow a large amount of freedom to the user to customize them. The Motif widgets (and the Motif window manager) allow applications to have the look-and-feel of IBM's Common User Access (note though that IBM is only one member of the Open Software Foundation which produces Motif, so the look-and-feel may differ in some respects).

With regard to versions of C: in general, X and the widgets have been written under the Kernighan and Ritchie version of C. Prototypes that allow them to be run under the ANSI–C style are often available, but whether or not you can use them depends on the state of your local compiler and on the completeness and accuracy of the prototypes. Noone seems to have attempted to rewrite X in the object oriented language C++, but there are a number of 'widget wrapper' libraries that provide a C++ shell around widgets. These are often a curious mix of object-oriented styles, and do not give all the advantages of object-oriented programming.

Chapter 7

Basic techniques

*This chapter discusses the basic techniques of Motif programming. It shows how
to create programs with a single widget, how this may be configured, and how
application code is called from a widget.*

7.1 A single widget

The Xt toolkit style of programming is quite different from Xlib. Many of the tasks
common to Xlib programs are encapsulated in single Xt functions. The following
Motif program displays a triangle in a window. The triangle is intended to denote a
direction and is shaped like an arrow. When the arrow is selected (by pressing on it
with the left button) it appears to become pressed into the surface. The arrow widget
is a very simple widget, so forms a good point from which to discuss the differences
between the Xlib and Xt programming methods. Following programs will expand
and explore in more detail both the Xt programming methods and the Motif widget
library. The program is called `arrow.c`.

Program 10: arrow.c

```
#include <Xm/ArrowB.h>

char Class_name[] = "Arrow";

main(argc, argv)
int argc;
char **argv;
{
        Widget toplevel, arrow_widget;
```

```
/* Initialize the intrinsics  with
   a toplevel widget
*/
toplevel = XtInitialize (NULL, /* application
                                   name     */
                 Class_name,    /* class name */
                 NULL,          /* options */
                 0,             /* number of
                                   options */
                 &argc, argv); /* command line
                                  args */
  /* Create an arrow widget with the
     toplevel as manager */
arrow_widget = XmCreateArrowButton (
                 toplevel,    /* parent */
                 "an_arrow", /* name of
                                widget*/
                 NULL,        /* resource
                                arguments */
                 0);          /* number of
                                args */
XtManageChild (arrow_widget);

/* display all of the widgets */
XtRealizeWidget (toplevel);

/* enter the main processing loop */
XtMainLoop ();
}
```

Compilation of this program depends on your system. It needs the libraries for Motif, the Xt intrinsics and Xlib. Generally it will be something like:

```
cc -o arrow arrow.c -lXm -lXt -lX11
```

Note that the order of libraries is important.

This program shows when run as in Figure 17. It shows an upward pointing arrow. Shading around the edges gives it a slight 3-D effect so that it appears to be standing up from the surface of the screen. If the left button is pressed on this arrow, the shading changes so that it appears pressed into the screen instead (this looks much more effective in color).

There is an include file for each type of widget used in the program. Since the program uses an arrow button widget it includes `<Xm/ArrowB.h>`. The abbreviation of names is due to the poor name-length capabilities of some operating systems. To ensure that the header files are portable, the length is restricted to eleven characters. The name of the include file to use is documented in standard Unix style under the manual entries for the widgets.

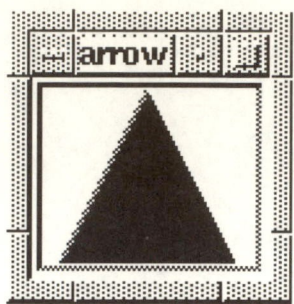

Figure 17:   The arrow program

There are other include files of interest to the Motif programmer that are auto-matically included if a widget include file is used. The first is `<Xm/Xm.h>`. This de-fines the major Motif constants. The file `<X11/Intrinsics.h>` is also included. This file defines various things to the Intrinsics layer. There are naming conventions in these include files: constants, macros and functions beginning with Xt belong to the Intrinsics set and those with Xm to the Motif toolkit. A book on Xt programming will often use constants beginning with `Xt` such as `XtNwidth`, which belong to the Intrinsics. In such cases, Motif defines equivalent constants which belong to Motif and begin with `Xm`, such as `XmNwidth`. This is simply to avoid having to remember whether things start with Xt or Xm. The appropriate Motif possibilities are given in the Motif documentation.

In Xlib a program begins with an initialization phase, establishing contact with the server and then going on to create windows. A toplevel window performs com-munications with the rest of the system to set things like geometry. Subsequent win-dows are created as children of this toplevel window, forming a tree of windows. In a similar manner Xt applications form a tree, but this time a tree of widgets. Toplevel widgets (called *shell* widgets) are used to interact with the rest of the system and the rest of the application's widgets have this widget as ancestor. (An application can have many shell widgets but we can ignore that for now.) This tree structure is not the same as the window-tree structure—in toolkit programming the actual window structure is maintained and manipulated by the toolkit itself.

In widget programming, much of the initialization is done by a single call `XtInitialize()`. This creates a single toplevel widget between the application and the system. Because of the nature of the other tasks it has to do, it is only allowed a single child.

The Xt libraries make full use of the resource database discussed in Section 3.4. To identify resources for an application, both an instance name and a class name are required.The first two parameters to `XtInitialize()` set the application name and class name. The first parameter gives the application name. The special value

NULL is used by Xt to mean the name of the binary executable file with any leading directory names removed. The class name of the application is given explicitly as Arrow. XtInitialize() gets the resource values from the standard places as discussed in the next section. The next two arguments can be ignored for quite some time: they allow an application to define its own resources. The final two arguments carry the actual command-line arguments. The user may set command-line resource values (such as width) which override any obtained from the standard places. XtInitialize() reads the ones it knows about from argv and sets them appropriately. It modifies argv and argc to remove the ones it finds. Thus, for example, the application could be run using the command-line arguments:

```
arrow -display jan:0
```

This would run the arrow using jan:0 as server. Before the call to XtInitialize(), argc would be three and argv would contain the -display jan:0. After the call, argc would be reduced to one and the arguments would be removed from argv.

The arrow widget is created by a call to XmCreateArrowButton(). The arguments to the call are first the parent widget, to establish it in the widget tree, a string name an_arrow (so that it can be used in resource files) and two further arguments. These can be used to control the widget's appearance and behavior and will be discussed in the next section.

The widget now has been created as part of the widget tree. The geometry of the widget now has to be dealt with. An arrow widget has a dynamic width and height, and its size at any time will be determined not by the arrow button but by its parent in the widget tree. Widget sizing is a complex matter with, for example, labels trying to be large enough to contain all of their text, whereas at the other end, a window manager may be insisting that the application fit into a particular size. This negotiation is done by the 'container' objects, such as the shell widget. The call XtManageChild(), which takes the arrow widget as argument, places the arrow under the control of its parent for any size and location calculations that might be done.

Even though much of the work to create the widget has been done, it is not yet showing on the screen because no windows have yet been created! This task is performed by XtRealizeWidget(), which starts at the top of the widget tree and recursively descends it, creating windows and performing final setup work.

Finally an Xlib program would have entered the event-processing loop. All of the work of this loop is performed by the single call XtMainLoop() with no parameters. From now on, the program runs itself! Of course, it does not appear to do anything particularly exciting as it is only a simple program and we have not written much application code that does anything. However, there is in fact a mass of functionality in the program. Click the left mouse button over the arrow: it will appear to move into the surface and back up when the button is released. Stretch the widget by using one of the resize mechanisms of the window manager: the arrow will grow or shrink to still fill the window. Cover the window with another and then uncover it: it will be redrawn for you.

7.1.1 Summary

This section has shown how to set up a simple application containing a single user-defined widget. Each application establishes a connection to the server, creates a toplevel shell and reads the resource database by:

```
XtInitialize ()
```

Each widget is created and managed by:

```
XmCreate<widget>
XtManageChild ()
```

Windows are created and the program enters the event processing loop by:

```
XtRealize ()
XtMainLoop ()
```

Exercises

1. Use a Push Button widget instead of the Arrow Button by `XmCreatePushButton()` with include file `<Xm/PushB.h>`.

2. Use a Label widget instead of the Arrow Button by `XmCreateLabel()` with include file `<Xm/Label.h>`.

7.2 Configuring widgets

7.2.1 Resources

Widgets have a number of resources such as foreground and background colors, font, etc. with default values which can be changed either by the user or the application. The handling of user preferences in Xlib is rather cumbersome. The resource database was taken from Xt into Xlib but it remains tedious. Xt offers full support for the resource database, to the extent that it becomes a major mechanism for both user and programmer control of Xt-based applications.

A typical widget such as the arrow button has over thirty resources, documented in the manual entry. Usually you will only need to worry about a small number of them as most will use either the default value or be set by other widgets. Most resources can be set by the user using the usual resource mechanism or by the programmer.

There is a delicate tradeoff in setting resources. Motif, as with most toolkits, is attempting to give the user as much control as possible (while still being workable) over the behavior and appearance of the application, while defaulting to reasonable values if the user does not specify values. The programmer must take great care not to impose his or her own beliefs or conveniences upon the user. For example, every application writer believes that his or her application should occupy the center of the screen, whereas users typically put them all over the place; every application writer would like his or her application to occupy a large portion of the screen, whereas the user will often iconify or shrink it; it may be easier for the application writer to use a particular fixed font, but screen resolutions and sizes vary dramatically and some people have visual disabilities requiring large fonts; there is often an attitude that 'everybody should speak English,' even if a button saying *Close* is less intuitive to a French speaker than one saying *Fermé*. These are arguments in favour of allowing the user as much control as possible over the appearance and behavior of an application.

Nevertheless, the amount of control offered by Motif can allow a user to ruin a program by allowing too much freedom. If the user labels every 'Save' button as 'Load', the program is bound to seem to function incorrectly. Thus the programmer must tie down resources sufficiently for the program to function correctly but still be configured by the user.

Each widget is separately documented in the Motif Programmer's Manual. The arrow widget has a manual entry under 'XmArrowButton.' Each widget has a set of resources documented in this manual entry. Some of these resources will be new and some inherited from superclasses. New resources are given in a table in the Section of this entry entitled 'New Resources':

XmArrowButton Resource Set				
Name	**Class**	**Type**	**Default**	**Access**
XmNactivateCallback	XmCCallback	XtCallbackList	NULL	C
XmNarmCallback	XmCCallback	XtCallbackList	NULL	C
XmNarrowDirection	XmCArrowDirection	unsigned char	XmARROW_UP	CSG
XmNdisarmCallback	XmCCallback	XtCallbackList	NULL	C
XmNmultiClick	XmCMultiClick	unsigned char	dynamic	CSG

There are five new resources for an arrow button (only four in Motif 1.0): `XmNactivateCallback`, `XmNarmCallback`, `XmNarrowDirection`, `XmNdisarmCallback` and `XmNmultiClick`. The remaining resources are inherited from a class `XmPrimitive`, including:

XmPrimitive Resource Set				
Name	**Class**	**Type**	**Default**	**Access**
XmNforeground	XmCForeground	Pixel	dynamic	C
XmNhighlightColor	XmCHighlightColor	Pixel	dynamic	C

and `Core`, including:

Core Resource Set				
Name	**Class**	**Type**	**Default**	**Access**
XmNbackground	XmCForeground	Pixel	dynamic	CSG
XmNheight	XmCHeight	Dimension	dynamic	CSG
XmNwidth	XmCWidth	Dimension	dynamic	CSG

There are five entries in each row of each table. The first gives the name of the resource. The second gives the class name of the resource. The third gives the type. You should pay attention to a number of types. Motif uses ordinary arrays of char (type `String`) and a type called `XmString` and these are not interchangeable. This is discussed in Section 7.3. A range of numeric types is used, such as `Dimension` and `Position`. It is easy to assume that they are integers, but often such types are not (they may be shorts or longs). You can discover this in a spectacular way on occasions when you try to store such a value in an `int` variable, only to discover that C has failed to do the type conversion for you and there is only garbage in the variable. To avoid this you should use the types given in the table.

The fourth column gives the default value of the resource. Default values given as dynamic are often set by other widgets. The final column in the table is labelled Access and entries are combinations of the letters C, S and G. These stand for Creation, Set and Get. The presence of C means that the resource can be set at *creation time*. S means that it can be *set* at any time, whereas G means that the program can *get* the value of the resource from the widget at any time. Thus the callback resources for the arrow button with access C can only be set when the arrow is created, but the direction with access CSG can be accessed or set at any time.

The new resources are described in more detail in the 'New Resources' section following the resource table. For example, for `XmNarrowDirection` the description is:

XmNarrowDirection
Sets the arrow direction. The following are values for this resource:

- **XmARROW_UP**
- **XmARROW_DOWN**
- **XmARROW_LEFT**
- **XmARROW_RIGHT**

These names are sufficiently obvious for no further description to be given. The default is sometimes given here; however it is also given in the last column in the resource table and for the direction it is `XmARROW_UP`—the direction it should show when the arrow program is run.

7.2.2 User control

Owing to the history of X, resources can be set in a number of files. Some system is needed to arbitrate which files are used and which take precedence in case of clashes. The `XtInitialize()` function picks up resources according to the following algorithm, where later resources override earlier ones whenever they are identical.

```
Load /usr/lib/X11/app-defaults/<Class–Name>
If XAPPLRESDIR is set then
    load $XAPPRESDIR/<ClassName>
else load $HOME/<ClassName>
If there are resources on root window
    load them
else load $HOME/.Xdefaults
If XENVIRONMENT is set
    load file specified by it
else
    load $HOME/.Xdefaults-<hostname>
Load command line options.
```

This allows a large measure of both application-designer and user control. The application designer should create system-wide resources in `/usr/lib/X11/app-defaults/<ClassName>` and the installation process should put it there. Typically the user will store resources in `.Xdefaults`. Whenever the same resource is set by both, the user value will override the application-defaults value because it occurs later in the resource-loading process.

In a program such as the arrow program, we need to be able to find the name of the resource so that it can be set. The first component is the application's name or class. These are set by the program as the first two arguments to `XtInitialize()`. For the arrow program, if the source is compiled to the executable file 'arrow' then the resource name of the application is 'arrow' and the class name is 'Arrow.' The resource name given to the arrow button is 'an_arrow' because that was the name given to it in the creation call. The class name from the widget documentation is 'XmArrowButton.' Thus any resources affecting this widget could be accessed via the patterns:

```
arrow.an_arrow
arrow.XmArrowButton
Arrow.an_arrow
Arrow.XmArrowButton
```

Suppose we want to set the arrow direction to 'right' using a resource file. That is, we want to set the value of `XmNarrowDirection` to `XmARROW_RIGHT`. `XmARROW_RIGHT` is defined as an integer constant in the include file `<Xm/ArrowB.h>`. This cannot be used, as there is no reasonable way in which the user could (or should) know this value. Motif adopts a simple convention for both the resource name and the resource value. For the resource name, drop the `XmN` and use the rest of the string as the name. For the resource value, drop the Xm and use the remaining characters in any mixture of upper and lower case. Thus the direction could be set to right by:

```
arrow.an_arrow.arrowDirection: arrow_right
```

Note that each time the application is run, the resource database is examined. To experiment, you can edit .Xdefaults, run the application, re-edit the file, re-run the application, etc. There is no need to recompile the application.

7.2.3 Program control

Resources may be set at Creation time, may be changed dynamically by Setting them, or may be obtained by Getting them. Each resource is documented as CSG or some subset.

To set values at creation time, use the third and fourth arguments to the creation routine XmCreate<*Widget*>(). The third argument is an array of resource name/ resource value pairs and the fourth argument is the number of resources being set. The array is of type Arg. One could set fields individually but a macro XtSetArg() is usually used which takes an array element, the resource name and the resource value[4]. For example, to create a very large arrow button, change the creation routine to include setting the height and width resources:

```
Arg args[2];
int n = 0;

XtSetArg (args[n], XmNwidth, 200); n++;
XtSetArg (args[n], XmNheight, 300); n++;
arrow_widget = XmCreateArrowButton(toplevel, "an_arrow",
                                   args, n);
```

Some comments on this program style are in order. First, note that the n cannot be incremented within XtSetArg() as it is a macro that uses its first argument twice and that would increment n twice. Why use n at all and not just number the array indices 0, 1, 2...? This is because you will probably spend quite a lot of time with each widget, adding, subtracting and modifying resources to get them right. This style allows lines to be added and deleted without having to renumber the indices each time.

To set values dynamically, i.e. at any time after the widget has been created, an array of type Arg is used again, with the resource names and values set as before. A call is then made to XtSetValues() with the widget, the array and number of resources:

---

[4] Programs that perform much resource manipulation unfortunately can get very cluttered with XtSetArg() statements. There is a substantially cleaner method based on the varargs facility of C, but this is not available in Motif 1.0 and is only poorly integrated into Motif 1.1.

```
Arg args[2];
int n = 0;

XtSetArg (args[n], XmNwidth, 200); n++;
XtSetArg (args[n], XmNheight, 300); n++;
XtSetValues(arrow_widget, args, n);
```

The call to `XtSetValues()` must be made after the widget has been created but apart from this there is no restriction on its use.

If a resource is labelled as Gettable, the application may query the widget at any time for the value of the resource. To get the value of a resource, an array of type `Arg` is again used, but this time to a call to `XtGetValues()`. Here the C function argument limitation comes into action: because parameters are passed by value, to change (set) a value you have to pass the *address* of variables in which to store the values. Thus the addresses of the width and height variables are set in the `args` array rather than the variables themselves:

```
Arg args[2];
int width, height;

n = 0;
XtSetArg (args[n], XmNwidth, &width); n++;
XtSetArg (args[n], XmNheight, &height); n++;
XtGetValues(arrow_widget, args, n);
```

7.2.4 Summary

This section has shown a number of ways of controlling widget resources. The user can set resources using the `.Xdefaults` file. Program methods involve an array of type `Arg` manipulated by the macro:

```
XtSetArg ()
```

Resources of a widget may be set by:

```
XmCreate<widget> ()
XtSetValues ()
```

Resource values in a widget may be found by:

```
XtGetValues ()
```

Exercises

---

1. Change the direction of the arrow using the `.Xdefaults` file.

2. Change the direction of the arrow by hard-coding.

3. Determine what direction the arrow is set to by `XtGetValues()`. Write the information to standard output.

7.3   Strings

Motif uses two types of strings. The first type is the ordinary array of characters. The type `String` is a synonym for this:

```
typedef char * String;
```

Ordinary strings are used for names of widgets. For example, consider the push-button widget which displays text in a box and changes appearance to look depressed into the surface when the left mouse button is pressed in it. Like every widget it requires a name to be given at creation time, a name by which it can be referred to in resource files.

```
button_widget = XmCreatePushButton(parent, "Push Here",
                                    args, n);
```

creates the widget with the name 'Push Here'. To set the width of this push button, use:

```
*Push Here.width:        200
```

By default, the width of the push button is set to the label it shows and by default, the label shown is the name of the widget, so the above creation and width values would give a widget with label 'Push Here' and width overridden to 200. One of the resources for the push button is `XmNlabelString`, which is represented in a resource file by 'labelString'. To set the label to say 'Really Push Here', use:

```
*Push Here.labelString: Really Push Here
```

The resource `XmNlabelString` is actually of type `XmString` rather than `String`. We cannot place an `XmString` in a resource file because it is a data type that no user of an application should need to know. Motif uses what is called a 'converter' to change the `String` into an `XmString` when it reads the resource database. Resource converters are advanced Xt programming and will not be needed further in this book. Motif performs the conversion for the user but in most other instances, using a `String` for an `XmString` will not be so well tolerated.

So what is an `XmString`? We saw in the part on Xlib that text is actually drawn using a font. With the desire to support international character sets, Motif adopts a string representation that allows strings with both an associated character set and a direction (Arabic writes from right to left). An `XmString` is a set of 'segments' each containing font-related information called 'character sets', or direction information, or the text itself (see Figure 18). Thus a 'string' of this type could contain a mixture of font-related information and directions, as well as the text.

charset	text	charset	direction	text	end

Figure 18:   Structure of an `XmString`

It would be poor practice to hard-code any particular font into the program. The particular font may not be available on the server, or the user may wish to use a different one. A character set is a way of 'soft-coding' font information. A character set is a label that can be associated with one or more fonts, either by the program or by the user. Both Motif 1.0 and 1.1 supply a character-set label that will match any font that the user may wish to use. This character-set label is XmSTRING_DE-FAULT_CHARSET, and will be the character set identifier used by most Motif programs[5]. Whatever font is chosen by the user will be matched by this identifier, so that XmStrings will be drawn in the user's choice of font. What it usually means is the program is a bit messier in that conversions have to be performed from the ASCII string representation to the XmString representation and back.

To create an XmString from an ASCII string in the simplest way, with the default direction of left-to-right, use the function XmStringCreateLtoR(). This will create an XmString containing the text 'Really Push Here':

```
XmString xmstr;
String asciistr = "Really Push Here";
xmstr = XmStringCreateLtoR(asciistr,
                            XmSTRING_DEFAULT_CHARSET);
```

A large number of resources use XmStrings instead of ordinary ASCII strings. For example, the resource XmNlabelString for a label or push button is really of type XmString. In resource files we could use ASCII strings but if we want to set the resource directly in the program we must use an XmString:

```
XtSetArg (args[n], XmNlabelString, xmstr); n++;
```

XmStrings are essentially opaque objects. If you want to find out what is in one, there is a range of functions to decode it. If the string has been created from an ASCII string with no embedded carriage returns by using XmStringCreateL-toR(), you can use XmStringGetLtoR() to give a NULL terminated ASCII string from it:

```
XmStringGetLtoR(xmstr, XmSTRING_DEFAULT_CHARSET,
                &asciistr);
```

(If the string has embedded returns, each line would have been placed in a separate segment and you would have to use the more complex calls that extract segments one at a time.)

For example, to find out what the label is in a string:

```
Arg args[1];
XmString xmstr;
String asciistr;

XtSetArg (args[0], XmNlabelString, &xmstr);
XtGetValues (button_widget, args, 1);
XmStringGetLtoR(xmstr, XmSTRING_DEFAULT_CHARSET,
```

---

[5] This may disappear in later versions of Motif.

```
                    &asciistr);
    printf("Button label was %s\n", asciistr);
```

There are several convenience routines for use with `XmStrings` such as:
```
Bool XmStringCompare (xmstr1, xmstr2)
XmString XmStringConcat (xmstr1, xmstr2)
XmString XmStringCopy (xmstr)
```
The most important of the additional `XmString` routines is `XmString-Free()` which takes an `XmString` and reclaims the space used for it. If an application continually creates `XmStrings` and does not free them when they are no longer needed, it will eventually run out of space[6].

7.3.1 Summary

Motif uses the the the types `String` and `XmString`. To convert between them, use:
```
XmStringCreateLtoR ()
XmStringGetLtoR ()
```
In resource files ordinary strings are used but in programs, resources are usually of the type `XmString`. There are a few convenience routines to manipulate `XmStrings`.

7.4 Callbacks

A widget should be regarded as an object which is a window and all its associated semantics. It is self-contained with its own internal state, and it knows how to respond to messages sent to it. An arrow widget displays an arrow with a direction, foreground and background colors; changes appearance when the pointer is pushed and released in it; and responds to requests from the window manager to move, change size, etc. Its internal state includes the direction, foreground and background. The messages it understands include button pushes from the user when the pointer is in the arrow and requests from other widgets to change size. These actions are all performed opaquely with the applications programmer not seeing (nor worrying about) the internals of its performance. The applications programmer is not involved at all with these actions, in that all of the code to handle them is supplied either by the object or by the Intrinsics layer.

However, it is necessary for the application to have more interaction with a widget than this. The widget so far is completely uncontrollable by the application once it has been created. In fact we do not have any mechanism yet to place application specific code in the program—we have set up the visible geometry of the appli-

---

[6] Having said that, there are 'memory leaks' with the implementation of `XmStrings` in Motif 1.0, so a Motif 1.0 application will possibly run out of space in any case.

cation by creating the widgets, but once the application enters the main loop it is totally under the control of the user, who chooses things to do, with the widgets responding to the user choices.

It is common in object-oriented systems for objects to *reply* to certain messages, thereby giving external information. X widgets do something vaguely similar to this: when a widget enters certain internal states it can 'inform' the rest of the system by calling application code.

A widget internally performs *actions* in response to external events. The actions associated with these changes are documented for each widget in the Motif Programmers's Manual. In the text we describe the Motif 1.1 documentation and in footnotes, how the the Motif 1.0 documentation differs. For any widget, the section on Action Routines in the manual entry for that widget describes each of the actions the widget can perform. For example, for the arrow widget the section documents the `Arm()` action[7] by:

Arm( ): Draws the shadow in the selected state and calls the callbacks for **XmNarmCallback**.

'Drawing the shadow in selected state' means that the shadow around the arrow is redrawn so that it appears depressed into the surface. The phrase 'calls the callbacks for XmNarmCallback' will be explained shortly. To find out how this action occurs, look at the Translations section. This states that `BSelectPress` (i.e. press the left button, usually) invokes the `Arm()` action. This associates a user action (pressing the left button) with an internal widget action `Arm()`. Similarly, releasing the button invokes the `DisArm()` action, which redraws the button in deselected state and calls the callbacks for `XmNdisarmCallback`. This establishes the connection between user actions and widget actions. (The reason you have to look in two places, the Actions and the Translations sections, is that the connection may be configured. This is dealt with in Section 11.1.)

To inform the rest of the system, a roundabout mechanism must be used because C is not an object-oriented language. We would like the application to be able to do something when the internal action `Arm()` takes place. In a pure object-oriented language a message would be sent to the object containing the application code. This is not possible in C. To overcome this, at some stage a widget is passed the

---

[7] In the Motif 1.0 Programmer's Reference manual they are documented in a rather roundabout way and you have to work at finding them from the documentation. For example, for the arrow-button widget the Behavior section of its manual page includes the following: '<Btn1Down> This action causes the arrow to be armed and the arrow to be drawn in the selected state. The callbacks for XmNarmCallback are called' and the Default Translations section includes '<Btn1Down>: Arm( )'. From this, deduce that one of the internal actions of the arrow button is `Arm()` and it causes the arrow to be drawn in the selected state.

addresses of a set of functions to execute whenever one of these actions must be performed. The object 'sends a message' by calling the application-specific code contained in the functions. These functions are named *Callback* functions, which are placed on callback lists associated with callback names.

An arrow widget has a number of callbacks. They are documented under the Resource Set section(s) of the widget manual entry as XmN<*name*>Callback. The callbacks for the arrow are: *activate, arm, disarm*, which are new to that widget; *help* which is inherited from the Primitive widget; and *destroy* from the Core widget. An application function will be placed on one of these callback lists and when an action is performed by the widget the functions on the appropriate callback lists will be executed[8].

Note this complex route: the user does things like pressing keys and buttons to make the widget do things. Some of these user actions invoke internal actions of the widget. Some of these internal actions may in turn call application code (see Figure 19). Let us look at some of the variations. Look first in the Translations section of the arrow widget documentation to see what various key and button presses do. For example, pressing the `<BExtend>` button (the right button, button three) is not documented as doing anything, so it does not. Pressing the `<BExtend>` button in the arrow has no effect on the arrow and no application code is ever called. However, pressing the `<BSelect>` button (the left button, button one) *is* documented: it invokes the action `Arm()`. Turn now to the Actions section of the arrow widget documentation to both see the effect on the arrow and find the callback lists called. In this case (as already noted) it calls all of the application functions on the arm callback list. Similarly, the `<KActivate>` key (the `<return>` key) invokes the action

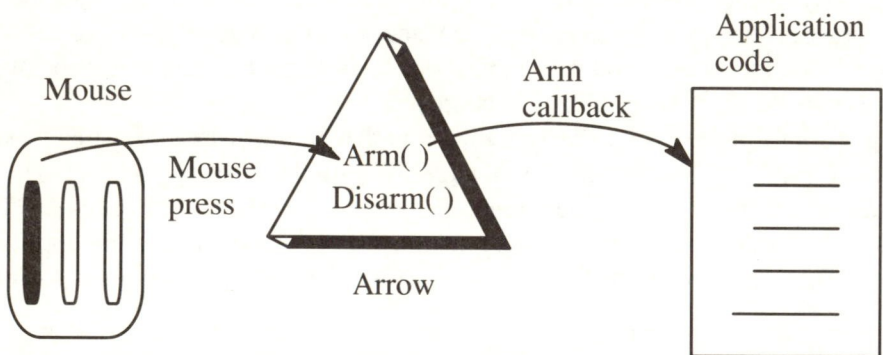

Figure 19:   Relating user actions to application code

---

[8] You can compare the documentation for Behavior and Default Translations in Motif 1.0 and make this assumption: when the widget internally performs the Arm( ) action, it also calls the callback functions on its armCallback list.

`ArmAndActivate()`. The action `ArmAndActivate()` invokes application code via two sets of callbacks: all the functions on the arm and activate callback lists are executed.

The missing steps in this route are first, how you actually place the application functions on these callback lists and second, what does their invocation look like? Application functions are added to these lists by the function `XtAddCallback()`, which takes the widget, the name of the callback, the address of your application specific C function and an argument which is usually `NULL`. The arrow program does not terminate. We can make it do so by adding an exit procedure (`quitX()`) to the arm callback:

```
XtAddCallback(arrow_widget, XmNarmCallback,
              quitX, NULL);
```

where `quitX()` (in this case) does an `exit(0)`. (*NB:* the function named in the `XtAddCallback()` must have been declared *before* the call because otherwise the C compiler will not have an address for it.) The `XtAddCallback()` statement generally appears directly after the widget creation statement. (The program appears on page 104 if you want to look ahead and see in stages the result of this quite complex set of ideas).

The functions called have a number of arguments. The callback function is invoked with three arguments:

```
void <Callback_func>(w, client_data, call_data)
    Widget w;
    caddr_t client_data;
    caddr_t call_data
```

The widget given as the first argument to the function is the widget with the action that invoked the function (here, our arrow widget). The `client_data` is a pointer to some application-defined structure. This pointer should have been passed to the widget at the time the callback was established (the last argument to `XtAdd-Callback()`, which was `NULL`) and is passed through unchanged. It can be used to pass information through from the time the callback was added to the time the callback function was invoked. It will be shown used in later programs (for example, in the pop-up editor of Section 10.2.2) where it forms a very effective mechanism for localizing data. The `call_data` is some widget-dependent structure which may give extra information about the callback. Most applications do not use this structure. The structure passed is documented in the widget entry. Note that although the documentation implies that a structure is passed in, this is not allowed in Kernighan and Ritchie C; it is actually a *pointer* to the structure that is the function argument. For the arrow widget it is, in Motif 1.1[9],

```
typedef struct
{   int reason;
```

---

[9] Motif 1.0 passes in a structure of type `XmAnyCallbackStruct` which only has the two fields shown of the 1.1 structure.

```
        XEvent *event;
        ....
} XmArrowButtonCallbackStruct
```

The 'reason' field is documented in the widget that first defines the callback; e.g. for an arrow a callback resource is `XmNarmCallback`. If this callback is invoked, the reason is `XmCR_ARM`. In a deep inheritance hierarchy this may involve looking up a large number of manual pages. For example, to find the reason for a destroy callback, the manual for `Core` widget must be consulted. The reasons are all defined in `<Xm/Xm.h>`. The event field allows extraction of information about the event that caused the callback to be invoked. This is an ordinary Xlib event, with a type field and so on. It is rarely used.

Callbacks are the principal means of getting application actions to be performed by widgets. A program illustrating this is `arrow_quit.c`.

Program 11: arrow_quit.c

```c
#include <X11/Intrinsic.h>
#include <Xm/Xm.h>
#include <Xm/ArrowB.h>

char Class_name[] = "Arrow";

void quitX (w, client_d, call_d)
Widget w;
caddr_t client_d, call_d;
{
        printf ("arrow was pushed\n");
        exit (0);
}

main (argc, argv)
int argc;
char **argv;
{
        Widget toplevel, arrow_widget;
        Arg wargs[2]; /* wargs not really used here */

         /* Initialize the intrinsics  with
            a toplevel widget */
        toplevel = XtInitialize (NULL, /* application
                                          name */
                      Class_name,  /* class name */

                      NULL,          /* options */
                      0,             /* number of
```

```
                                              options */
                    &argc, argv);

        /* Create an arrow widget with the
           toplevel as manager;
        */
        arrow_widget = XmCreateArrowButton (
                           toplevel,    /* parent */
                           "an_arrow",  /* name */
                           wargs,       /* resource
                                           arguments */
                           0);          /* number
                                           of args */
        XtManageChild (arrow_widget);
        XtAddCallback (arrow_widget, XNarmCallback,
                       quitX, NULL);  m

        /* display all of the widgets */
        XtRealizeWidget (toplevel);

        /* enter the main processing loop */
        XtMainLoop ();
}
```

This program creates a toplevel widget and a child arrow-widget. No resources are set. The arrow is managed, windows are created by `XtRealizeWidget()` and then the program enters the event processing loop. A callback to the function `quitX()` is added to the arrow so that whenever the arrow is pressed the `quitX()` function is called.

It is important to stop here and consider what has been accomplished. This is a simple program in that it has only a single arrow showing. However, the user has control over the environment in a *modeless* way. The user can ignore this application and interact with others, or choose to interact with the application in whatever manner desired. All the application can do is respond in a suitable way when the user performs an action. Thus the application has lost control of the interaction, which is as it should be. When the user wishes the application to perform some action he or she signals by some appropriate action, which for our program is to press the left button on the arrow. The application code should then act according to the following principle: it has been handed control to perform a user-desired action. It should perform that action, and that alone, and then relinquish control to the user. That is, the callback function should do as little as it needs to do, and then return, so that the user can resume control. (Here the function terminates the application and never returns—a special case.)

7.4.1 Summary

User events are related to internal widget actions through the Translation Table.
Internal actions are related to callback lists through the Action routines. When an
appropriate user event occurs, all the functions on the corresponding callback lists
are executed. Application functions are placed on callback lists by:

```
XtAddCallback ()
```

Exercises

1. Add a callback procedure to the arrow widget for the 'arm' callback which
   writes 'Ouch!' to standard output when the button is pressed, and another to the
   'disarm' callback that writes 'That's better!' when released.

2. What happens when the <return> key is pressed?

7.5 Motif key and button bindings

If you are using Motif 1.0, the key and button bindings are fairly straightforward:
`<Btn1Down>`, `<Btn1Up>`, `<Key>Return`, `<Key>A`, etc.

In Motif 1.1, a layer of abstraction (in fact two layers) was placed above this for
arguable reasons. First, keys and buttons are described in terms of their *function*
rather than by what they are. Thus, for example, in describing the key to move up by
an item in a list, the key is called `KUp` (rather than `<Key>Up`) and the button that is
pressed to select an item is `BSelect` (rather than `<Btn1Down>`). The actual binding
of these virtual keys and buttons to real keys and buttons is documented in the manual entry VirtualBindings(3Xm). The second layer is that some keys are known by
names which are not part of the X system and begin with 'osf' such as `<Key>osfUp`,
`<Key>osfBeginLine`. There is a default mapping of these to keys that X knows
about. For example, `<Key>osfUp` is mapped to `<Key>Up`, `<Key>osfBeginLine`
to `<Key>Home`. This default is also given in VirtualBindings, which also describes
how these can be configured using the resource `defaultVirtualBindings`.

Exercise

1. What is the help key in Motif?

7.6 Reading the documentation

In this section we will look at the Motif 1.1 manual entry for a typical widget, in this case the PushButton. (The Motif 1.0 entry is similar but less clear.) The reason for doing this is simple: any Motif programmer will need to spend many hours reading the actual manuals, so a guided walkthrough should be beneficial. A manual page has the following format:

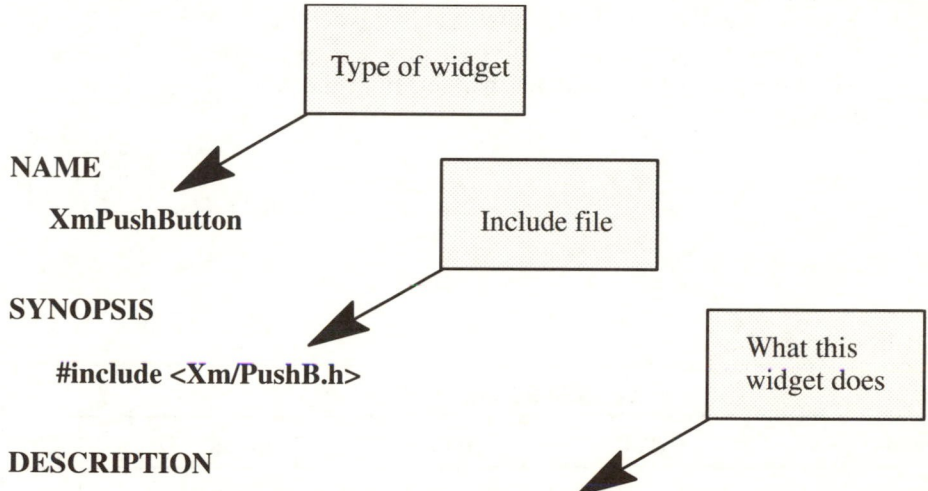

NAME

    XmPushButton

SYNOPSIS

    #include <Xm/PushB.h>

DESCRIPTION

    PushButton issues commands within an application. It consists of a text label or pixmap surrounded by a border shadow. When a PushButton is selected, the shadow changes to give the appearance that it has been pressed in. When a PushButton is unselected, the shadow changes to give the appearance that it is out.

Classes

    PushButton inherits behavior and resources from **Core**, **XmPrimitive**, and **XmLabel** Classes.

    The class name is **XmPushButton.**

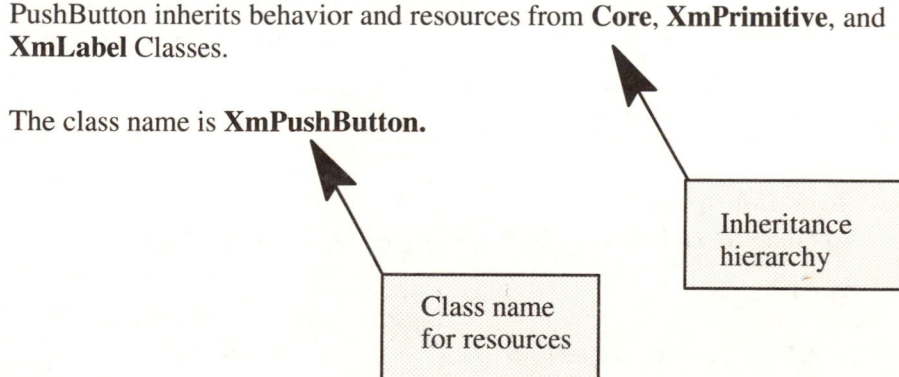

New Resources

XmPushButton Resource Set				
Name	**Class**	**Type**	**Default**	**Access**
XmNarmCallback	XmCCallback	XtCallbackL...	NULL	C
XmNarmColor	XmCArmColor	Pixel	dyn...	...G

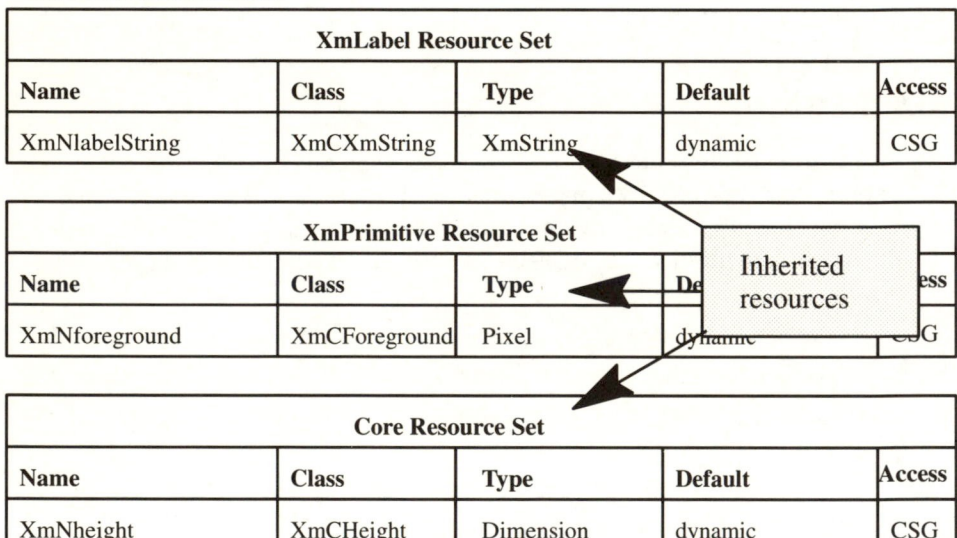

New resource
table

XmNarmCallback

Specifies the list of callbacks that is called when Pus...
PushButton is armed when the user presses the active mouse button
while the pointer is inside that widget. For this callback the reason is
XmCR_ARM.

New resource
description

Inherited Resources

XmLabel Resource Set				
Name	**Class**	**Type**	**Default**	**Access**
XmNlabelString	XmCXmString	XmString	dynamic	CSG

XmPrimitive Resource Set				
Name	**Class**	**Type**	**De...**	**...ss**
XmNforeground	XmCForeground	Pixel	dynamic	...G

Inherited
resources

Core Resource Set				
Name	**Class**	**Type**	**Default**	**Access**
XmNheight	XmCHeight	Dimension	dynamic	CSG

Callback Information

A pointer to the following structure is passed to each callback:

```
typedef struct
{ ...
} XmPushButtonCallbackStruct
```

Structure returned
as call data

Translations

BSelectPress:	**Arm( )**
BSelectClick:	**Activate( )**
	Disarm( )

> User actions to widget actions

Action Routines

Activate( );

> This action draws the shadow in the unarmed state. If the pointer is still within the button, this action calls the callbacks for **XmNactivateCallback**.

> Widget actions and callbacks invoked

What can we learn from this? From the widget type, there is a routine `XmCrea-tePushButton()`. To use this, the include file `<Xm/PushB.h>` must be included. The 'DESCRIPTION' section, in true Unix style, gives a potted version of what a PushButton will do. In the 'Classes' section, the inheritance hierarchy is given. This hierarchy is vital but quite daunting to begin with. It is discussed in more detail both later in this section and in the next chapter.

The classname is given as `XmPushButton`. Every PushButton created has both an instance name and a class name. The class name can be used in resource files to give generic behavior:

```
*XmPushButton.foreground:       red
```

The 'New Resources' section tells you what is new about PushButtons that is not inherited. For example, the PushButton has a number of new callbacks such as `XmNarmCallback`. The 'Inherited Resources' section fills in the rest of the resources from the inheritance hierarchy. For example, every Button can show a label—this comes from the Label widget; each PushButton has a foreground color, from XmPrimitive; every PushButton has a height from Core. As you become more familiar with the hierarchies, you will get to know where the resources come from. For example, every widget has a width and height because every widget inherits from Core which has these resources. Every Primitive widget has a foreground color because they draw something against the background.

The next section, on 'Callback Information' gives information about the structure that is the call-data parameter in each callback function. This allows the program to get extra information about the circumstances that caused it to be executed.

The Translations section links user actions to widget actions. For example, when the left button is clicked within the widget, it takes two actions: `Activate()` and `Disarm()`. To find out what each of these does look at the 'Action Routines' section, where the effect of each action on the widget is described, and the callbacks executed are listed.

Chapter 8

Multiple widgets

This chapter discusses the basic techniques needed to write multiple-widget programs. It discusses the major geometry management widgets that control how widgets are placed next to each other.

8.1 Multiple-widget programs

So far we have dealt with programs containing only a single widget (apart from a toplevel shell widget). This has been the ArrowButton widget in the examples and both the Label and PushButton widgets in the exercises. The ArrowButton displays a triangular arrow that can be pressed. The Label displays a static piece of text and the PushButton displays a piece of text and can also be pressed by clicking the mouse on it. There are many other widgets which will be surveyed in the next chapter. In the meantime, it is more important to look at how applications containing more than one widget are created and controlled.

Any non-trivial application will contain many widgets. All widgets have to be created with other widgets as parents, forming a tree of widgets. This is controlled by the creation routines.

Programs using many widgets have the following format:

```
#include<Xm.widget.h>

XtInitialize(...)
for each widget
    /* set up argument lists for the widget */
    XtSetArg(...)
    /* create widget */
    XmCreate<widget>(...)
    /* and manage it */
    XtManageChild(...)
```

```
          /* add callback routines */
          XtAddCallback()
   /* realize widgets and loop */
   XtRealizeWidget(main_widget)
   XtMainLoop()
```

In addition to parenting, the widgets have a particular geometric relation to each other so the window(s) of one widget will appear next to, or above, etc, the window(s) of another. This is controlled by resources on the individual and on *container* widgets. A container widget is specifically designed to hold other widgets. There are a number of these, varying in their capability. Some are also *constraint* widgets that also control the positioning and size of the widgets they contain. The most commonly used of these container widgets are the RowColumn and Form widgets.

The following program `four.c` places four PushButton widgets together in a window. It uses a RowColumn container to place the four widgets. Each PushButton displays a piece of text in a rectangular window, as in Figure 20. The widget hierarchy is shown in Figure 21.

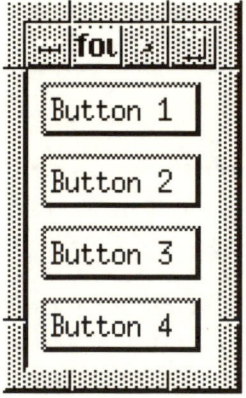

Figure 20:   Four buttons in a RowColumn

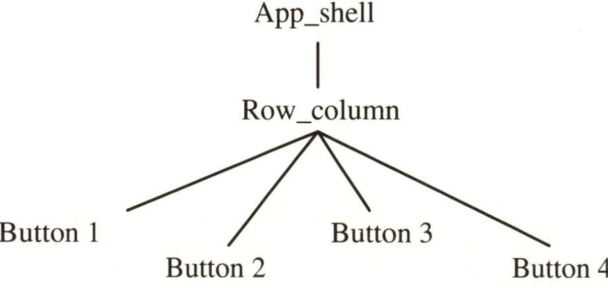

Figure 21:   Widget tree for `four.c`

Program 12:   four.c

```
#include <stdio.h>

#include <Xm/PushB.h>
#include <Xm/RowColumn.h>

/*-----------------------------------------------------
**          Forward Declarations
*/

void main ();                      /*  main logic for
                                       application  */

void CreateApplication ();     /*  create main window */
void QuitCB ();                /*  callback for
                                   quit button     */

/*-----------------------------------------------------
**          Global Variables
*/

#define MAX_ARGS 20
#define Class_name "FourButtons"

main (argc,argv)
    int     argc;
    char    **argv;
{
    Widget  app_shell;

    /* Initialize toolkit, open the display
       and create the toplevel widget. */
    app_shell  =  XtInitialize(NULL,   /*  application
                                           name */
                      Class_name,  /* class name */
                      NULL,        /* options */
                       0,          /* number of
                                      options */
                      &argc, argv);

    /* set up all the sub-widgets */
    CreateApplication(app_shell);
    XtRealizeWidget (app_shell);
```

```
          /* Get and dispatch events. */
          XtMainLoop ();
}


/*---------------------------------------------------------
**          CreateApplication          - create main window
**          This must be customized
**          for each application.
*/
void CreateApplication (parent)
     Widget  parent;        /*  parent widget */
{
     Widget row_column;  /* RowColumn            */
     Widget  button;        /*  PushButton         */

     Arg       args[MAX_ARGS]; /*  arg list      */
     int    n;         /*  arg count      */

     /*       Create RowColumn Window. */
     n = 0;
     row_column     =       XmCreateRowColumn      (parent,
                    "rowColumn", args, n);
     XtManageChild (row_column);

     n = 0;
     button = XmCreatePushButton (row_column,
                              "Button 1", args, n);
     XtManageChild (button);
     XtAddCallback (button, XmNactivateCallback,
                              QuitCB, NULL);

     n = 0;
     button = XmCreatePushButton (row_column,
                              "Button 2", args, n);
     XtManageChild (button);
     XtAddCallback (button, XmNactivateCallback,
                              QuitCB, NULL);

     n = 0;
     button = XmCreatePushButton (row_column,
                              "Button 3", args, n);
     XtManageChild (button);
     XtAddCallback (button, XmNactivateCallback,
                              QuitCB, NULL);

     n = 0;
```

```
        button = XmCreatePushButton (row_column,
                                  "Button 4", args, n);
        XtManageChild (button);
        XtAddCallback (button, XmNactivateCallback,
                                  QuitCB, NULL);
}


/*-----------------------------------------------------------
**        QuitCB              - callback for quit button
*/
void QuitCB (w, client_data, call_data)
    Widget      w;            /*  widget id   */
    caddr_t     client_data; /* data from application */
    caddr_t     call_data;   /* data from widget call */
{

    /*  Terminate the application. */
    printf("button was pressed\n");
    exit (0);
}
```

The widgets in this application have no resources set. In general, widgets have their resources set individually, so 'Button 1,' 'Button 2,' etc. are controlled separately. In programs, the previously discussed methods of setting resources by the creation routine or by `XtSetValues()` are used. In resource files, the path to a widget is used. This path consists of the application name, through all of the widget's ancestors down to the widget itself. (The shell widget is not included in this.) Thus to set the label of 'Button 1' to something else, use:

```
four.rowColumn.Button 1.labelString:    something else
```

or any of the Class names or '*' wildcards.

Is this really all there is to it? Well, yes and no. What is correct is the structure. What is missing is, first, serious application code. All of the widgets call the same callback, which does very little. In a real application the callbacks represent the programming interface between the application code and the widgets, so this should be much more substantial. The second component that is weak is the lack of control used over the widget behavior. Each widget has a large number of resources but we have set none of them. A real application would set many of them, either in the code or in one of the resource files.

The major weakness from the point of view of this section, though, is the lack of layout or geometry control. We have just placed four push-button widgets into a row column. Is this appropriate? What does it look like? How is it controlled? Everything has been left to defaults. The next section considers the RowColumn widget in more detail to answer these questions.

8.1.1 Summary

Multiple widgets are placed into the widget tree by the creation routine. Each widget must be managed. Each widget has its own callback list. Each widget can have resources individually set. The resource path to a widget consists of its name and those of all its ancestors. Many widgets can share a container as parent.

Exercises

1. What happens when the user resizes a RowColumn, for example, making it shorter and wider?

2. What happens in the RowColumn if different-size labels are used?

3. Place two buttons inside one RowColumn, two more inside another, and both inside a third. What does it look like? How does it behave on resizing?

8.2 Row Column

Geometry management controls how widgets are laid out on the screen and how they change shape and position when windows are resized. The two primary Motif geometry managers are RowColumn and Form. RowColumn is best used when all children are of the same type and are laid out in a regular fashion. Even so, there are many complexities to 'regularity' and it is important to find out how RowColumn can be configured. RowColumn unfortunately has a multiple role in Motif. It doubles as many kinds of objects, many of them related to menus. For example, it also acts as a 'menu bar' and as a 'pop-up menu pane.' This behavior should probably have been done in subclasses, but for now you simply have to accept a widget that changes behavior because it has the role of several objects.

The most important resource of RowColumn is `XmNorientation` which can take the values `XmHORIZONTAL` or `XmVERTICAL`. This controls the direction in which children are added to it. The default is given in the tables as 'dynamic,' but if you read about this resource you find that it is vertical (unless the RowColumn is being used in a menu bar). Each child is added below the last in vertical mode, in vertical columns. If you want them to be laid out side-by-side, set this resource to `XmHORIZONTAL`. The example of the last section did not set the resource, so it takes the default value. You can change this either by programming or in resource files. For example, to make the four widgets appear horizontally, put this in a resource file:

```
*XmRowColumn.orientation:    horizontal
```

(You may often wish to use a less general pattern — this changes *all* RowColumns unless they have the resource value specified.)

The next most important resource is `XmNpacking`. This, like many other Row-Column resources, depends on whether the orientation is vertical or horizontal. We will assume the default of vertical. If you set it to horizontal, swap all occurrences of horizontal to vertical and vice-versa. The default is given in the tables as dynamic because of the way RowColumn is used in menus and boxes. For direct use it defaults to `XmPACK_TIGHT`.

If the packing is set to `PACK_NONE`, no particular attempt is made to make the children look regular.

If the packing is set to `PACK_TIGHT`, it means that the children will be arranged in columns where within each column the children have the same width. Different columns may have different widths, so for example, the first column could be twenty pixels wide, the second thirty pixels wide and so on. The RowColumn may have a height set by other constraints. In this case it will start another column when it cannot fit any more children into the current column.

If the packing is set to `PACK_COLUMN` *all* children are made the same size (the maximum size needed for all children). This gives the most regular arrangement.

Following this is `XmNnumColumns`. This resource only has meaning when packing is set to `PACK_COLUMN`. It gives the number of columns to put the children into. Alas, there is no way to specify the number of rows even though I always find that to be the number I want to specify. For example, to put thirty children into columns, with three rows, you have to specify `XmNnumColumns` as ten.

The remaining resources are mainly concerned with menus or obscure uses. Two others, though, have a strong impact on the Motif programmer: `XmNisAligned` and `XmNentryAlignment`. Motif containers will sometimes change the behavior of their children, depending on what they are. RowColumn does things to Labels and descendants of Labels such as PushButtons. The default for a Label is to center the text. This can be controlled on a per-Label basis by the Label resource `XmNalignment`. RowColumn allows you to align the text of *all* label children with a single RowColumn resource. If `XmNisAligned` is set to `True`, the alignment of all Labels and descendants is controlled by the RowColumn resource `XmNentryAlignment`. The values and meaning of `XmNentryAlignment` are the same as those of the Label resource `XmNalignment`—aligned to the beginning, the end or centered. In general this is quite convenient, unless you get caught by it unexpectedly.

8.2.1 Summary

RowColumn imposes a simple geometry control on its children using the resources:

```
XmNorientation
XmNpacking
XmNnumColumns
```

Useful resources to control Label children are:

```
XmNalignment
XmNisAligned
```

8.3   Example: Noughts and crosses

This section illustrates many of the Motif concepts dealt with so far:

- Widget creation.

- Widget control through resources.

- The widget container RowColumn.

- Responding to user actions through callbacks.

- XmStrings.

The noughts and crosses problem has been set as a major assignment for Xlib. Ignoring the complexities (such as who won), let us re-examine this as a Motif problem. First, we will not bother drawing Xs and Os because they are not part of Motif. It is easier to use Labels and just put the characters X and O in them. You can draw in Motif, but only using the DrawingArea widget. The DrawingArea widget is designed for doing in Xlib the things you cannot do in Motif. While valuable, use of the DrawingArea widget is not a common activity so we use the Motif-supplied mechanisms instead. If you want to change the size of the Xs and Os, use a bigger font in the command-line option `-font` or in a resource file.

The geometry is regular as a three-by-three square of identical objects, so a RowColumn is suitable as a container. This must be configured to make each square of identical size, with three columns. If it contains labels, it would look neater if the text was centered, so this should also be set.

We will use a Label or label-derived widget for each square because it draws the text for us itself. The user would expect things to occur when the mouse is clicked in a square. Label does not handle this, but its descendant PushButton does: when the left button is pressed in the button the `Arm()` action is executed. Callback functions can be attached to this `Arm()` action which attempt to fill in an X or O. The function `pushed()` in the following program is designed to do this. It writes a nought or a cross into a square if it does not already have a value, and changes the player.

An Xlib noughts and crosses program has to maintain information about the content of each window because it is not possible to extract information easily from the window. A push button contains a label and it *is* easy to get it back from the button: just ask for it by `XtGetValues()`. The label is encoded as an `XmString` and it is set and retrieved using this datatype. We can use the XmString convenience function XmStringCompare() to find out if we have a space, a O or an X showing. Noughts and crosses in Motif is shown as a screendump in Figure 22.

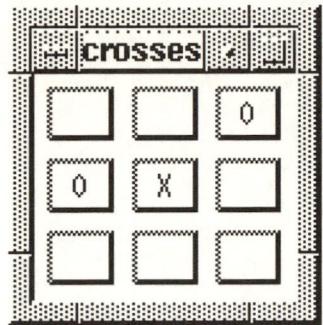

Figure 22: Motif noughts and crosses

The program to give this is:

Program 13: crosses.c

```
#include <Xm/PushB.h>
#include <Xm/RowColumn.h>

char Class_name[] = "Crosses";
XmString blank, nought, cross;
int turn;      /* 0 = nought, 1 = cross */

/* Callback invoked on Arm action when a
** button is pressed
*/
void
pushed (w, client_d, call_d)
     Widget w;
     caddr_t client_d, call_d;
{    XmString xmstr;
     char str[8];
     Arg args[16];
     int n;
     /* find the current label in the button */
     n = 0;
     XtSetArg (args[n], XmNlabelString, &xmstr); n++;
     XtGetValues (w, args, n);

     /* change the label if it is a blank */
     if (XmStringCompare (xmstr, blank))
```

```
        {       n = 0;
                if (turn == 0)
                        XtSetArg (args[n], XmNlabelString,
                                  nought);
                else    XtSetArg (args[n], XmNlabelString,
                                  cross);
                n++;
                XtSetValues (w, args, n);
                /* update the turn */
                turn = (turn + 1) % 2;
        }
}
main (argc, argv)
        int argc;
        char **argv;
{
        Widget toplevel, button, rowcol;
        Arg args[16];
        int i, n;

        turn = 0;       /* nought always starts */
        /* set up the XmStrings */
        blank = XmStringCreateLtoR ("      ",
                        XmSTRING_DEFAULT_CHARSET);
                        /* 3 blank spaces */
        nought = XmStringCreateLtoR ("0",
                        XmSTRING_DEFAULT_CHARSET);
        cross = XmStringCreateLtoR ("X",
                        XmSTRING_DEFAULT_CHARSET);
        /* Initialize the intrinsics
           with a toplevel widget  */
        toplevel = XtInitialize (NULL,        /* application
                                                name */
                        Class_name,    /* class
                                          name */
                         NULL,             /* options */
                         0,                /* number of
                                             options */
                        &argc, argv);
        /* Create a Row Column with the
           following resource values:
                all children the same size (PACK_COLUMN)
                3 columns (numColumns)
                all labels aligned the same way (isAligned)
                all labels centered (ALIGNMENT_CENTER)
        */
```

```
                n = 0;
                XtSetArg (args[n], XmNpacking, XmPACK_COLUMN); n++;
                XtSetArg (args[n], XmNnumColumns, 3); n++;
                XtSetArg (args[n], XmNisAligned, True); n++;
                    /
                XtSetArg (args[n], XmNentryAlignment,
                                        XmALIGNMENT_CENTER); n++;
                rowcol = XmCreateRowColumn (
                                        toplevel,/* parent */
                                        "rowcol", /* name     */
                                        args,     /* resource
                                                    arguments */
                                        n);       /* number of
                                                        args   */
            /* create 9 pushbutton children of rowcol with
                blank labels.
                all buttons are given the same name and
                have the same callback, because we don't
                need to distinguish them at all.
            */
            for (i = 0; i < 9; i++)
            {      n = 0;
                    XtSetArg (args[n], XmNlabelString, blank);
    n++;
                button = XmCreatePushButton (rowcol,
                                        "button", args, n);
                XtAddCallback (button, XmNarmCallback,
                                        pushed, NULL);
                XtManageChild (button);
            }
        XtManageChild (rowcol);

                /* display all of the widgets */
                XtRealizeWidget (toplevel);

                /* enter the main processing loop */
                XtMainLoop ();
    }
```

A walkthrough is again in order. Three XmStrings are created for each possible value in a square. These variables have to be global because they need to be accessed by the callback functions. The Xt style of programming unfortunately encourages many global variables because of this. We have used a blank square value of three spaces. First, this looks nicer on the screen. Second (the real reason for not using only one space) on my current machine running mwm with a fairly small font, the size of the final application window is quite small. It is too small for the window manager mwm to put a title and all of its buttons along the top, so mwm resizes it and spoils the regular appearance (because RowColumn does not manage resizing very well). The easy way to solve this is to make the application window larger by making each square larger.

The RowColumn widget is created with resources to make all its buttons the same size, with three columns, and with centered text on all labels. Nine PushButton children are created with blank labels. They all have the same name and the same callback. The implications are twofold: first, since they have the same name, they can all be controlled simultaneously in the resource files. Of course this can be done through the class name, but this is another way. Second, when the callback is invoked it will not have much information to distinguish which button is pushed. It has the widget as a parameter, but that does not convey much in this program. It is left to the exercises to show how the last argument to XtAddCallback() can be used to convey useful information.

The callback function extracts the current label from the button. This is of type XmString, so the function XmStringCompare() is used to check that it is blank before resetting it to the new value with XtSetValues(). This is all that is required to change the label.

Finally, some comments are in order about the appearance of this version of noughts and crosses. An inspection of Figure 22 shows that it is not the 'classical' board. Each square is a button raised to show that it can be pushed, and they are all separated from each other. Part of the Motif style is that anything that can be pushed should be raised, to show that this can happen. If the widgets were flat (like Label widgets) then pushing them would not succeed in doing anything! (Despite this, you can make the buttons appear flat—see the Exercises.)

8.3.1 Summary

An example has been discussed illustrating the following:
1. Multiple widgets in a RowColumn.

2. Setting and getting widget resources.

3. Use of XmString.

4. Use of callback functions.

Exercises

1. The program checks whether or not the button is blank before adding to it: blank buttons can still be pressed. Xt can make buttons *insensitive* so that they cannot be activated. Use `XtSetSensitive()` to disallow buttons instead.

2. Encode the widget number as the last parameter to `XtAddCallback()` so that it can be extracted as client information in the callback. Watch type casts, as you will be passing in an integer when the function call expects a pointer.

3. Make the crosses screen look like the normal game (flat buttons with an edge, etc.) by setting the push-button resources `XmNshadowThickness`, `XmNhighlightThickness` and `XmNborderWidth`, and the RowColumn resource `XmNspacing`.

8.4 Form

Form is the other major geometry manager besides the RowColumn. It can handle widgets of differing sizes and attempts to place them in quite complex geometric arrangements. If you look at a typical real-life form of any kind and attempt to work out how the components are related, you will often end up with something non-trivial. The power and the complexity of Form comes at a cost: it can be quite hard to drive Form and ensure that it gives the geometry you really want. Unfortunately, early versions of Form often could not cope with this. The Form would fail to show widgets, put them in the wrong place or just give up with a message 'bailing out...'. Many of these problems have been removed in later versions. By itself, the improvements in Form during the Motif releases are almost sufficient to justify switching from Motif 1.0 to Motif 1.1.

Widgets are placed in a Form by giving the Form as the parent. The default location is in the top-left corner, so the default will place all widgets on top of each other in this corner. The actual placement of each widget must be specified to avoid this. Form handles the *edges* of widgets. The positioning of the top, the bottom, the left and the right-hand edge of each widget can be specified. These are controlled by the resources `XmNtopAttachment`, etc.

Up to this point resource control has been done by looking at the resources of an individual widget and setting them. With Form, this changes. Each widget has its own set of resources as before, but in addition it must have the resources that Form requires. Resources such as `XmNtopAttachment` are put on the widget that is a child of the Form rather than on the Form itself. Form queries its children to find the values.

Widgets can be attached to the edge of the Form on any side. To do this, set the value of the appropriate attachment (top, bottom, left, right) to `XmATTACH_FORM`:

```
XtSetArg (args[n], XmNtopAttachment, XmATTACH_FORM); n++
```

You can set more than one side to be attached to the Form and if you set an opposing pair of sides, the child widget will have its size controlled in that direction. For example, if both the left and right sides are attached, the width of the widget is controlled by the Form. Often it will let the widget be the size it wants to be (e.g. big enough to hold its label) but sometimes it will override this and set the size to what it thinks is appropriate.

Another common attachment is to another widget. The value of the appropriate attachment is set to `XmATTACH_WIDGET` and then another resource is set to the widget the attachment is made to:

```
XtSetArg (args[n], XmNtopAttachment,
                        XmATTACH_WIDGET); n++;
XtSetArg (args[n], XmNtopWidget, the_other_widget); n++;
```

This setting can be used to place widgets next to each other (in any direction).

Instead of this, suppose we wanted two edges to have a common edge (say the left one) lined up together. For this, attach one widget's left edge *opposite* the other one:

```
XtSetArg (args[n], XmNleftAttachment,
                        XmATTACH_OPPOSITE_WIDGET); n++;
XtSetArg (args[n], XmNleftWidget,
                        the_other_widget); n++;
```

Another common setting is to place edges at proportionate positions in the Form. This can be used to attach an edge to say 30 per cent of the way along the Form. This is controlled by three resources. First, `XmNfractionBase` controls the units for positioning. The default is 100, so any position is set in hundredths of the distance across the Form (a percentage setting). If finer control is required, such as down to thousandths, reset this resource. Second, the attachment is set to `XmATTACH_POSITION` and the appropriate position is then set:

```
XtSetArg (args[n], XmNtopAttachment,
                        XmATTACH_POSITION); n++;
XtSetArg (args[n], XmNtopPosition, 50); n++;
```

Why are there so many possibilities? They allow a fine tuning of geometry as you try to get exactly what you want. For example, consider placing four widgets in a box in a rectangular arrangement as in Figure 23. In many circumstance a RowColumn may be the best bet, but not always. We will discuss the later in this chapter.

There are a number of ways of getting this geometry. The first, which we call Form1 is:

- Attach Widget 1 to the Form at the top and left.

- Attach Widget 2 to the Form on the left and bottom and Widget 1 at the top.
- Attach Widget 3 to the Form on the top and right, and to Widget 1 on the left.
- Attach Widget 4 to the Form on the right and bottom, to Widget 2 on the left and to Widget 3 on the top.

Widget 1	Widget 3
Widget 2	Widget 4

Figure 23:   Four widgets in a form

Form 1, and two others, are shown in Figure 24.

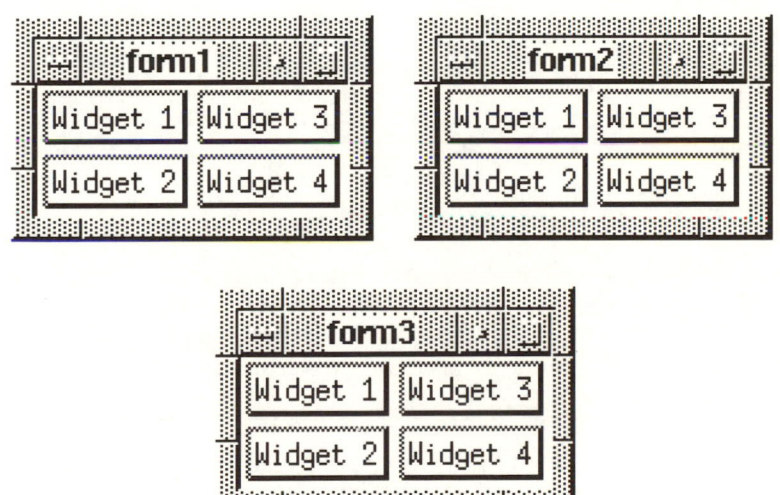

Figure 24:   The three Form programs

The code for geometry arrangements always looks messy:

Program 14:   form1.c

```
n = 0;
XtSetArg (args[n], XmNtopAttachment,
               XmATTACH_FORM); n++;
```

```
XtSetArg (args[n], XmNleftAttachment,
                   XmATTACH_FORM); n++;
XtSetValues (widget1, args, n);

n = 0;
XtSetArg (args[n], XmNtopAttachment,
                   XmATTACH_WIDGET); n++;
XtSetArg (args[n], XmNtopWidget, widget1); n++;
XtSetArg (args[n], XmNleftAttachment,
                   XmATTACH_FORM); n++;
XtSetArg (args[n], XmNbottomAttachment,
                   XmATTACH_FORM); n++;
XtSetValues (widget2, args, n);
n = 0;
XtSetArg (args[n], XmNtopAttachment,
                   XmATTACH_FORM); n++;
XtSetArg (args[n], XmNrightAttachment,
                   XmATTACH_FORM); n++;
XtSetArg (args[n], XmNleftAttachment,
                   XmATTACH_WIDGET); n++;
XtSetArg (args[n], XmNleftWidget, widget1); n++;
XtSetValues (widget3, args, n);
n = 0;
XtSetArg (args[n], XmNbottomAttachment,
                   XmATTACH_FORM); n++;
XtSetArg (args[n], XmNrightAttachment,
                   XmATTACH_FORM); n++;
XtSetArg (args[n], XmNtopAttachment,
                   XmATTACH_WIDGET); n++;
XtSetArg (args[n], XmNtopWidget, widget3); n++;
XtSetArg (args[n], XmNleftAttachment,
                   XmATTACH_WIDGET); n++;
XtSetArg (args[n], XmNleftWidget, widget2); n++;
XtSetValues (widget4, args, n);
```

An alternative method of achieving the same geometry appearance is Form 2, where widgets are attached to the Form as before but the inside edges are set to half-way across (or down) the Form. Part of the resource setting (for Widget 1) looks like:

Program 15:   form2.c

```
n = 0;
XtSetArg (args[n], XmNtopAttachment,
                   XmATTACH_FORM); n++;
XtSetArg (args[n], XmNleftAttachment,
                   XmATTACH_FORM); n++;
```

```
XtSetArg (args[n], XmNrightAttachment,
                   XmATTACH_POSITION); n++;
XtSetArg (args[n], XmNrightPosition, 50); n++;
XtSetArg (args[n], XmNbottomAttachment,
                   XmATTACH_POSITION); n++;
XtSetArg (args[n], XmNbottomPosition, 50); n++;
XtSetValues (widget1, args, n);
```

Yet another possibility is Form 3 where we attach Widget 1 and Widget 2 as in Form1, but also attach the right-hand side of Widget 2 to the right-hand side of Widget 1 using XmATTACH_OPPOSITE_WIDGET. Similarly, the left-hand side of Widget 4 is attached to the left-hand side of Widget 3:

Program 16: form3.c

```
n = 0;
XtSetArg (args[n], XmNtopAttachment,
                   XmATTACH_FORM); n++;
XtSetArg (args[n], XmNleftAttachment,
                   XmATTACH_FORM); n++;
XtSetValues (widget1, args, n);
n = 0;
XtSetArg (args[n], XmNtopAttachment,
                   XmATTACH_WIDGET); n++;
XtSetArg (args[n], XmNtopWidget, widget1); n++;
XtSetArg (args[n], XmNleftAttachment,
                   XmATTACH_FORM); n++;
XtSetArg (args[n], XmNbottomAttachment,
                   XmATTACH_FORM); n++;
XtSetArg (args[n], XmNrightAttachment,
                   XmATTACH_OPPOSITE_WIDGET); n++;
XtSetArg (args[n], XmNrightWidget, widget1); n++;
XtSetValues (widget2, args, n);
n = 0;
XtSetArg (args[n], XmNtopAttachment,
                   XmATTACH_FORM); n++;
XtSetArg (args[n], XmNrightAttachment,
                   XmATTACH_FORM); n++;
XtSetArg (args[n], XmNleftAttachment,
                   XmATTACH_WIDGET); n++;
XtSetArg (args[n], XmNleftWidget, widget1); n++;
XtSetValues (widget3, args, n);
n = 0;
XtSetArg (args[n], XmNbottomAttachment,
                   XmATTACH_FORM); n++;
XtSetArg (args[n], XmNrightAttachment,
```

```
                                XmATTACH_FORM); n++;
XtSetArg (args[n], XmNtopAttachment,
                    XmATTACH_WIDGET); n++;
XtSetArg (args[n], XmNtopWidget, widget3); n++;
XtSetArg (args[n], XmNleftAttachment,
                    XmATTACH_OPPOSITE_WIDGET); n++;
XtSetArg (args[n], XmNleftWidget, widget3); n++;
XtSetValues (widget4, args, n);
```

We have three versions, as shown in Figure 24. They all look the same. What then are the differences? The differences are twofold and depend upon the initial preferred sizes of the widgets and what happens to them on resizing. Any widget has its 'preferred size.' For a Label, this is the width needed to draw the text of the widget, which is the same for each widget in this case. The first point to note is that any widget with both sides attached to something will have its width totally controlled by the Form, rather than using its preferred size. Similarly, its height is controlled if it is attached at the top and the bottom. Usually Form does a reasonable job of sizing the widgets, but odd things can happen. Figure 25 shows the attachments of each of the three geometry arrangements.

Figure 26 shows what happens to each widget when its containing Form is enlarged. For the widgets of Form1, Widget 1 is left to its preferred size as it is only attached on the top and left. Widget 2 is attached at the top and bottom, so it stretches vertically. Its width stays unaltered as it is only attached on the left. Widget 3

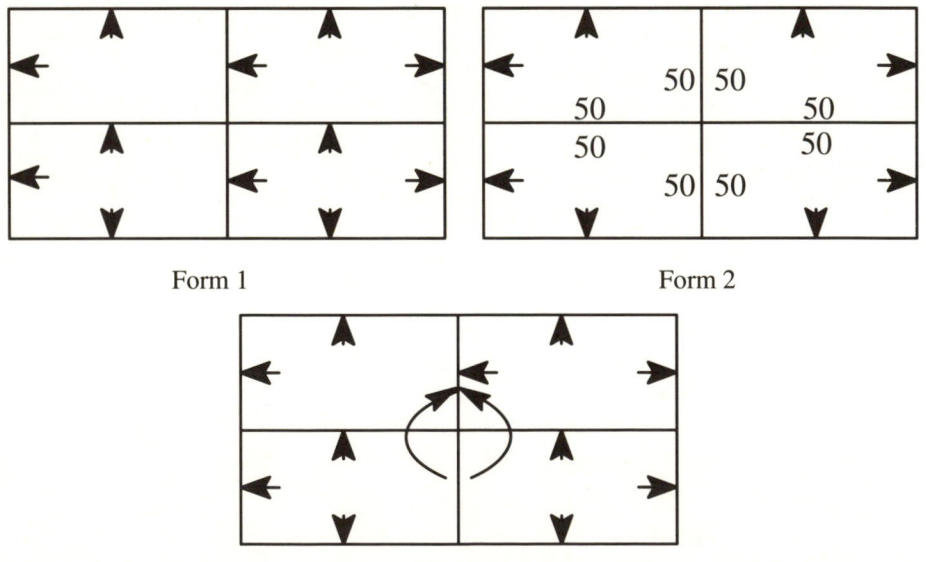

Form 1   Form 2

Form 3

Figure 25:   Edge attachments of buttons in the forms

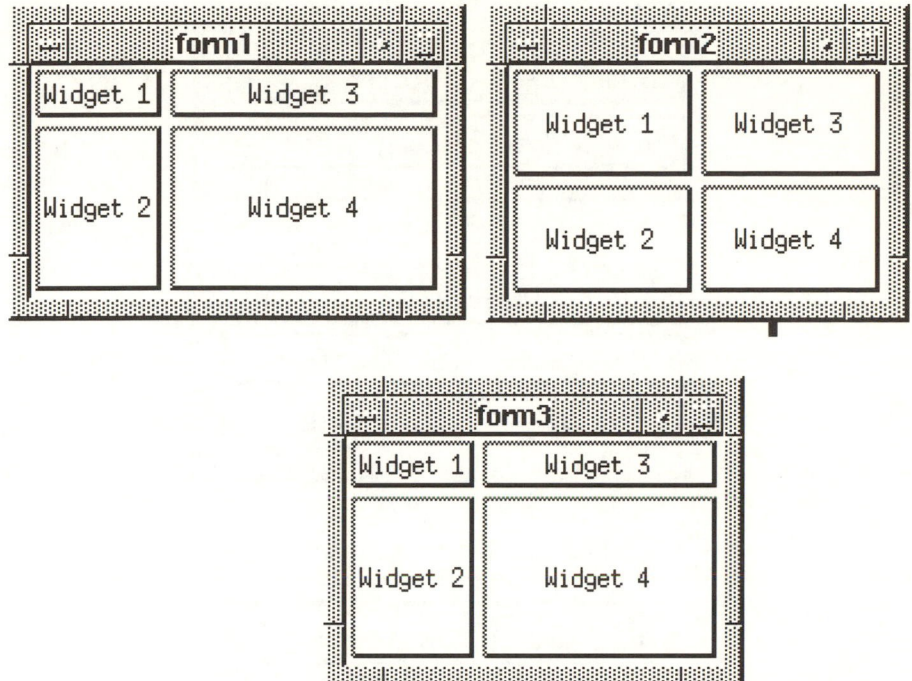

Figure 26:   The three forms resized

stretches horizontally because it is attached on the left and right, but not vertically. Widget 4 is attached on all four sides, so stretches in both directions.

For the widgets of Form 2, they are all attached on all four sides and so they all stretch. This maintains the proportions because they are all attached to the middle of the Form.

The widgets of Form 3 stretch in the same way as Form 1, but for different reasons. Widget 1 is unchanged in size, as in Form 1, because it is only attached at the top and left. Widget 2 changes its height as before but retains the same width for a different reason: it is attached on the left and right, but neither the left nor the right attachments move. Widget 3 changes as in Form 1. Widget 4 changes height as in Form 1 but it changes width because it is attached on the left to Widget 3's left, and this has changed.

Another consequence is seen if you have widgets with different preferred sizes. Figure 27 shows what happens if different size labels are set in the widgets. For the widgets of Form 1, Widget 1 and Widget 2 take their preferred width. Widgets 3 and

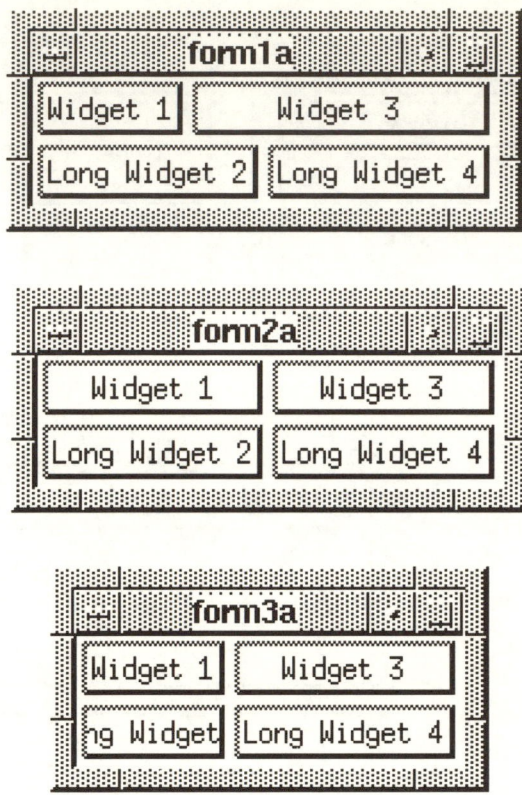

Figure 27:   The three forms with different labels

4 are made at least as big as their preferred width (to show all of their labels), but Widget 3 is then stretched further.

For the widgets of Form 2, the 50 per cent geometry makes all of them the same size, but Form makes them all big enough to contain their labels.

Form 3 is more complex. Widget 1 takes its preferred size. Widget 2 is constrained on the left by the Form and on the right by the edge of Widget 1. It does not have enough room to show its label completely. Both Widgets 3 and 4 have their size constrained on both sides and Form allows them to show their labels.

8.4.1 Summary

Positions of widgets within a Form are controlled by resources of each widget. Positions are controlled by attachments of the edges `XmNleftAttachment`, etc. Possible attachments include to the Form, to another widget, to the corresponding edge of a widget or to a proportion across (or down) the Form. If a widget is attached on two opposite edges, its size in that direction is controlled by the Form.

Exercises

1. What happens if all widgets are bound to the Form only, but not to positions or to each other?

2. What arrangement will allow Widgets 3 and 4 to maintain their size, with Widget 4 immediately below Widget 3?

3. Print out the sizes of all widgets after they have been managed.

4. What happens if you reset the width and length of widgets after they have been managed?

5. What happens if you reset the x,y coordinates of widgets after they have been managed?

8.5   Example: A realistic form

A real form is shown in Figure 28. It is a typical data-entry form with a list of field names down the left and a set of text-entry fields down the right. The names are right adjusted and are only Labels. The data-entry fields are single-line Text widgets. What Form constraints give this arrangement?

First, let us look at the Labels. The text is all right-aligned. This can be done using the Label resource `XmNalignment` set to `XmALIGNMENT_END`, assuming the Labels have their right-hand sides aligned. This can be done, showing all of the text,

Figure 28:   A typical data-entry form

if each of the Label widgets is attached-opposite to the Label with the longest string (we will do it hard-coded because we can see which string is longest: if you want to find out which string is longest, use XmStringLength().)

We do not particularly want the Labels to grow or shrink when the form is stretched horizontally, so leave the Label with the longest string unattached on the right-hand side. Form will then leave its horizontal size alone and that of all the widgets attached to it. In the vertical direction we would want the Label widgets to occupy the same proportion of the form. Set the top and bottom attachments to the relative position desired in the form, that is to the Form, to 33 or to 66. Do not attach the Labels to each other or the one with the last attachment will be stretched and the others left alone.

Turning to the Text widgets, set the resource XmNeditMode to single-line mode. This is the default, but it can also be set in user-resource files, which produces quite a substantial change in its behavior and geometry. (In Motif 1.1 you could use the TextField widget.) The geometry for these widgets is quite easy: since the Labels are pinned down, attach on the left to the corresponding Label, on the right to the Form, and vertically by position. Since these widgets will be attached on all four sides, when the Form is resized they will be resized with it. This would probably be the desired behavior, to stretch or shrink the text-entry area to what the user desires.

Program 17:   realform.c

```
Widget      form;       /*  Form              */
Widget      label[3], text[3];

Arg         args[MAX_ARGS];    /*  arg list        */
int         n;                 /*  arg count       */

/*      Create Form Window.
*/
n = 0;
form = XmCreateForm (parent, "aForm", args, n);
XtManageChild (form);

n = 0;
label[0] = XmCreateLabel (form, "Name", args, n);
n = 0;
label[1] = XmCreateLabel (form, "Address", args, n);
n = 0;
label[2] = XmCreateLabel (form, "Telephone", args, n);

n = 0;
text[0] = XmCreateText (form, "nameText", args, n);
n = 0;
```

```
text[1] = XmCreateText (form, "addressText", args, n);
n = 0;
text[2] = XmCreateText (form, "telephoneText", args, n);


/* geometry for label 2
*/
n = 0;
XtSetArg (args[n], XmNalignment, XmALIGNMENT_END); n++;
XtSetArg (args[n], XmNleftAttachment,
                   XmATTACH_FORM); n++;
XtSetArg (args[n], XmNbottomAttachment,
                   XmATTACH_FORM); n++;
XtSetArg (args[n], XmNtopAttachment,
                   XmATTACH_POSITION); n++;
XtSetArg (args[n], XmNtopPosition, 66); n++;
XtSetValues (label[2], args, n);

/* geometry for label 1
 */
n = 0;
XtSetArg (args[n], XmNalignment, XmALIGNMENT_END); n++;
XtSetArg (args[n], XmNbottomAttachment,
                   XmATTACH_POSITION); n++;
XtSetArg (args[n], XmNbottomPosition, 66); n++;
XtSetArg (args[n], XmNtopAttachment,
                   XmATTACH_POSITION); n++;
XtSetArg (args[n], XmNtopPosition, 33); n++;
XtSetArg (args[n], XmNleftAttachment,
                   XmATTACH_FORM); n++;
XtSetArg (args[n], XmNrightAttachment,
                   XmATTACH_OPPOSITE_WIDGET); n++;
XtSetArg (args[n], XmNrightWidget, label[2]); n++;
XtSetValues (label[1], args, n);

/* geometry for label 0
*/
n = 0;
XtSetArg (args[n], XmNalignment, XmALIGNMENT_END); n++;
XtSetArg (args[n], XmNbottomAttachment,
                   XmATTACH_POSITION); n++;
XtSetArg (args[n], XmNbottomPosition, 33); n++;
XtSetArg (args[n], XmNtopAttachment,
                   XmATTACH_FORM); n++;
XtSetArg (args[n], XmNleftAttachment,
                   XmATTACH_FORM); n++;
```

```
XtSetArg (args[n], XmNrightAttachment,
                   XmATTACH_OPPOSITE_WIDGET); n++;
XtSetArg (args[n], XmNrightWidget, label[1]); n++;
XtSetValues (label[0], args, n);

/* geometry for text 0
*/
n = 0;
XtSetArg (args[n], XmNtopAttachment,
                   XmATTACH_FORM); n++;
XtSetArg (args[n], XmNbottomAttachment,
                   XmATTACH_POSITION); n++;
XtSetArg (args[n], XmNbottomPosition, 33); n++;
XtSetArg (args[n], XmNrightAttachment,
                   XmATTACH_FORM); n++;
XtSetArg (args[n], XmNleftAttachment,
                   XmATTACH_WIDGET); n++;
XtSetArg (args[n], XmNleftWidget, label[0]); n++;
XtSetValues (text[0], args, n);

/* geometry for text 1
*/
n = 0;
XtSetArg (args[n], XmNtopAttachment,
                   XmATTACH_POSITION); n++;
XtSetArg (args[n], XmNtopPosition, 33); n++;
XtSetArg (args[n], XmNbottomAttachment,
                   XmATTACH_POSITION); n++;
XtSetArg (args[n], XmNbottomPosition, 66); n++;
XtSetArg (args[n], XmNrightAttachment,
                   XmATTACH_FORM); n++;
XtSetArg (args[n], XmNleftAttachment,
                   XmATTACH_WIDGET); n++;
XtSetArg (args[n], XmNleftWidget, label[1]); n++;
XtSetValues (text[1], args, n);

/* geometry for text 2
*/
n = 0;
XtSetArg (args[n], XmNtopAttachment,
                   XmATTACH_POSITION); n++;
XtSetArg (args[n], XmNtopPosition, 66); n++;
XtSetArg (args[n], XmNrightAttachment,
                   XmATTACH_FORM); n++;
XtSetArg (args[n], XmNleftAttachment,
                   XmATTACH_WIDGET); n++;
```

```
XtSetArg (args[n], XmNleftWidget, label[2]); n++;
XtSetArg (args[n], XmNbottomAttachment,
                   XmATTACH_FORM); n++;
XtSetValues (text[2], args, n);
```

8.6   Form versus RowColumn

RowColumn has simple geometry arrangements and is correspondingly simpler to drive. In fact, the example of the last section cannot be done in a reasonable way using RowColumn: it needs the complexity of Form in Motif, or use of a non-OSF widget from other sources (such as Table widgets). If the example of the last section is attempted using a RowColumn, problems show up quickly.

On the problem is that the Label and Text widgets have different preferred sizes in the vertical direction. Text has the resource XmNmarginHeight which controls the distance between the text itself and the top and bottom of the widget and this defaults to five pixels. So Text is taller than Label. You can experiment with some of the size resources, but it is not pleasant. It gets worse if you start mixing fonts, which can often happen in Forms: the Labels are frequently in a different font to the Text. The only way RowColumn handles this easily is to force all widgets to be the same size (XmNpacking to XmPACK_TIGHT) but this negates the possibility of fixing the size of the Labels and letting the Text widgets vary in size. RowColumn works best in a homogeneous situation and even has a resource that can be set to ensure that all of its children are of the same type.

On the other hand, Form can cause many worries. The example of the last section was discussed on UseNet for quite some time before a satisfactory solution arose. The difficulties with Form stem primarily from its complexity. Users of Form have to become used to two error messages: 'Circular constraint encountered' and 'bailing out after 1000 tries.' The first of these occurs when you make attachments in both directions, such as attaching Widget 1 to Widget 2 on the left, and Widget 2 to Widget 1 on the right. Remove one of the attachments and the problem disappears. This may occur in more complex arrangements as Form does not like chasing itself round a loop. The second error message occurs in the most complex arrangements where Form has been unable conclusively to find a loop but has nevertheless been around the same loop a thousand times without being able to work out the geometry. On the assumption that an error has occurred, it gives up. On other occasions it will just not show a widget. This may well be a bug in an early version of Form and you will have to try other possibilities or get a later version of Motif.

Note, however, that containers can be nested: you can have a Form within a RowColumn within a Form, and so on. Regular structures can be contained within irregular ones and can themselves contain irregular ones. The ability to put complicated structures inside, or next to other ones can give you even more flexibility.

Exercise

1. Experiment with other arrangements that may give the geometry of Figure 28. For example, two RowColumns inside a Form, or two Forms inside a RowColumn. Try to determine why some arrangements work but others do not.

Chapter 9

Widget classes

This chapter briefly surveys the range of Motif widgets. Some are discussed in more detail than others because they are more useful.

9.1 Introduction

The previous sections have covered the major mechanisms for controlling widget and application behavior and apply to all widget sets. From now on we deal with detail: the range of widgets, their resources and callbacks, the widget actions and the default translations. An intimate knowledge of each widget is required for effective Motif programming because each is an extremely complex object with nuances of behavior that can be quite entertaining (particularly to masochists!). A Motif application consists of a large number of widgets interlocked in a complex geometric and behavioral pattern. It contains a broad 'splash' of objects with detailed attention to the minutiae of behavior and interaction. This section considers a number of widgets in varying detail—those used later (or in the exercises) are dealt with in more detail than others. In successive sections the reader will see this interplay between broad and narrow detail.

The Motif toolkit is still being developed. While it is a massive achievement to have such a complex set of widgets available, it is perhaps inevitable that there are errors in the software and behavioral patterns occur that should not happen but were unforeseen at the design stage. Of course, it has to happen—the coding or design errors impact on whatever you try to do and the frustration is proportional to the level of achievements made until then. That is, a 'trivial' problem will seemingly threaten what has been a complex and smoothly functioning product. In addition to the broad 'splash' and the fine detail, attention also has to be given to these errors. Even in this book, at an introductory level, 'workarounds,' or comments on these bugs, sometimes have to be made.

The set of widget classes comes partly from the Xt Intrinsics, which gives a number of superclasses, the rest coming from any particular widget set such as the Motif widgets. The purpose of the superclass widgets from Xt is to set up general properties, behavior and characteristics of all widgets. The superclass hierarchy is shown in Figure 29. `Core` is at the top of this widget hierarchy and it gives resources like the background, width, height and coordinates.

Although `Core` is a widget from the Intrinsics, the resource names and values begin with *Xm* rather than *Xt*. This is simply because Motif has supplied values in the include file `<Xm/Xm.h>` that begin with *Xm*. There is an Xt widget called `Composite` which acts as a container for other widgets. Composite widgets contain things.

To organize geometry there are `Constraint` widgets which provides real-estate management to their children. These handle sets of widgets in groups, trying to arrange them in ways that fit constraints of size and relative location, etc. The `Shell` widget forms a shell around the application, handling the interface with the window manager. Two Motif widgets are `XmManager` and `XmPrimitive`. The Motif widget `XmManager` is a subclass of `Constraint` and adds visual resources and keyboard traversal mechanisms required for Motif. `XmPrimitive` is the superclass of all widgets that cannot contain any other widgets. The programmer would not use these superclass widgets directly unless he or she had to design new widgets and this is not a common activity. The exception is the `shell` widget because a widget of this type is returned from the call `XtInitialize()`.

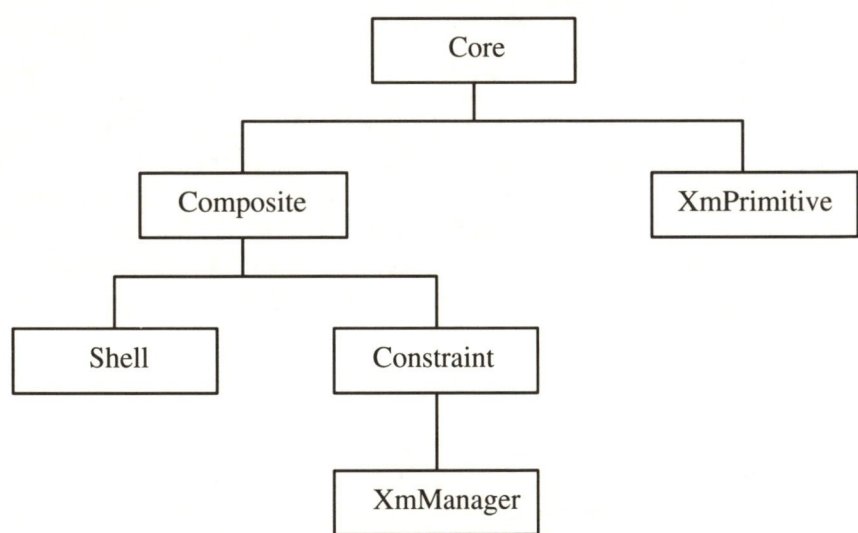

Figure 29: Toplevel of widget hierarchy

Primitive widgets cannot contain any other widgets. They are subclassed from `XmPrimitive`. They form buttons, scrollbars, etc. Although they cannot have children, they may be quite complex and appear to be built out of many components, such as the List widget which contains many distinct items. The *widget* programmer will be interested in the internals—the applications programmer need not worry.

Gadgets are widgets without windows and are used to improve efficiency. They behave like their corresponding widget siblings but without the window overheads. I avoid using them because there are some traps with them, and hopefully gadgets may disappear as the Xlib, Xt and Xm implementations become more efficient. They are not considered further in this book.

Motif supplies a number of convenience functions which wrap up combinations of widgets into packages. These are the scrollbar functions and the dialog functions. They are not widgets themselves as they have a role amalgamating a number of widgets.

9.2   Shell widgets

Shell widgets control the interface between an application's toplevel windows and the window managers. The shell-widget hierarchy is shown in Figure 30.

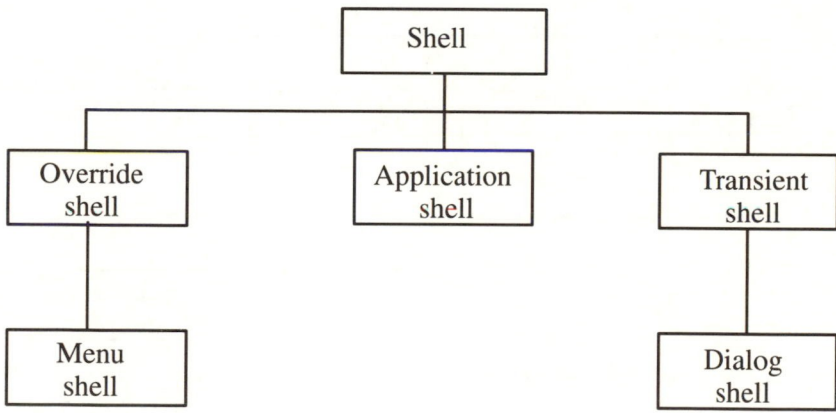

Figure 30:   Shell widgets

9.2.1   ApplicationShell

This is the normal toplevel shell for an application. It is created by `XtInitialize()` and is used as the root of the widget tree.

9.2.2   OverrideShell

This is required for pop-up menus that may be at the toplevel but which must not be interfered with by the window manager. The Motif programmer will not often use them directly. A descendant is the menu shell.

9.2.3 TransientShell

This may be manipulated by the window manager but should not have window bars, etc. placed around it. The Motif programmer will not often use them directly. TransientShell widgets are used for dialog interactions which are of limited duration. Motif uses convenience functions to package the transient shell with other widgets. It uses the subclass DialogShell for this.

9.3 Primitive widgets

The primitive widgets will be the most common ones used by the Motif programmer. They are widgets such as we have already seen. They cannot contain any other widgets and form functional objects in their own right. The primitive widget set is shown in Figure 31. Some of these widgets are shown in Figure 32.

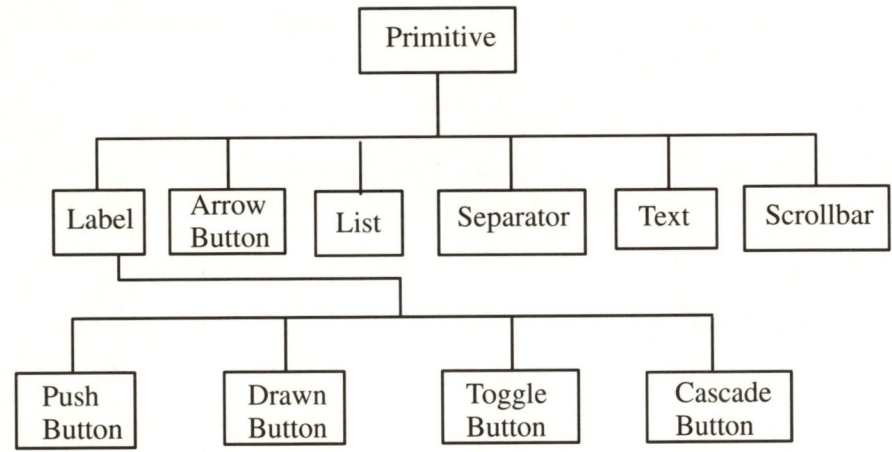

Figure 31:   The primitive widgets

9.3.1 ArrowButton

Displays an arrow pointing in some direction. The arrow appears to move when the left button is clicked in it. It is created by `XmCreateArrowButton()`. It has been discussed several times.

9.3.2 Label

This shows a piece of text (or a bitmap) only. Clicking on it has no effect. Its purpose is simply to show a static or infrequently changing message. It is created by `XmCreateLabel()`. It is shown in Figure 32. Note that it does not have the three-dimensional appearance of many widgets. This is to remove the temptation to press

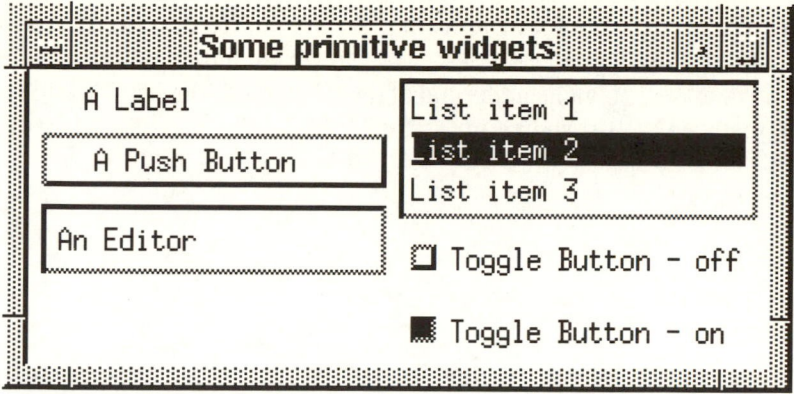

Figure 32:   Some of the Motif primitive widgets

it—Motif takes the view that only raised objects can be usefully pressed and there is no point in pressing a label, because it will not react to it.

Label has nearly fifty resources. The programmer or user will be interested mainly in one: XmNlabelString—the string shown in the label. This may be set by resource files or by the program. If it is not set, it defaults to the name of the widget. This is very useful, particularly for foreign-language environments: let the label default to the name of the widget (probably in English, since C has standardized on English) but allow the user to customize the labels in their resource files[10]. A resource that may be used for Label, but less frequently, is XmNalignment. This controls the placement of the string within the Label and may be set to left-justified, centered or right-justified. (Actually if your text runs right-to-left as in Hebrew, these directions are reversed.)

9.3.3   PushButton

PushButton is a button with a message. It is raised and can be pushed with the left button. When it is pushed it appears to sink in by changing colors. It is created by XmCreatePushButton(). PushButton inherits from Label, so the label shown is either set from the resource XmNlabelString or the widget name. PushButton has a number of callbacks. The major one is XmNarmCallback which is invoked when button one is pressed within the widget.

9.3.4   List

This allows selection from a list of items. The items can be selected by means of the left button. The list widget is created by XmCreateList(). Two resources control the list items: XmNitems and XmNitemCount. XmNitems is of type

---

[10] There is a minor drawback at present: hard-coding of labels is faster than extracting the information from resource files.

`XmStringTable`, that is, a 'table' of strings. The word 'table' uniformly means an array, so to create this resource an array of `XmString` is declared and the strings are set one at a time. The value `XmNitemCount` *must* match the number of strings set. There is no magic `NULL` value at the end of the table to tell the list when to stop. For example, to create the list shown in Figure 32:

```
XmString items[3];
Arg args[2];

items[0] = XmStringCreateLtoR ("List item 1",
                    XmSTRING_DEFAULT_CHARSET);
items[1] = XmStringCreateLtoR ("List item 2",
                    XmSTRING_DEFAULT_CHARSET);
items[2] = XmStringCreateLtoR ("List item 3",
                    XmSTRING_DEFAULT_CHARSET);
n = 0;
XtSetArg (args[n], XmNitems, items); n++;
XtSetArg (args[n], XmNitemCount, 3); n++;
list = XmCreateList (parent, "list", args, n);
```

Resources may be used to set the list to allow selection of only one item at a time, or multiple items. Other resources may be used to find out which items have been selected. The resource `XmNselectionPolicy` should be set to `XmSINGLE_SELECT` (the default) for single selection only of items. When the resource has this value, the callback list `XmNsingleSelectionCallback` is invoked when an item is selected. A pointer to the `XmNlistCallbackStruct` is passed to the callback functions in the third parameter. This structure contains:

```
typedef struct
{   int       reason;
    XEvent    *event;
    XmString  item;
    int       item_position;

    ....
} XmListCallbackStruct;
```

This allows the program to find the selected item.

The resource `XmNitems` can be manipulated like any other resource. When you set it, any previous list of items is replaced by the new list. When you get the list from the widget by `XtGetValues()` you must, however, be a little careful: when a Motif widget returns a list of things, it returns a pointer to its internal list and does not provide a copy. You must not get the list of items from a List widget and then free them, for that will give the List widget a 'touch of indigestion.'

Motif 1.1 has a set of functions to manipulate the list, for example, inserting an item into a list.

9.3.5   Text

Text is a single or multiline text editor. This handles a large set of basic editing operations such as inserting and deleting text and moving around by the arrow keys. Text can also be selected for cutting or pasting, but these operations and others require extra work by the programmer. The text widget is created by `XmCreateText()`. The actual text in the widget can be set programmatically by `XmTextSetString()` which takes an ordinary ASCII string, not an `XmString`.

```
void XmTextSetString (text_widget, string)
```

A copy of the text can be obtained at any time by `XmTextGetString()` which creates an ordinary ASCII string.

```
char *XmTextGetString(text_widget)
```

The text widget has two roles: one as a single-line editor, the other as a multiline editor (Motif 1.1 has a special single-line editor called `XmTextField`). The resource to control this is `XmNeditMode` and is by default set to `XmSINGLE_LINE_EDIT`. The alternative value is `XmMULTI_LINE_EDIT`. For simple multiline editing, the three functions `XmCreateText()`, `XmTextSet-String()` and `XmGetString()` are usually enough to manipulate the Text widget.

There are some additional callbacks associated with Text, as well as those inherited from Core and XmPrimitive. They are mainly concerned with monitoring and altering text as it is entered. The callbacks for `XmNmodifyCallback` are called before any text is inserted or deleted. This allows the application to check and maybe change what the text is before it is entered. This is particularly useful for such things as password entry, where the text needs to be typed in but not 'echoed' to the user. For a widget in single-line mode, callbacks on the `XmNactivateCallback` list are called when the <enter> key is pressed.

The callbacks for `XmNvalueChangedCallback` are called *after* text is added or deleted. An application can monitor the result of any changes using this callback.

The Text widget has a range of edit functions similar to the text widget of the Athena toolkit, as used in `xedit`. The default bindings are given in the following table. Many Unix-based people like to use `emacs` editing keystrokes: some of these are given in Section 11.1.1. I doubt that it would be possible to configure Text to look like `vi` because of the modal nature of `vi`.

Table 2:   Editing functions for the Text widget

Function	Virtual key	Actual key	Default binding
Start of line	KBeginLine	osfBeginLine	Home
End of line	KEndLine	osfEndLine	End
Next page	KPageDown	osfPageDown	Next
Previous page	KPageUp	osfPageUp	Prior
Beginning of file	KBeginData	Ctrl osfBeginLine	Ctrl Home
End of file	KEndData	Ctrl osfEndLine	Ctrl End
Delete selection	KPrimaryCut	Mod1 Shift osfDelete	Alt Shift Delete
Copy selection	KPrimaryCopy	Mod1 osfCopy	<unbound>
Insert selection	KPrimaryPaste	osfPrimaryPaste	<unbound>

9.3.6   Others

The Separator widget acts as a 'line' that can be drawn between widgets. The direction of drawing is controlled by the resource `XmNorientation` which is set to vertical or horizontal. The resource `XmNseparatorType` controls the style of line: no line, single line, double line, single- dashed or double-dashed line, or a shadow line. I find it useful for drawing a line across a form and attaching widgets to this line so that they all line up nicely.

The Scrollbar widget allows data to be viewed in a work area by scrolling up and down, or left and right. There is a set of convenience routines combining scroll bars with other widgets such as lists, which will be described later. These reduce the amount of time that a programmer has to spend with scroll bars, which is just as well because this is a complex area.

The CascadeButton widget is only used in menus. Pulldown menus are hung from it.

The DrawnButton widget acts like a PushButton widget but instead of having an `XmString` to set the label, it supplies an area in which the application can draw arbitrary graphics.

The ToggleButton widget is used for non-transitory information. When pushed, it stays pushed until it is pushed again. It can thus show two states in a permanent manner. It is shown in Figure 32 with a square button. It can also be set to show a diamond shape instead.

9.4   Manager widgets

There are a number of container widgets, even though one would not expect some of them to contain anything. They belong in the widget hierarchy under XmManager. They are shown in Figure 33.

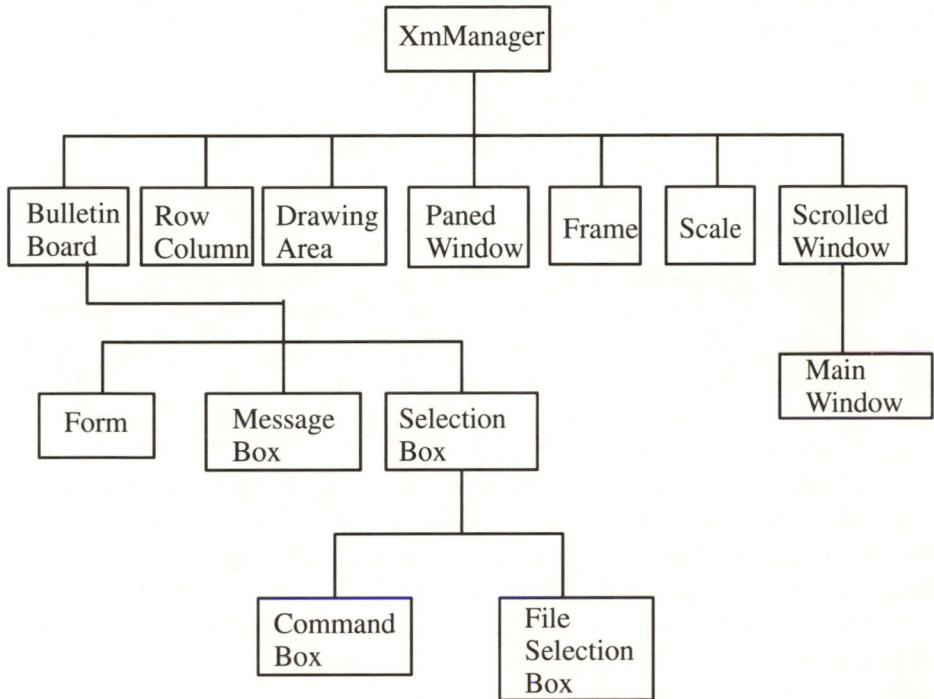

Figure 33:   Manager widgets

9.4.1   Frame

This provides a frame with a border. It is used to give other widgets a three dimensional effect. For example, if you really wanted to, you could make a three-dimensional version of Label by putting one in a Frame.

9.4.2   MainWindow

This is typically used as the toplevel container for the application's windows. It can contain a menu bar along the top, an area for typing 'commands' below this, and scrollbars around some 'work area,' which can be any other widget. MainWindow has resources to control these areas, such as `XmNmenuBar`, but it is often simpler to set them all at once using `XmMainWindowSetAreas()`. An example of its use is shown in Section 10.3.

9.4.3   DrawingArea

This provides an area in which to draw lines and text. It is misnamed. It does not provide any drawing functions of its own but is really the only place where many of the Xlib drawing functions can be used. The principal callbacks are `XmNexpose-Callback` and `XmNinputCallback`. These are invoked on exposure and keyboard/mouse events, respectively. The callback structure allows the program to examine both the event and the window it occurred in:

```
typedef struct
{   int         reason;
    XEvent      *event;
    Window      window;
}
```

An example of this widget is considered in Section 11.5.

9.4.4   Dialog widgets

These are widgets designed to be used in dialogs with the user. They inherit behavior from BulletinBoard. The MessageBox gives information to the user. This displays a symbol such as a question mark or a big 'i', a message, and three buttons set up as OK, Cancel and Help. It allows display of warning, question, information dialogs, etc. with suitable buttons to press for more interaction. Some convenience routines make this even easier to use. Figure 34 shows a typical warning dialog. The SelectionBox gets a selection from a list of alternatives. This has two children. The Command widget gives an entry area for commands and a command history. The FileSelectionBox displays files in a directory and allows file selection. A FileSelectionBox is shown in Figure 35.

Figure 34:   A warning dialog

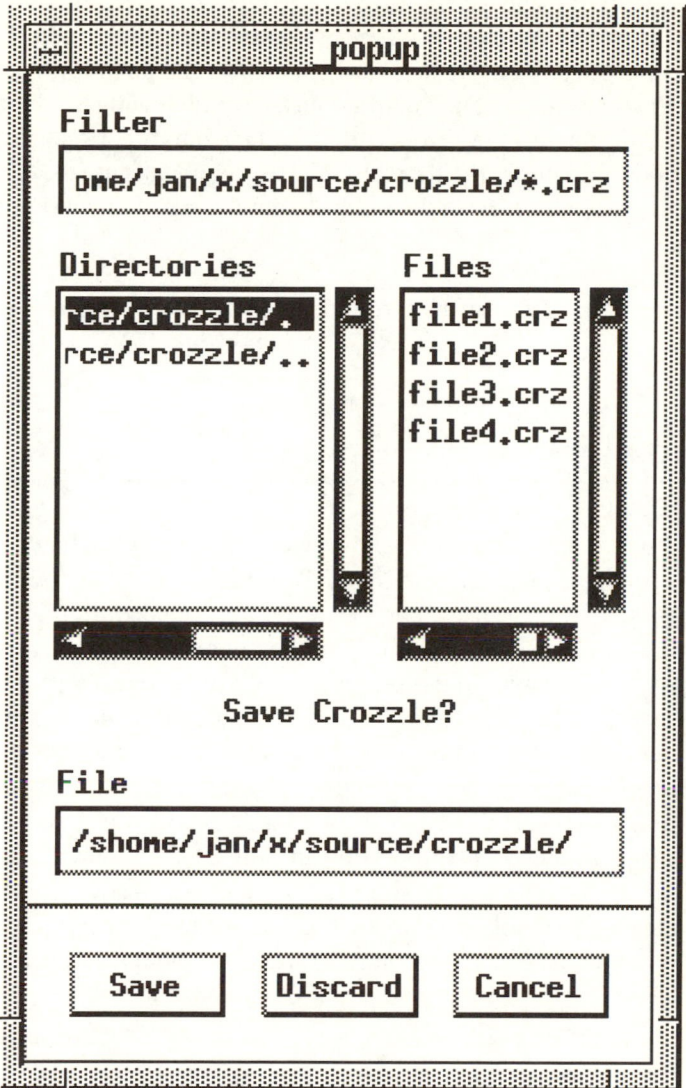

Figure 35:   A FileSelectionBox

9.4.5   Others

RowColumn and Form have been dealt with already. The Scale widget gives a sliding scale that can be manipulated by the user or application. A PanedWindow lays out its children vertically, separating them with a 'sash' so that each window can be resized vertically. A ScrolledWindow manages any widget (called a 'work-area' widget) with scrollbars around it, to give a view onto a part of the widget. Two common work area widgets are Text and List, and there are special routines `XmCrea-`

`teScrolledText()` and `XmCreateScrolledList()` for these. Resources are set for both the ScrolledWindow and the workarea in the Create call. The work-area widget is returned from the Create call, with the ScrolledWindow as its parent (see Figure 36).This can cause a bit of confusion, as to which widget is being dealt with. For example, in placing the scrolled text widget into a form, you must put the scrolled window into the form. To modify the text, you must use the text widget. It is relatively easy to find one from the other: to get the scrolled window from the text widget, use:

```
XtParent (text)
```

and to get the text widget from the scrolled window, use the resource `XmNworkWindow`.

9.5 Summary

This section has attempted to give an overview of the major Xt and Motif widgets without attempting to do much with them. This contrasts with earlier sections of the book where I have tried to use a concept as it is introduced. In this section, I have done a survey for two reasons: (a) to show the range of Motif widgets; (b) to show the finiteness of this range. In the sections to follow, widgets with appropriate behavior may appear to be pulled out of a hat. This section is trying to counter any complaints of that kind: at least I hinted that such a widget might be available....

The list of widgets is neither functionally complete nor a complete listing. There are situations where the Motif widget set does not quite give the programmer what is required. In these situations you can turn to other sources: there is a Table widget which can handle many common geometry organizations, and a set of field-entry widgets commercially available which can be used for type checking of data entry. In the future one can expect more Motif-based widgets to become available.

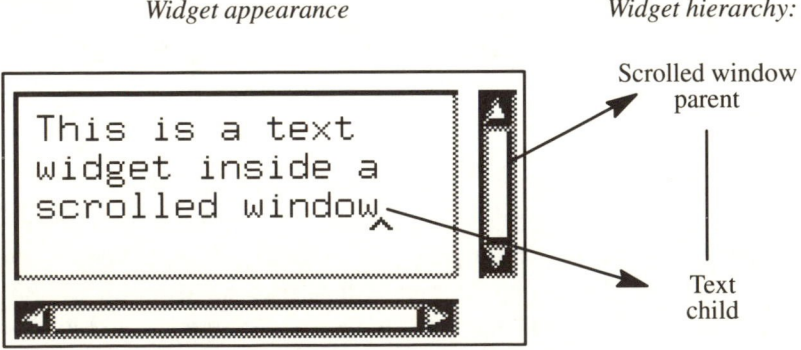

Figure 36:   A scrolled text object

Exercise

1. The game of Crozzle is a word game in which lists of 3, 4, 5,... letter words are given that have to be fitted into a 10×10 grid. A score is calculated from the number of words and the intersecting letters. Figure 37 shows a Motif application that aids in playing Crozzle by allowing the user to pick up words and drop them onto the grid. Various areas are used to show messages about the score, direction of word insertion, error messages and word selected. What widgets would be used to give this appearance? What geometry arrangements would be required? (Ignore the menu bar for now.)

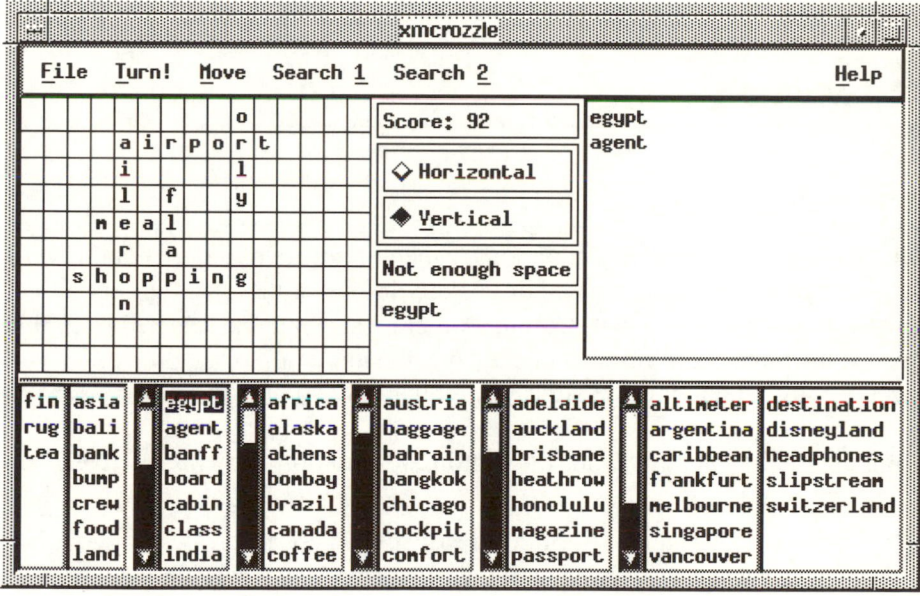

Figure 37: A Crozzle screen

Chapter 10

Application techniques

This chapter discusses some additional techniques required to build full applications. This includes menus and dialogs and concludes with an extensive example.

10.1 Menus

10.1.1 Pulldown menus

Pulldown menus are extremely common. A menu consists of a horizontal row of buttons. When the mouse is pressed or clicked in one of these buttons, a vertical column of buttons 'drops down' from it. A menu entry may be selected from this column. If the mouse is released or clicked outside this column, the drop down disappears. In Motif a pulldown menu is a combination of a number of widgets:

- A menu bar that holds all the buttons in the top row. This is created by `XmCreateMenubar()`.
- A set of cascade buttons, forming the top row. These are created by `XmCreateCascadeButton()`, and are Labels specialized for use in menus.
- A set of pulldown menu panes. Each one of these has the menu bar as parent widget but is associated with a particular cascade button. These are created by `XmCreatePulldownMenu()`.
- A set of push buttons for each menu pane.

The container widgets are in fact RowColumn widgets in a specialized role. Many of the RowColumn resources that you do not have to deal with are set for these widgets.

Consider the pulldown menu system of Figure 38 where the Help button also has two options when pulled down—About and Application (not shown in the figure).

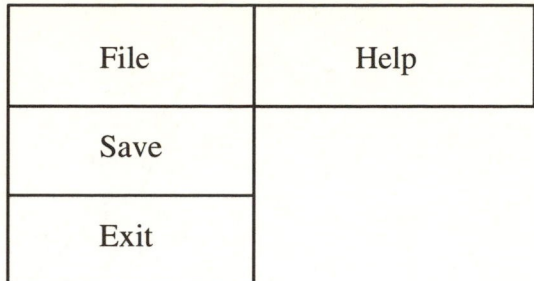

Figure 38:   A simple menu

To get a clearer view of what is going on in the widget structure of a menu, look at a 'blown-apart' version of the menu where the widgets are separated (Figure 39).

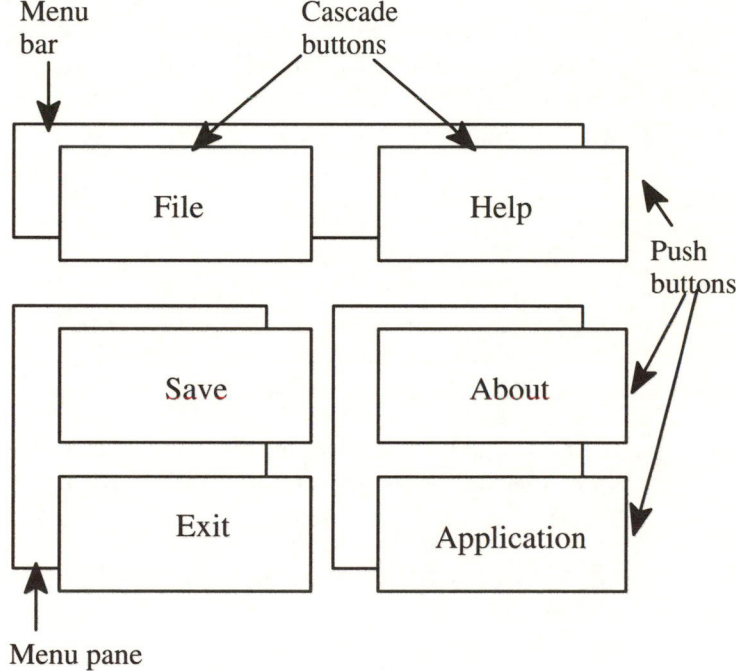

Figure 39:   Exploded structure of a menu

The menu bar parents the File and Help cascade buttons and also the two menu panes file_pane and help_pane. Each pane holds its own buttons. In order that the correct pane is shown when one of the menu-bar buttons is selected, a link has to be established between the two. This is done by setting the resource XmNsubMenuId of the cascade button to the corresponding pane.The widget hierarchy for this is given in Figure 40.

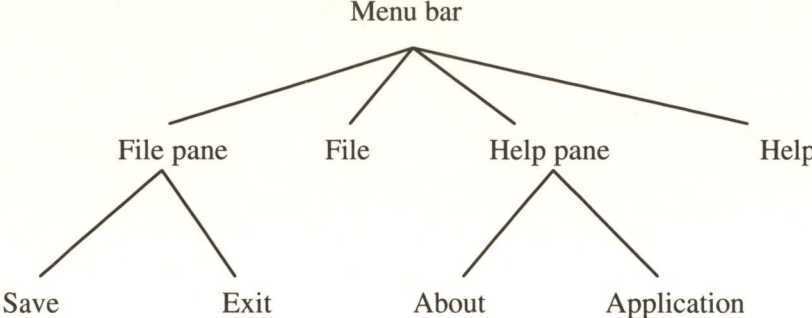

Figure 40:   Widget creation hierarchy for a menu

Motif treats the Help button in a special way. It is placed to the right of all others. In Motif 1.0, pressing the F10 key in the application posts the Help submenu, but in Motif 1.1, pressing the F10 key only posts the menu bar. To inform the system as to which button actually is the Help button, the resource `XmNmenuHelpWidget` is set in the menu bar to be the help button.

The following schema creates the pulldown menu:

```
/* create the menu bar */
menubar = XmCreateMenuBar(..)
XtManageChild(menubar)
/* create pulldown menu panes */
for each pane
    pulldown-n = XmCreatePulldownMenu(menubar, ...)
    /* create cascade buttons,
       associated with menu  panes */
    for each cascade button
       XtSetArg(args[0], XmNsubMenuId, pulldown-n)
       cascade[n] = XmCreateCascadeButton(menubar,
                                            .., args, 1)
    XtManageChildren(cascade)
/* create all of the menu pane buttons */
for each pane m
   for each button n in each
      button-m[n] = XmCreatePushButton(pulldown-m,
                                         ...)
   XtmanageChildren(button-m)
```

The following sets up the above simple pulldown menu in program `menu.c`:

Program 18:   menu.c

```
#include <Xm/CascadeB.h>
#include <Xm/PushB.h>
```

```
#include <Xm/RowColumn.h>

/*-------------------------------------------------------
**  Forward Declarations
*/

void main ();     /*  main logic for application  */

void CreateApplication (); /* create main window     */

/*-------------------------------------------------------
**      Global Variables
*/

#define MAX_ARGS 20
#define Class_name "SampleMenu"

/*-------------------------------------------------------
**      main       - main logic for application
*/
void
main (argc,argv)
    int     argc;
    char    **argv;
{
    Widget  app_shell;

    app_shell = XtInitialize (NULL,     /* application
                                           name */
                      Class_name,    /* class name */
                      NULL,          /* options */
                      0,             /* number of
                                        options */
                      &argc, argv);

    /* Create and realize main
       application window.
    */
    CreateApplication (app_shell);
    XtRealizeWidget (app_shell);

    /*      Get and dispatch events.
    */
    XtMainLoop ();
}
```

```
/*-----------------------------------------------------
**          CreateApplication       - create main window
*/
void CreateApplication (parent)
    Widget  parent;     /*  parent widget     */
{
    Widget  menu_bar;   /*  MenuBar   */
    Widget  menu_pane;  /*  MenuPane */
    Widget  cascade;    /*  CascadeButton */
    Widget  button;     /*  PushButton    */

    Arg     args[MAX_ARGS]; /* arg list   */
    int     n;              /*  arg count */

    /* Create MenuBar in parent
    */
    n = 0;
    menu_bar = XmCreateMenuBar (parent, "menu_bar",
                                  args, n);
    XtManageChild (menu_bar);

    /* Create "File" PulldownMenu.
    */
    /* Create the file pane
    */
    n = 0;
    menu_pane = XmCreatePulldownMenu (menu_bar,
                                "file_pane", args, n);
  /* The Save button
    */
    n = 0;
    button = XmCreatePushButton (menu_pane,
                                  "Save", args, n);
    XtManageChild (button);

    /* The Exit button
    */
    n = 0;
    button = XmCreatePushButton (menu_pane,
                                    "Exit", args, n);
    XtManageChild (button);

    /* Create the cascade button for the menu bar.
    Link the menu pane and cascade button by
    subMenuId resource
    */
```

```
n = 0;
XtSetArg (args[n], XmNsubMenuId,
             menu_pane);  n++;
cascade = XmCreateCascadeButton (menu_bar,
                          "File", args, n);
XtManageChild (cascade);

/* Create "Help" menu in a similar way.
*/

n = 0;
menu_pane = XmCreatePulldownMenu (menu_bar,
                          "help_pane", args, n);
 n = 0;
button = XmCreatePushButton (menu_pane,
             "About", args, n);
XtManageChild (button);

n = 0;
button = XmCreatePushButton (menu_pane,
                    "Application", args, n);
XtManageChild (button);

n = 0;
XtSetArg (args[n], XmNsubMenuId,
             menu_pane);  n++;
cascade = XmCreateCascadeButton (menu_bar,
                          "Help", args, n);
XtManageChild (cascade);

/* tell the menu bar which is the help button
*/
n = 0;
XtSetArg (args[n], XmNmenuHelpWidget,
             cascade);  n++;
XtSetValues (menu_bar, args, n);
}
```

This menu does not actually do anything, as no application behavior has been attached to it. This is done by the usual callback mechanism of each of the PushButton widgets Save, Exit, About and Application. For example, invoke the function `ExitCB` when the Exit button is pressed by adding this line after the creation of the Exit button:

```
XtAddCallback (button, XmNactivateCallback,
                ExitCB, NULL);
```

10.1.2 Accelerators and mnemonics

The method of using menus—and all applications—so far has been mouse driven;
click the mouse in the menu bar and drag to the appropriate entry before releasing. If,
instead, the user presses and releases the mouse while in the menu bar, keyboard
mechanisms can be used as well: the arrow keys can be used to move around and the
<enter> key will select an item. In addition to this mechanism, Motif supports *mne-
monics* to move around menus (usually a single key such as 'E' to exit) and 'hot'
keys to select menu items without bothering to go through popping up or pulling
down a menu.

Mnemonics are only accessible while in a menu. The mnemonic for a button is
a single letter which must occur in the label displayed by the button. This letter will
be displayed underlined. Typing the letter will select the button. The programmer
sets this resource by two calls: one to set the label, one to set the mnemonic:

```
XtSetArg(args[n], XmNlabelString,
            XmStringCreateLtoR("Exit",
                    XmSTRING_DEFAULT_CHARSET)); n++;
XtSetArg(args[n], XmNmnemonic, 'E'); n++;
button = XmCreatePushButton (menu_pane,
                "Exit", args, n);
```

Menus have default hot keys (accelerators). The pressing of these hot keys
anywhere inside the parent or a child widget will invoke the menu directly, without
having to move the pointer into the menu bar. For a pulldown menu, the accelerator
is <F10>. This is controlled by the resource XmNmenuAccelerator. To associate
an accelerator with an individual button, perform the following:

```
XtSetArg(args[n], XmNacceleratorText,
        XmStringCreateLtoR("F3",
                XmSTRING_DEFAULT_CHARSET)); n++;
XtSetArg(args[n], XmNaccelerator, "<Key>F3:"); n++;
button = XmCreatePushButton (menu_pane, "Exit",
                            args, n);
```

Figure 41 shows the menu when both of these changes have been made to the Exit
button.

10.1.3 Summary

This section has shown how to create a pulldown menu using the calls:

```
XmCreateMenuBar ()
XmCreateCascadeButton ()
XmCreatePulldownMenu ()
XmCreatePushButton ()
```

and the resources:

Figure 41:   The menu with accelerators and mnemonics on the Exit button

```
XmNsubMenuId
XmNmenuHelpWidget
```
Accelerators and mnemonics are set using the resources:
```
XmNmnemonic
XmNacceleratorText
XmNaccelerator
```

Exercise

1. Most applications have a File pulldown, containing Save, Save as..., New, Open, Exit and Print buttons. Write a function `CreateFileMenu()` to create this pulldown menu. Include suitable accelerators and mnemonics.

10.2   Dialogs

10.2.1   Pop-up dialog

When users select Help, they expect to get at least a box with a message in it. If a user attempts to perform an irrevocable action, such as exiting an application with unsaved work, a warning box should appear asking for confirmation or cancellation. Motif supplies a number of these often short-lived *dialogs*. They are not widgets but are, instead, a set of widgets packaged in a pop-up shell. The main dialogs are error, file selection, information, message, prompt, question, selection, warning and working dialogs. There is a function to create each one, for example:
```
Widget XmCreateWarningDialog (parent, name,
                              args, argcount)
```
Each dialog contains a widget of some type to which the resource arguments refer. The error, information, message, question, warning and working dialogs all contain a message box; the file selection dialog contains a file selection widget; the prompt and selection dialogs contain a selection box. The widget returned from the

creation routine is the message box, file selection or selection box. Each dialog sets some of the resources of the widget but the others are left to the program (or the user) to set.

Consider the type of dialog that would arise from the user selecting a help option. Clearly the intention is to get information, so use an information dialog. Such a dialog shows an information symbol (a big 'i'), a message of some text, and three buttons: OK, Cancel and Help.

Resources set for the dialog are actually set for the MessageBox, so one would have to look at its resource list to see what can be done. For example, to set or change the label in the OK button, one would use the resource `XmNokLabelString` of the MessageBox. When the OK button is pressed, callbacks on the MessageBox's `XmNokCallback` list are invoked.

Although Motif supplies three buttons, they may not always be needed. If the dialog is invoked from a help button it is hardly necessary to have another Help button showing. All that the user would want to do is to read the message and then to close the dialog. The Help button should be removed from the dialog. We could also remove the Cancel button. Widget children can be removed by unmanaging them. They are found by the function:

```
Widget XmMessageBoxGetChild (widget, child)
```

where `child` is one of `XmDIALOG_CANCEL_BUTTON`, `XmDIALOG_HELP_BUTTON`, etc.

The message given to the user is set in the resource `XmNmessageString`, of type `XmString`. This can be a multiline message by embedding the C new-line character '\n' in the string. The dialog simply becomes large enough to contain it all. (However, it does not give scroll-bars if the message is too large for the screen!)

To close the dialog the user would push the OK button. We need to attach a callback to this. MessageBox overrides certain actions of its children. When a button is pressed, you would expect from what we have done so far that the callbacks of the button itself would be called. In fact, the callbacks on the MessageBox's lists are called. When the callback is invoked, the widget in the first argument is not the OK button but the MessageBox.

Remove the dialog from the screen by unmanaging the widget that you get in the button-press callbacks. This removes, it but does not destroy it or reclaim space for it. To show the same dialog again, the MessageBox can be simply remanaged. To reclaim space for the whole dialog the parent of the MessageBox is destroyed. This is the pop-up shell containing the MessageBox and destroying the shell destroys it and all of its children.

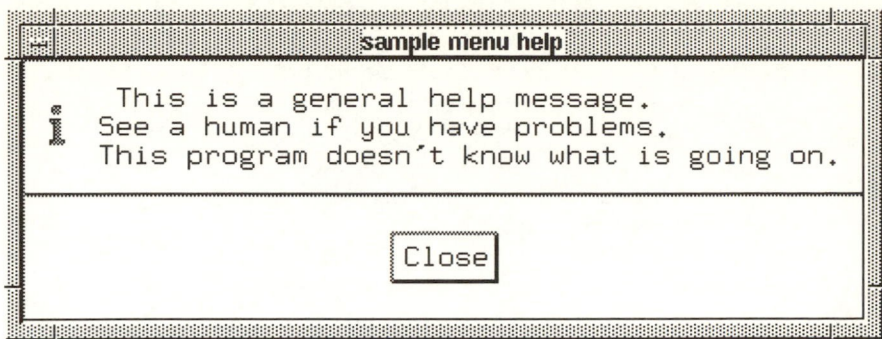

Figure 42:   An information dialog

The code to implement the dialog shown in Figure 42 is:

Program 19:   help.c

```
#include <Xm/MessageB.h>
#define MAX_ARGS 20
#define BUFSIZ   1024
void  CloseCB();
/*-----------------------------------------------------
**      CreateHelp                - create help window
*/
Widget CreateHelp (parent)
    Widget  parent;         /* parent widget */
{
    Widget  button;
    Widget  message_box;   /* Information Dialog */
    Arg     args[MAX_ARGS]; /* arg list    */
    int  n;                 /*  arg count */

    static char  message[BUFSIZ]; /* help text */
    XmString        title_string;
    XmString        message_string;
    XmString        button_string;

    /*      Generate message to display.
    */
    sprintf (message, "\
This is a general help message.  \n\
See a human if you have problems. \n\
This program doesn't know what is going on.");
    message_string = XmStringCreateLtoR (message,
                  XmSTRING_DEFAULT_CHARSET);
```

```
button_string = XmStringCreateLtoR ("Close",
                XmSTRING_DEFAULT_CHARSET);
title_string = XmStringCreateLtoR (
                "Help dialog",
                XmSTRING_DEFAULT_CHARSET);

/*      Create Information Dialog
**      using a MessageBox
*/
n = 0;
XtSetArg (args[n], XmNdialogTitle,
            title_string);  n++;
XtSetArg (args[n], XmNokLabelString,
            button_string);  n++;
XtSetArg (args[n], XmNmessageString,
            message_string);  n++;
message_box = XmCreateInformationDialog (parent,
            "helpbox", args, n);
XtAddCallback (message_box, XmNokCallback,
            CloseCB, NULL);

/* Get rid of unwanted buttons  */
button = XmMessageBoxGetChild (message_box,
            XmDIALOG_CANCEL_BUTTON);
XtUnmanageChild (button);
button = XmMessageBoxGetChild (message_box,
            XmDIALOG_HELP_BUTTON);
XtUnmanageChild (button);

/* Free strings and return MessageBox.
*/
XmStringFree (title_string);
XmStringFree (message_string);
XmStringFree (button_string);
return (message_box);
}

/*--------------------------------------------------------
** CloseCB   - callback for close button
*/
void CloseCB (message_box, client_data, call_data)
    Widget  message_box;    /*  widget id */
    caddr_t client_data;    /*  NULL */
    caddr_t call_data;      /*  data from
                               widget class  */
{
```

```
    Widget shell = XtParent (message_box);

    /* Unmanage and destroy widgets.
    */
    XtUnmanageChild (message_box);
    XtDestroyWidget (shell);
}
```

10.2.2 Pop-up editor

The dialog functions such as `XmCreateInformationDialog()` can be used for many common situations to give an easily programmed pop-up. Others such as `XmCreateFileSelectionBoxDialog()` can be used for some more complex dialogs. One that is missing, but is fairly commonly used, is a pop-up dialog containing a text editor widget. It is a good example of how to deal with pop-ups in general. Unfortunately, in Motif 1.0 the implementation of dialogs has meant that a pop-up text editor has a serious problem, and almost no one gets it right first time. It is due to an interaction between BulletinBoard and its children, which arguably should never have been there in the first place and had to be worked around in Motif 1.1 to *not* apply to text-widget children. It was in fact this problem that led me to compile a list of Frequently Asked Questions (and answers) for Motif, since I narrowly avoided being seriously caught by this only by a timely UseNet posting by someone else. The solution is given in the program but is discussed later in Section 11.1.3. All parts of the solution are enclosed in preprocessor commands (`#ifdef MOTIF_1_0`) so may be readily ignored until then.

A pop-up editor will consist of a text widget inside some kind of dialog. There must be a means of terminating an edit session and this could be either by a menu or by pressing a quit button. The Motif dialogs give buttons to press, so to conform with them we will also use buttons. What buttons should we have? At least a 'quit' button. A 'help' button is always handy, to explain what is going on, or perhaps to document edit functions. It should be possible to cancel any dialog so there should be a 'cancel' button. The edited text could be saved on exit, but to increase a user's security it may be better to have an explicit 'save' button. Thus four buttons and a text widget inside a dialog are needed. Such a dialog is not given by the Motif widget set, so it must be constructed. Motif does have a BulletinBoard dialog (by `XmCreateBulletin-BoardDialog()`) or a Form dialog (by `XmCreateFormDialog()`) which give bulletin board or form containers inside a dialog shell and the contents can be built inside one of these. For example, a form could be used with the edit widget at the top and four push buttons in a row along the bottom. This is not hard, but if the result is compared with the supplied dialogs, it probably will not look very good. In the supplied dialogs the buttons are spread out nicely from each other and from the edges of the container; the selected button is nicely highlighted; when the dialog is resized, the dialog spreads out or contracts nicely. Trying to do the same with one's own form or bulletin board is possible, but it takes a lot of work. A more devious approach gives a much nicer result: take one of the Motif dialogs and warp it as required.

The prompt dialog in its normal configuration has a message string, a text input region (a single-line editor) and three buttons. This may not seem to be a brilliant candidate but let us look further. The message string and text-input region are not wanted but they will effectively disappear if they are just unmanaged. The buttons are OK, Cancel and Help. The first has the wrong name, so we would reset its label-String resource to 'Quit'. We need an extra button. The prompt dialog has an additional button called the Apply button which is usually unmanaged. Set its label to 'Save' and manage it and we have the four buttons desired. The dialog can have an extra 'work-area' widget added to it. Make this the scrolled text widget and all the geometry is done (note that the work-area child is actually the scrolled window rather than the text widget). Figure 43 shows a standard prompt dialog and the edit pop-up so that the reader can see the effect of these quite simple changes.

The behavior is more complex. For simplicity we assume simple sources and sinks for the initial and final text as global strings `in_text` and `out_text` (since we want a save button, we must save the text *somewhere*). In other situations a file for source and sink may be better. The program sets `in_text`, invokes the dialog, and when it is over, the result of the edit will be in `out_text`. If the dialog is cancelled, the `out_text` will point to `NULL`. (This can be changed to read from a file and save in the file, for example.) So on creation, the text of the widget should be set by `XmTextSetString()` and the callback for the save button should save the text in `out_text` using `XmTextGetString()`, whereas the cancel button callback should set `out_text` to `NULL`. The help button should invoke some help message in a pop-up, as in the menu program given earlier. When the quit button is pressed, the dialog should exit. There is a minor complexity in this: each time `XmTextGetString()` is called, it returns a *copy* of the text, so if it is called many times, there could be many different copies, only one of them current, the rest being garbage. Old copies should be freed first. To ensure that `XtFree()` works correctly, the `out_text` should be initialized to `NULL` when the dialog is created.

This method would appear to use two global variables, `in_text` and `out_text`. If we wanted multiple edit-dialogs this would be a bad idea. We can make `in_text` a function parameter quite easily as it would only be used by the dialog creation routine in setting the editor's text. Fixing `out_text` is more complex since it would need to be passed into the creation routine, but is actually used by the Save and Cancel callback functions. Xt fortunately supplies a way out: the last argument to `XtAddCallback()` may be used by the application to carry its own data. Use this parameter to pass the address of `out_text` around and then it can be a parameter to the creation function, and not have to be a global variable after all. This is shown in Figure 44.

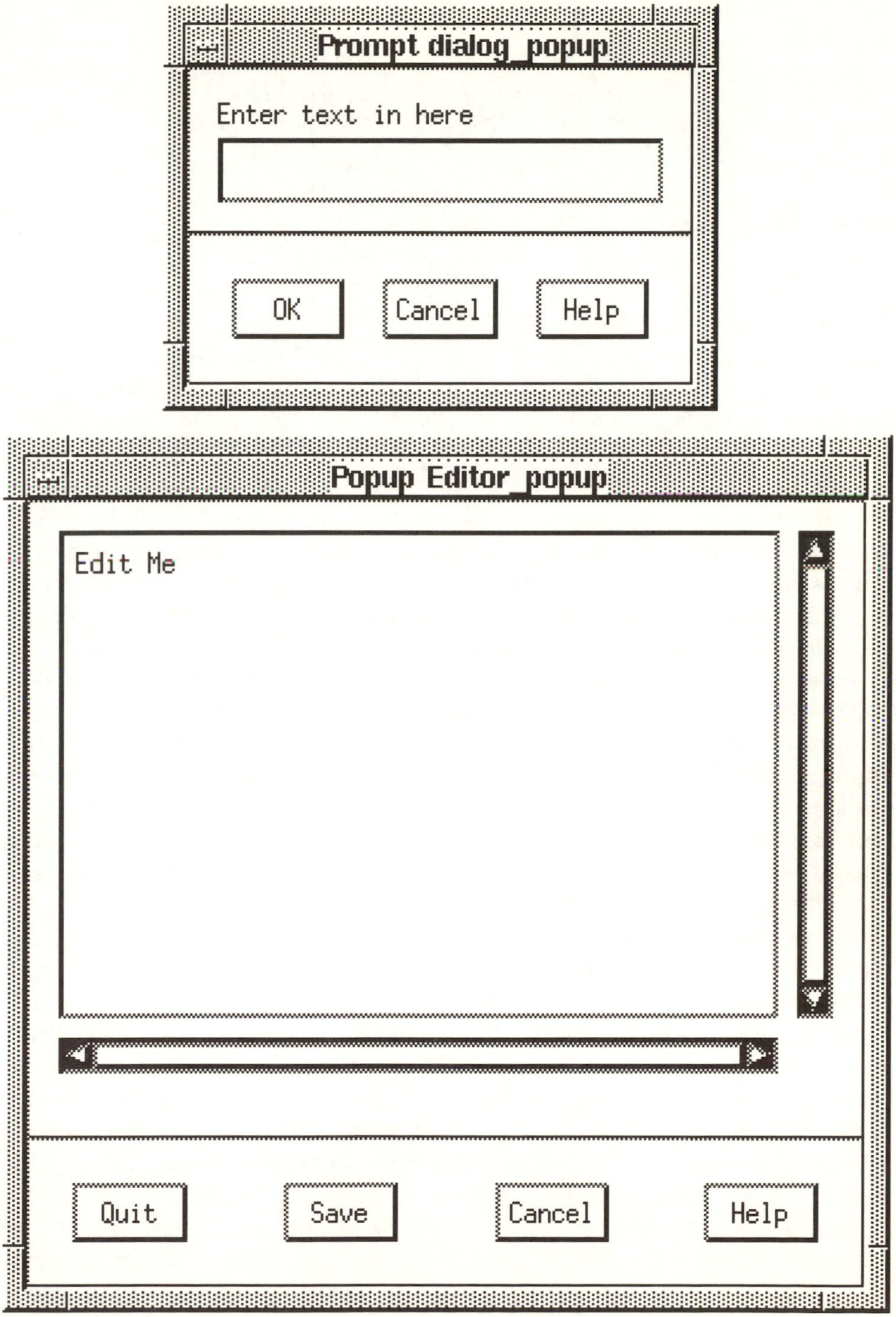

Figure 43:   A pop-up editor derived from a prompt dialog

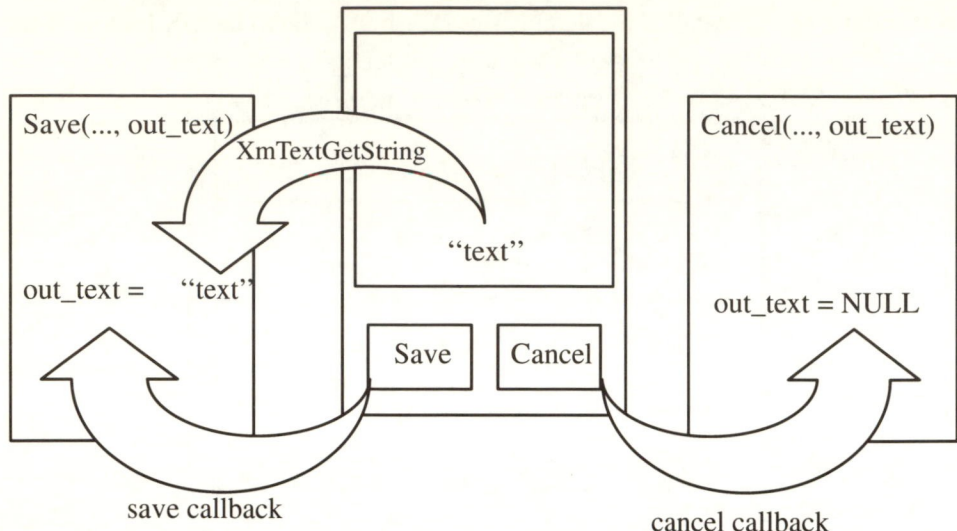

Figure 44:   Returning text values from a pop-up editor

The above description covers the general behavior. Unfortunately we have to delve a little deeper to get other parts of the behavior correct. The prompt dialog actually uses a SelectionBox and this is a subclass of BulletinBoard. BulletinBoard modifies the behavior of its children when it occurs in a dialog and is usually the place to look when the dialog behaves in an unexpected way. First, it has a resource called `XmNautoUnmanage`. This defaults to `True`, and the effect is that when a button is pushed it unmanages the BulletinBoard widget. That is, the dialog disappears from the screen so that pressing the Quit or Cancel buttons will terminate the dialog without further action. However, it will happen for *any* button, including the Help and Save buttons! We usually want the dialog to remain after these have been pushed, so this resource must be set to `False`. The widget must then be unmanaged explicitly by the program when the Quit or Cancel buttons are pressed.

Use of the convenience function `XmCreatePromptDialog()` returns the SelectionBox widget in an unmanaged state. To show the dialog, it must be managed. When a button is pressed in the dialog, the callbacks of PushButton are not invoked but rather one of the callbacks of the SelectionBox. These are the `XmNapplyCall-back`, the `XmNcancelCallback`, the `XmNhelpCallback` and the `XmNokCall-back`. The widget given in the first argument to each of the callback functions is also the SelectionBox rather than a PushButton. If we wanted to, say, destroy the dialog when the Cancel or Quit button is pressed, we destroy the pop-up shell. This is given by `XtParent()` of the SelectionBox widget returned in the callback.

Many widgets are set up so that they can respond to the keyboard as well as to the mouse. For example, if the return key is pressed in a PushButton widget, the activateCallbacks are invoked. BulletinBoard also looks for the return key. Bulletin-

Board has a resource called the defaultButton, which is set to the OK button. If the return key is pressed anywhere in the dialog, the default button is activated. Unfortunately, in Motif 1.0 the BulletinBoard applies this rather liberally, to the extent that pressing Return while in the text widget does not result in a new line, but in the default button being activated! This has been fixed in Motif 1.1 so that return works 'properly' in a Text widget, even when within a BulletinBoard. There is a workaround in Motif 1.0—the correct behavior has to be restored to Text by using *translation tables*. The action usually invoked for the return key for a multiline editor is `newline()`. This action will have been removed by BulletinBoard. Put it back again by creating a translation table for the return key/newline( ) combination and installing it in the widget. This topic is discussed further in Chapter 11. Ignore the parts enclosed by preprocessor `#ifdef` statements for now.

We put all this together in the following program which consists of a single PushButton with the label 'Edit Me'. When pushed, an editor is popped up with the same message. We put some pretty naive behavior in the cancel and quit callbacks: both of them print a message to an `xterm` saying what has happened and how the text ended up. More intelligent behavior is discussed after the program.

Program 20: popupedit.c

```
#include <stdio.h>
#include <Xm/PushB.h>
#include <Xm/Text.h>
#include <Xm/SelectioB.h>

#define MAX_ARGS 20

#if XmVersion == 1000
#define MOTIF_1_0
#endif
char Class_name[] ="XmPopupEditor";
char *in_text  = "Edit Me";
char *out_text = NULL;
#ifdef MOTIF_1_0
/* to fix a "feature" of a bulletin board in a dialog */
char transLine[] = "<Key>Return: newline()";
#endif
/*-----------------------------------------------------
**      Save
*/
void edit_saveCB(w, out_text, call_data)
Widget w;
char **out_text;
caddr_t call_data;
```

```
{   Arg args [MAX_ARGS];
    Widget   scrolled_window, edit_text;
    /* reclaim space from the old string */
    XtFree (*out_text);

    /* find the scrolled window */
    /* find the text widget */
    scrolled_window = XmSelectionBoxGetChild (w,
                        XmDIALOG_WORK_AREA);
    /* the text widget is the scrolled window's
       work area child. Get the child from the
       workWindow resource */
    XtSetArg (args[0], XmNworkWindow, &edit_text);
    XtGetValues (scrolled_window, args, 1);
    /* get the text string */
    *out_text = XmTextGetString(edit_text);
}
void edit_helpCB(w, client_data, call_data)
    Widget w;
    caddr_t client_data;
    caddr_t call_data;
{

    /* Should use the CreateHelp routine of earlier.
       This is a pretty stupid method, guaranteed to
       annoy users:
    */
    fprintf(stderr, "help not implemented\n");
}
void edit_cancelCB(w, text, call_data)
    Widget   w;
    char     **text;
    caddr_t call_data;
{
    Widget shell = XtParent(edit_dialog);
    *text = NULL;
    printf("Edit dialog cancelled\n");
    XtUnmanageChild(edit_dialog);
    XtDestroyWidget(shell);
}
void
edit_quitCB(w, text, call_data)
    Widget   w;
    char     **text;
    caddr_t call_data;
{
    Widget shell = XtParent(edit_dialog);
```

```
        printf("Quitting popup edit dialog.\n");
        if (*text == NULL)
            printf("no edited text saved\n");
        else
            printf("Edited text was:\n\n%s", *text);
        XtUnmanageChild(w);
        XtDestroyWidget(shell);
}
PopupEdit(parent, in_text, out_text)
        Widget  parent;
        char    *in_text;
        char    **out_text;
{
        int n;
#ifdef MOTIF_1_0
        XtTranslations transTable;
#endif
        Arg args[MAX_ARGS];
        Widget w;
        Widget edit_text;
        Widget edit_dialog;          should be global.
        /* create the display window with
        ** a text widget as
        ** a popup window
        */
        n = 0;
        XtSetArg(args[n], XmNautoUnmanage, False); n++;
        edit_dialog = XmCreatePromptDialog(parent,
                        "Popup Editor", args, n);
        XtAddCallback (edit_dialog, XmNapplyCallback,
                        edit_saveCB, out_text);
        XtAddCallback (edit_dialog, XmNcancelCallback,
                        edit_cancelCB, out_text);
        XtAddCallback (edit_dialog, XmNhelpCallback,
                        edit_helpCB, NULL);
        XtAddCallback (edit_dialog, XmNokCallback,
                        edit_quitCB, out_text);

        n = 0;
        XtSetArg(args[n], XmNscrollingPolicy,
                        XmAUTOMATIC); n++;
        XtSetArg(args[n], XmNeditMode,
                        XmMULTI_LINE_EDIT); n++;
        edit_text = XmCreateScrolledText(edit_dialog,
                        "edit text",
                        args, n);
```

```
    XmTextSetString (edit_text, in_text);
    XtManageChild(edit_text);

#ifdef MOTIF_1_0
    /* edit_text is a child of a selection box
       in a dialog.
       A form is a subclass of a bulletin board which
       "redefines" the return key in this context.
       Fix the return key back to what it should be:
    */
    transTable = XtParseTranslationTable(transLine);
    XtOverrideTranslations(edit_text, transTable);
#endif

    /* Show the apply button
    */
    w = XmSelectionBoxGetChild (edit_dialog,
                   XmDIALOG_APPLY_BUTTON);
    XtManageChild (w);
    /* and lose the input area
    */
    w = XmSelectionBoxGetChild (edit_dialog,
                     XmDIALOG_TEXT);
    XtUnmanageChild (w);

    XtManageChild(edit_dialog);
}
void
PushCB(w, client_data, call_data)
Widget w;
caddr_t client_data;
caddr_t call_data;
{
    PopupEdit (w, in_text, &out_text);
}

main(argc, argv)
int argc;
char **argv;
{
    Widget toplevel;
    Widget button;

    /* Initialize the intrinsics
       with a toplevel widget */
    toplevel = XtInitialize(NULL,
```

```
                    Class_name,
                    NULL,
                    0,
                    &argc, argv);
    /* Create a widget, with the
        toplevel as manager;
     */
    button = XmCreatePushButton(toplevel,
                    "Edit Me",
                    NULL,
                    0);
    XtAddCallback (button, XmNactivateCallback,
                    PushCB);
    XtManageChild (button);

    /* display all of the widgets */
    XtRealizeWidget(toplevel);

    /* enter the main processing loop */
    XtMainLoop();
}
```

In the discussion of the program prior to presenting it we said that the OK button should have its label set to 'Quit' and the apply button to 'Save'. Lines to do this did not appear in the program. Also, if an attempt is made to run the program as it is, the editor will probably be constrained to be too small to be useful and so should have its width and height set to something reasonable. If these pieces of information were hard-coded into the program, it would reduce user flexibility for configuration. On the other hand it would be too much to expect every user to modify his or her own `.Xdefaults` file. The solution is to use a system-wide application-defaults file. The application-defaults file for this application should contain:

```
XmPopupEditor*applyLabelString:    Save
XmPopupEditor*okLabelString:       Quit
XmPopupEditor*Text.width:          300
XmPopupEditor*Text.height:         200
```

This file should be installed as `/usr/lib/X11/app-defaults/XmPopupEditor`. Application defaults files are generally stored in this directory and the actual file name is the class name of the application. During development it is common to call the local copy of the application-defaults file `<Class-name>.ad`.

Before leaving this section we should discuss some of the issues raised in using pop-ups. There is an increase in complexity since each pop-up has its own callbacks, which all need their own callback functions. In C, this complexity can be localized by using multiple files, hiding all the functions of a dialog in a file and marking them all as static, to avoid clashes elsewhere. Because data must often be shared among functions it is all too tempting to make it global. If only one instance of a dialog using this shared data will be active at any time, it is satisfactory to use global data. If not, steps must be taken to pass the address of the data into the dialog creation routine, passing this around through the `client_data` component of callbacks.

The behavior when the Quit button is pressed has a serious flaw: the text in the output-text parameter may not be the current text in the text widget. We should keep track of changes to the text. The text widget supplies a resource for this: the callbacks on `XmNvalueChangedCallback` are invoked each time a change is made to the text. If a variable (global to this callback, the Save callback and the Quit callback) is set to an 'unsaved' value each time by the `XmNvalueChangedCallback`, but reset to 'saved' in the Save callback, the Quit callback can detect unsaved text. It should then post a warning dialog.

10.2.3   Modal dialogs

The dialogs considered so far have been *modeless*. The user can interact with the dialog or with any other part of the application. This is the norm for any component of a Motif application. For example, if a Help dialog has been popped up, the user may close it or may move it off to one side so that the rest of the application can be continued while the Help dialog can still be read.

A *modal* or *blocking* dialog, on the other hand, requires a response from the user before it will allow the user to continue with the rest of the application. Programmers tend to like modal dialogs—they give a single execution thread that is easy to follow. They are also easier to program if no special support is given. X is an event-driven system that *does* give this support and in fact most dialogs that traditionally would have been modal are simpler to write and easier to use if they are modeless.

For example, consider an editor where the user already has a file opened, but wishes to open another. An Open dialog would give a text-entry area for the filename, and OK and Cancel buttons. A modeless dialog would allow the user to get half-way through typing the filename and then do something else before completing (or cancelling) the dialog. This could be a task such as closing the first file, or even a major edit of the first file, before they resume the dialog. The modeless dialog allows the user to maintain a multithreaded use of the system. On the other hand, a modal dialog would force the dialog to completion, releasing control only when the OK or Cancel buttons are pressed. Microsoft's Word for Windows for example is full of such modal dialogs and thus can be very annoying and frustrating to use.

Despite these words of caution, there are a few occasions when modal dialogs are required. For example, if Exit has been selected from an editor, and the file has not been saved, a warning dialog should prompt the user to either Save or Abandon the changes. This dialog should be modal, because there should be no other interaction with the application—all it is going to do is exit.

Modal dialogs hold some pitfalls for the Motif programmer because they run counter to the normal modeless style. The method described here requires the cooperation of the Motif window manager mwm. It only works when mwm is running (test for this by `XmIsMotifWMRunning()`).

Any one of the dialog-creation routines creates a widget such as `MessageBox` (a subclass of `BulletinBoard`) that is parented by a `DialogShell`. This `DialogShell` has resources of its own but it also uses resources of its `BulletinBoard` child. One of the `BulletinBoard` resources is `XmNdialogStyle` which can be set to `XmDIALOG_MODELESS` (the default) or `XmDIALOG_FULL_APPLICATION_MODAL`[11] (the other values you are unlikely to need). Setting this resource is basically all that needs to be done to control the modality of the dialog:

```
XtSetArg (args[n], XmNdialogStyle,
               XmDIALOG_FULL_APPLICATION_MODAL); n++;
w = XmCreateWarningDialog (parent, "warning", args, n);
XtManageChild (w);
```

Callbacks need to be set as usual.

That was the easy part. Since the dialog is now modal, and must be completed before anything else can be done, it is very tempting to write the following for an application that may be posting a warning dialog before exiting:

```
/* ERRONEOUS CODE FOLLOWS! */
if (!file_saved)
{   XtSetArg (args[n], XmNdialogStyle,
               XmDIALOG_APPLICATION_MODAL); n++;
    w = XmCreateWarningDialog (parent, "warning",
                                  args, n);
    XtAddCallback (w, XmNokCallback, OkCB, NULL);
    XtAddCallback (w, XmNcancelCallback,
               CancelCB, NULL);
    XtManageChild (w);
}
exit (0);

OkCB(...)
{
    ...
}

CancelCB(...)
{
    ...
}
```

---

[11] Use Xm_DIALOG_APPLICATION_MODAL in Motif 1.0.

Alas, the program will exit every time with the file unsaved, with perhaps a flash of the warning dialog. What happens is this: the `XtManageChild()` call starts the dialog. This will inform the window manager that the dialog is modal so that mwm can enforce the modal style on the application. However, while the server and mwm— asynchronous processes—are sorting out all of this, the `XtManageChild()` call completes and falls through to `exit(0)`. This promptly terminates the application, often before the dialog even gets its windows drawn!

The Motif window manager enforces the modality through the delivery of events. It cannot interfere with the normal execution of code and can only take control when the application is waiting for events. So after creating the dialog as modal, no more application code should occur. Instead, control should be returned to event-loop processing. From then on, events will only be sent to the dialog.

The dialog will have some buttons such as OK, Cancel and Help. Interaction is limited to the dialog, and generally means that only these buttons can be pressed. When this occurs, application code is called through the appropriate callback. This code may unmanage or destroy the dialog, at which point the modal dialog will terminate, allowing normal modeless interaction to resume. If there had been some code intended to follow the modal dialog (such as the `exit()` statement in the erroneous code of the previous page) it would have to be moved and duplicated among all of the callback functions:

```
if (!file_saved)
{   XtSetArg (args[n], XmNdialogStyle,
                XmDIALOG_APPLICATION_MODAL); n++;
    w = XmCreateWarningDialog (parent, "warning",
                            args, n);
    XtAddCallback (w, XmNokCallback, OkCB, NULL);
    XtAddCallback (w, XmNcancelCallback,
                CancelCB, NULL);
    XtManageChild (w);
}
else
    exit (0);

OkCB(...)
{
    ...
    exit (0);
}

CancelCB(...)
{
    ...
    exit (0);
}
```

Such duplication is reasonable when there is only one modal dialog followed by modeless interaction. However, this is not always the case. Later in this chapter an example of a calendar with twenty-eight days is considered. Associated with each day is a file and upon exit, the application should check that all twenty-eight files have been saved, using up to twenty-eight modal dialogs. It is tempting to write:

```
for (day = 1; day <= 28; day++)
    if (!text_saved[day])
        modal_save_dialog (day);
```

This does not work as hoped, because when it is expanded it is:

```
if (!text_saved[1])
    modal_save_dialog (1);
if (!text_saved[2])
    modal_save_dialog (2);
...
```

and this does contain any return of control to the event loop. The Motif window manager has no chance to enforce modality so up to twenty-eight modal (!) dialogs are created at once.

This problem can be resolved by simulating the `for` loop by passing the loop counter into the callback functions, which in turn call `modal_save_dialog()` with the next value of the loop counter. The flow of control is not at all simple to follow and makes this an unsatisfactory method.

What is needed is a means to have an event loop after creation of the dialog. The Xt toolkit has a function `XtProcessEvent()` which waits for the next event and dispatches it to the appropriate widget. Put a loop around this and modality can be enforced by the Motif window manager:

```
while (?)
    XtProcessEvent (XtIMAll);
```

How can such a local loop terminate? It should terminate when one of the dialog callbacks unmanages or destroys the dialog. No events are generated by this. The event loop and the callback functions must share a 'flag' which the callback function can set to terminate the loop. This flag can be a global variable but it is more elegant to make it local and pass it around as a parameter. The modal dialog to check on a single file now becomes:

```
Bool dialog_over = False;

if (!file_saved)
{   n = 0;
    w = XmCreateWarningDialog (parent, "warning",
                                args, n);
    XtAddCallback (w, XmNokCallback, OkCb,
                    &dialog_over);
    XtAddCallback (w, XmNcancelCallback, CancelCB,
```

```
                              &dialog_over);
        modal_dialog_loop (w, &dialog_over);
        exit (0);
    }
    void
    modal_dialog_loop (w, dialog_over)
        Widget w;
        Bool *dialog_over;
    {   int n = 0;

        XtSetArg (args[n], XmNdialogStyle,
                  XmDIALOG_FULL_APPLICATION_MODAL); n++;
        XtSetValues (w, args, n);
        XtManageChild (w);
        while (*dialog_over == False)
            XtProcessEvent (XtIMAll);
        exit (0);
    }


    OkCB (w, dialog_over, call_data)
        Widget w;
        Bool *dialog_over;
        caddr_t call_data;
    {
        ...
        *dialog_over = True;
    }


    CancelCB (w, dialog_over, call_data)
        Widget w;
        Bool * dialog_over;
        caddr_t call_data;
    {
        ...
        *dialog_over = True;
    }
```

10.2.4 Summary

This section has considered a number of dialogs. Motif-supplied dialogs can be created using calls such as:

```
XmCreateMessageDialog ()
XmCreateInformationDialog ()
XmCreateWarningDialog ()
```

Individual components of a dialog may be found by calls such as:

```
XmMessageBoxGetChild ()
XmFileSelectionBoxGetChild ()
```

Dialogs using other widgets may be created by using a PromptDialog with the other widget added as a 'work-area' widget.

Dialogs default to modeless. To change the modality, use the resource:

```
XmNdialogStyle
```

(This only works under mwm.) Modal dialogs are usually undesirable and Motif does not make it very easy to use them. It is sometimes necessary to set up a local event-processing loop using:

```
XtProcessEvent ()
```

Exercises

1. Add a warning dialog to the pop-up editor that is invoked if the user tries to leave without saving the file. It should give options to save the file, to cancel the exit, or to exit without saving changes.

2. Create a personal details pop-up that contains a form to fill in name, address and telephone number.

3. Justify every modal dialog you use with a one-page document clearly explaining why it cannot be modeless.

10.3   Example: A calendar

In this section we consider a non-trivial Motif program to give a simple calendar with diary-entry facilities for each day. As we want to look at Motif code rather than lots of other C code, we make a few simplifying assumptions for the calendar: there are only twenty-eight days in the month and the first is always a Monday. This will allow us to avoid computations of the current month, the number of days in the month and the starting day—important enough but not necessary for our purposes. We can lay out the calendar in a fairly standard way: the names of the days along the top and a number for each day in a four-by-seven grid below this. The appearance is shown in Figure 45. The program should not only show the days, but also allow us to make diary entries for each day. When the left button is clicked over a day, a pop-up window should appear, containing an editor. This should show any text entered previously and allow it to be changed. This program is only a toy because it does not get the days right. However, it should still be at least useable. Information entered into the diary editors should not be lost between invocations of the program. On start-up, previous information (if existing) should be read, and on finishing, current information should be written. The simplest way to manage this is to have one file per day and this is adopted here.

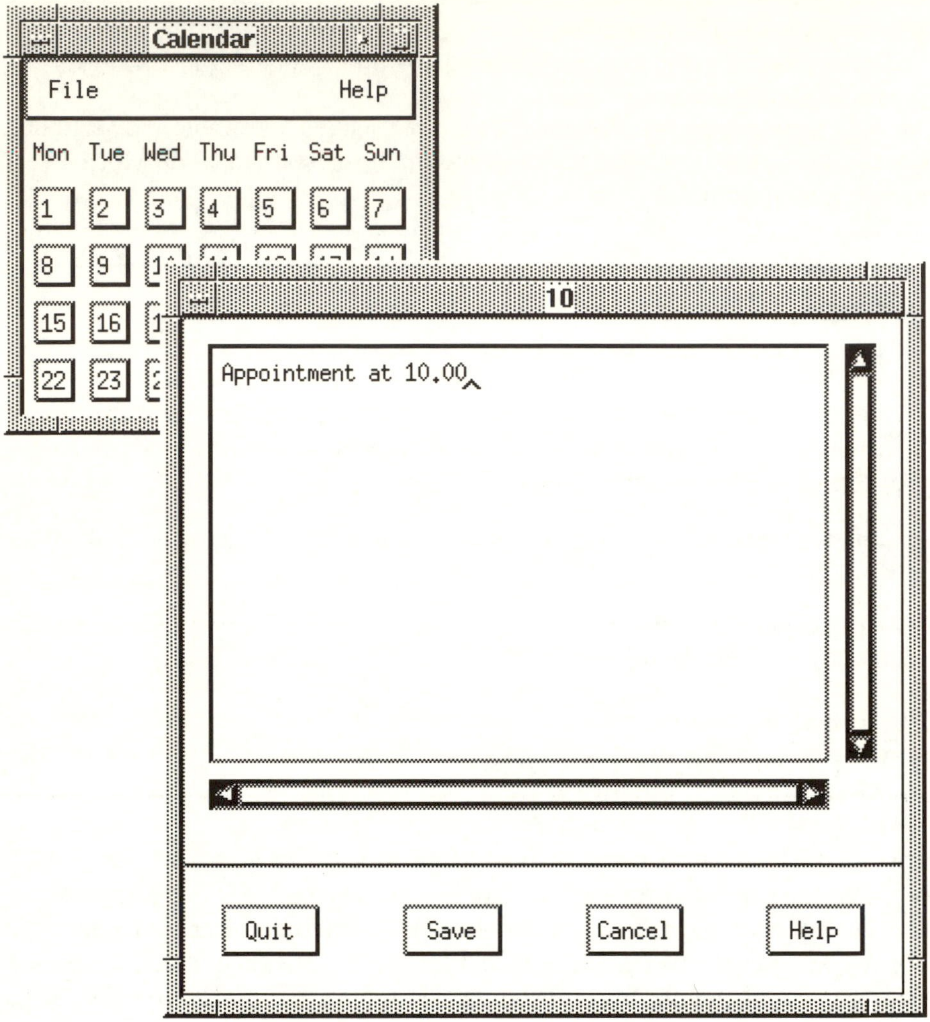

Figure 45:   The calendar program

Before going into the details of the program, let us look at what is involved. Along the top is a pulldown menu. Under this is the array of days and numbers. The days themselves have no input semantics, that is, there is no point in clicking on them or using the keyboard in them. They can be represented by seven label widgets. However, the numbers should respond, in that pressing the mouse button in them will invoke a pop-up. They can each be a push button. The two sets, days and numbers, are all in a rectangular array. Even though the components are of different types (labels and push buttons) they all fit together into the array. The array can most easily be done by a row column widget. The menu bar and the row column together make up the application. They could be placed in a form, a row column, a bulletin board, or a main window. A main window is probably the easiest to deal with. The pop-ups contain editors. For this, just use the pop-up editor of an earlier section.

There is the question of whether we should use one or twenty-eight pop-ups or as many as needed, and whether they should be created at the beginning or only as needed. If we use just one, we would have to swap text from one day to the next, retaining the text for undisplayed days somewhere. This is not particularly hard. However, if we only use one pop-up for all days, we could only edit one day at a time, whereas if we have more, we could allow several pop-ups to be active at once. This would give the user more flexibility. If we have exactly twenty-eight pop-ups, things are quite simple. It is neither time- nor space-consuming to set them up at the beginning and makes creation much easier than if we have to remember which ones have been created and which have not[12]. The last alternative, of creating pop-ups as needed, and perhaps discarding them on completion, has a minor problem: if the user clicks twice on one day, the program has to make sure that a second pop-up is not created for the same day! So we use twenty-eight pop-ups created at the beginning.

The broad structure of the program is first initialization, then creation of the main window to hold the other components. The menu is created in the same way as before, followed by the row column and the pop-ups. The menu and the row column are set into the main window, the whole lot is realized and then the main loop is entered. In creating the row column, first the row-column widget itself is created, followed by the seven day-labels and the twenty-eight push buttons for the days. Twenty-eight pop-ups are created, with text contents taken from the files '1' to '28'. These editors will be stored in an array of text widgets for later convenience. Callbacks on the push buttons pop-up the corresponding editor and a callback on the menu exit button saves the contents of the text widgets and exits. The resulting program is a typical Motif program: calls which perform complex tasks or create complex objects, mixed with a large amount of detail. This detail controls the behavior of the widgets and typically requires much browsing of the manual.

Program 21:   calendar.c

```
/*-----------------------------------------------------
**      Include Files
*/
#include <stdio.h>
#include <string.h>
#include <sys/types.h>
```

---

[12] On the other hand, if one had to set up, say, several thousand widgets, the application would start up very slowly if they were all created at once. It would be better to create them as needed.

```c
#include <Xm/BulletinB.h>
#include <Xm/CascadeB.h>
#include <Xm/DialogS.h>
#include <Xm/Form.h>
#include <Xm/Label.h>
#include <Xm/MainW.h>
#include <Xm/MessageB.h>
#include <Xm/PushB.h>
#include <Xm/RowColumn.h>
#include <Xm/ScrolledW.h>
#include <Xm/Text.h>
#include <Xm/SelectioB.h>

/* Motif version number */
#if XmVersion == 1000
#define MOTIF_1_0
#endif


/*---------------------------------------------------
**      Forward Declarations
*/
void main ();
void CreateApplication ();
Widget CreateHelp ();
Widget CreateMenu();
Widget CreateCalendar();
Widget CreatePopupEditor();
char *ReadFile ();

/* Close popup help callback */
void CloseCB ();

/* Help callbacks */
void AboutHelpCB ();
void ApplicHelpCB ();
void EditHelpCB ();

/* Editor callbacks */
void EditDayCB ();
void EditCancelCB();
void EditExitCB ();
void EditSaveCB ();
void EditChangedCB ();

/* Exiting application with
   unsaved files callbacks
```

```
*/
void ExitSaveCB();
void ExitDontSaveCB();
void ExitAnywayCB();
void QuitCB ();

/* File menu callbacks */
void FileSaveCB ();
void FileExitCB ();

/*-------------------------------------------------------
**     Global Variables
*/
#define MAX_ARGS 20
#define Class_name "XmCalendar"

Arg     args[MAX_ARGS];
Widget  popups[29];
char    *text[29];
Bool    text_saved[29];
char * daylabels[] = {"Mon", "Tue", "Wed", "Thu", "Fri",
                      "Sat", "Sun"};

/* Help texts */
char APPLIC_HELP_TEXT[] =
"Click on a day to see or \n\
edit messages for that day";
char ABOUT_HELP_TEXT[] =
"XmCalendar - version 1.0 \n\
J.D. Newmarch";
char EDIT_HELP_TEXT[] =
"A simple editor";

/*-------------------------------------------------------
**     main          - main logic for application
*/
void main (argc,argv)
    unsigned int    argc;
    char       **argv;
{
    Display    *display;    /* Display           */
    Widget     app_shell;   /* ApplicationShell     */

    app_shell = XtInitialize(NULL,
              Class_name,      /* class name */
              NULL,            /* options */
```

```
                0,            /* number of options */
                &argc, argv);

    /*    Create and realize main application window.
    */
    CreateApplication (app_shell);
    XtRealizeWidget (app_shell);

    /*    Get and dispatch events.
    */
    XtMainLoop ();
}


/*---------------------------------------------------------
**    CreateApplication    - create main window
*/
void CreateApplication (parent)
    Widget    parent;
{

    Widget    main_window;
    Widget    menu;
    Widget    calendar;
    register int    n;
    XmString    label_string;

    /*    Create MainWindow
    */
     n = 0;
    main_window = XmCreateMainWindow (parent, "main1",
                        args, n);
    XtManageChild (main_window);
    menu = CreateMenu(main_window);
    calendar = CreateCalendar(main_window);

    XmMainWindowSetAreas (main_window,
            menu,            /* menu bar */
            NULL,            /* command */
            NULL,            /* horizon scroll bar */
            NULL,            /* vert scroll bar */
            calendar);       /* work area */
}
Widget CreateMenu(parent)
    Widget parent;
{

    Widget        menu_bar;
    Widget        menu_pane;
```

```
Widget          cascade;
Widget          button;
int n;      /*    Create MenuBar in MainWindow.
*/
n = 0;
menu_bar = XmCreateMenuBar (parent, "menu_bar",
                              args, n);
XtManageChild (menu_bar);


/*    Create "File" PulldownMenu.
*/
n = 0;
menu_pane = XmCreatePulldownMenu (menu_bar,
                    "menu_pane", args, n);


n = 0;
button = XmCreatePushButton (menu_pane, "Save",
                      args, n);
XtManageChild (button);
XtAddCallback (button, XmNactivateCallback,
                    FileSaveCB, NULL);


n = 0;
button = XmCreatePushButton (menu_pane, "Exit",
                      args, n);
XtManageChild (button);
XtAddCallback (button, XmNactivateCallback,
                      FileExitCB, (caddr_t) 1);


n = 0;
XtSetArg (args[n], XmNsubMenuId, menu_pane);   n++;
cascade = XmCreateCascadeButton (menu_bar, "File",
                      args, n);
XtManageChild (cascade);


/*    Create "Help" PulldownMenu
*/
n = 0;
menu_pane = XmCreatePulldownMenu (menu_bar,
                    "menu_pane", args, n);


n = 0;
button = XmCreatePushButton (menu_pane, "About",
                      args, n);
XtManageChild (button);
XtAddCallback (button, XmNactivateCallback,
```

```
                                AboutHelpCB, NULL);

        n = 0;
        button = XmCreatePushButton (menu_pane,
                            "Application", args, n);
        XtManageChild (button);
        XtAddCallback (button, XmNactivateCallback,
                            ApplicHelpCB, NULL);

        n = 0;
        XtSetArg (args[n], XmNsubMenuId, menu_pane);  n++;
        cascade = XmCreateCascadeButton (menu_bar, "Help",
                            args, n);
        XtManageChild (cascade);

        n = 0;
        XtSetArg (args[n], XmNmenuHelpWidget,
                            cascade);  n++;
        XtSetValues (menu_bar, args, n);
        return (menu_bar);
}

Widget
CreateCalendar(parent)
    Widget parent;
{   Widget rowcol;
    Widget label;
    Widget button;
    int day, n;
    char daystr[4];

    n = 0;
    XtSetArg (args[n], XmNpacking, XmPACK_COLUMN); n++;
    XtSetArg (args[n], XmNorientation,
                    XmHORIZONTAL); n++;
    XtSetArg (args[n], XmNnumColumns, 5); n++;
    rowcol = XmCreateRowColumn(parent, "row col",
                                args, n);
    XtManageChild (rowcol);

    for (day = 0; day < 7; day++)
    {
        n = 0;
        label = XmCreateLabel (rowcol, daylabels[day],
                            args, n);
        XtManageChild (label);
```

```
        }

    for (day = 1; day <= 28; day++)
    {       popups[day] = CreatePopupEditor (rowcol,
                                                day);

        text_saved[day] = True;
        sprintf (daystr, "%d", day);
        n = 0;
        XtSetArg (args[n], XmNlabelString, NULL);
        button = XmCreatePushButton (rowcol, daystr,
                                        args, n);
        XtAddCallback(button, XmNactivateCallback,
                    EditDayCB, popups[day]);
        XtManageChild (button);
    }
    return (rowcol);
}


/*---------------------------------------------------
**      CreateHelp          - create help window
*/
Widget CreateHelp (parent, help_text, title_text)
    Widget          parent;
    char            *help_text;
    char            *title_text;
{
    Widget          button;
    Widget          message_box;
    Arg             args[MAX_ARGS];
    register int    n;
    XmString    title_string = NULL;
    XmString    message_string = NULL;
    XmString    button_string = NULL;

    /*  Generate message to display.
    */
    message_string = XmStringCreateLtoR (help_text,
                        XmSTRING_DEFAULT_CHARSET);
    button_string = XmStringCreateLtoR ("Close",
                        XmSTRING_DEFAULT_CHARSET);
    title_string = XmStringCreateLtoR (title_text,
                        XmSTRING_DEFAULT_CHARSET);

    /*  Create MessageBox dialog.
    */
```

```
        n = 0;
        XtSetArg (args[n], XmNdialogTitle,
                                title_string);   n++;
        XtSetArg (args[n], XmNokLabelString,
                                button_string);   n++;
        XtSetArg (args[n], XmNmessageString,
                                message_string);   n++;
        message_box = XmCreateMessageDialog (parent,
                                "helpbox", args, n);
        XtAddCallback (message_box, XmNokCallback, NULL);
                                                    CloseCB,
        button = XmMessageBoxGetChild (message_box,
                                XmDIALOG_CANCEL_BUTTON);
        XtUnmanageChild (button);
        button = XmMessageBoxGetChild (message_box,
                                XmDIALOG_HELP_BUTTON);
        XtUnmanageChild (button);

        /*    Free strings and return MessageBox.
        */
        XmStringFree (title_string);
        XmStringFree (message_string);
        XmStringFree (button_string);
        return (message_box);
}


/*-----------------------------------------------------
**    CloseCB              - callback for close button
*/
void
CloseCB  (w, client_data, call_data)
    Widget    w;      /*  widget id          */
    caddr_t    client_data;    /*  font pointer    */
    caddr_t    call_data;    /*  data from widget class
*/
{   /*    Unmanage widgets.
    */
    XtUnmanageChild (w);
    XtDestroyWidget (XtParent (w));
}

#ifdef MOTIF_1_0
/* to fix a "feature" of a bulletin board in a dialog */
char transLine[] = "<Key>Return: newline()";
#endif
```

```
Widget
CreatePopupEditor (parent, day)
    Widget    parent;
    int    day;
{
    Widget    edit_message_box;
    Widget    edit_dialog;
    Widget    edit_text;
    int    n;
#ifdef MOTIF_1_0
    XtTranslations    transTable;
#endif
    char daystr[4];
    sprintf (daystr, "%d", day);
    /* create the display window with a text widget as
    ** a popup window
    */
    n = 0;
    XtSetArg (args[n], XmNselectionLabelString,
                        XmStringCreateLtoR ("",
                            XmSTRING_DEFAULT_CHARSET));
    n++;
    XtSetArg(args[n], XmNautoUnmanage, False); n++;
    edit_dialog = XmCreatePromptDialog(parent,
                daystr, args, n);
    XtUnmanageChild (XmSelectionBoxGetChild (
                                    edit_dialog,
                        XmDIALOG_TEXT));
    XtManageChild (XmSelectionBoxGetChild (edit_dialog,
                        XmDIALOG_APPLY_BUTTON));
    /* Add callbacks for each button.
       The day value is passed in as client data.
       Note the type cast of int to pointer for this
    */
    XtAddCallback(edit_dialog, XmNapplyCallback,
                EditSaveCB, (caddr_t) day);
    XtAddCallback(edit_dialog, XmNcancelCallback,
                EditCancelCB, (caddr_t) day);
    XtAddCallback(edit_dialog, XmNhelpCallback,
                EditHelpCB, (caddr_t) day);
    XtAddCallback(edit_dialog, XmNokCallback,
                EditExitCB, (caddr_t) day);

    n = 0;
    XtSetArg (args[n], XmNtitle, daystr); n++;
    XtSetValues (XtParent(edit_dialog), args, n);
```

```
        n = 0;
    XtSetArg(args[n], XmNeditMode,
                          XmMULTI_LINE_EDIT); n++;
    edit_text = XmCreateScrolledText(edit_dialog,
                          "edit text",  args, n);
    XtAddCallback (edit_text, XmNvalueChangedCallback,
                      EditChangedCB, (caddr_t) day);
#ifdef MOTIF_1_0
    /* edit_text is a child of a form in a dialog.
       A form is a subclass o a bulletin board which
       "redefines" the return key in this context.
       Fix the return key back to what it should be: */
    transTable = XtParseTranslationTable(transLine);
    XtOverrideTranslations(edit_text, transTable);
#endif

    text[day] = ReadFile(day);
    XmTextSetString (edit_text, text[day]);
    XtManageChild (edit_text);
    return (edit_text);
}
/*
**    Read the contents of the file into
**    a string and return the string.
*    Returns NULL on any failure (eg no file)
*/
char *
ReadFile(day)
    int day;
{
    char filename[4];
    struct stat statbuf;  /* File Info. */
    int file_length;      /* File Length */
    char * file_string;   /* File Contents */
    FILE *fp = NULL;      /* File Pointer */
    int nread;    sprintf (filename, "%d", day);
    if ((fp = fopen(filename, "r+")) == NULL)
        if ((fp = fopen(filename, "r")) != NULL)
        {
                fprintf(stderr,
                    "Warning: file opened read only.\n");
        }
        else
        {
                return((char *) NULL);
```

```
                }       if (stat(filename, &statbuf) == 0)
                    file_length = statbuf.st_size;
            else
                    file_length = 1000; /* arbitrary file length */
            /* read the file string */
            file_string = (char *)
                            XtMalloc((unsigned)file_length + 1);
            nread = fread(file_string, sizeof(char),
                            file_length, fp);
            /* NULL terminate the string */
            file_string[nread] = (char) 0;
            /* close the file */
            if (fclose(fp) != NULL)
                fprintf(stderr,
                        "Warning: unable to close file.\n");
            return (file_string);
    }
    /*----------------------------------------------------
    ** Callbacks for each of the three help buttons
    */


    /*----------------------------------------------------
    **    ApplicHelpCB  - callback for help button
    */
    void
    ApplicHelpCB (w, client_data, call_data)
        Widget      w;
        caddr_t     client_data;
        caddr_t     call_data;
    {
        Widget          message_box;

        /*      Create help window.
        */
        message_box = CreateHelp (w, APPLIC_HELP_TEXT,
                                    "Application");
        /*      Display help window.
        */
        XtManageChild (message_box);
    }


    /*----------------------------------------------------
    **    AboutHelpCB                - callback for help button
    */
    void
    AboutHelpCB (w, client_data, call_data)
```

```
      Widget      w;
      caddr_t     client_data;
      caddr_t     call_data;
{
      Widget          message_box;

      /*    Create help window.
      */
      message_box = CreateHelp (w, ABOUT_HELP_TEXT,
                                "About");
      /*    Display help window.
      */
      XtManageChild (message_box);
}


/*-----------------------------------------------------
**    EditHelpCB              - callback for help button
*/
void
EditHelpCB (w, day, call_data)
      Widget      w;
      caddr_t     day;
      caddr_t     call_data;
{
      Widget          message_box;

      /*    Create help window.
      */
      message_box = CreateHelp (w, EDIT_HELP_TEXT,
                          "Edit");
    /*    Display help window.
      */
      XtManageChild (message_box);
}

void
SaveFile (day)
    int day;
{   char filename[4];
    FILE *fp = NULL;

    /* free the old string and get the current text
    */
    XtFree (text[day]);
    text[day] = XmTextGetString (popups[day]);
    sprintf (filename, "%d", day);
```

```
        if ((fp = fopen (filename, "w")) == NULL)
        {   fprintf (stderr,
                "Can't open file %s for writing\n",
                filename);
            return;
        }
        fputs (text[day], fp);
        if (fclose (fp) != NULL)
            fprintf (stderr,
                "Can't close file %s\n", filename);
        else
            text_saved[day] = True;
    }


    void
    EditSaveCB(w, client_data, call_data)
        Widget w;
        caddr_t client_data;
        caddr_t call_data;
    {   int day;     day = (int) client_data;
        SaveFile (day);
    }


    void
    EditCancelCB(w, client_data, call_data)
        Widget w;
        caddr_t client_data;
        caddr_t call_data;
    {   int day;

        /* extract the day value, casting it
           back to int from pointer
        */
        day = (int) client_data;

        /* restore text to last saved value
        */
        XmTextSetString (popups[day], text[day]);
        text_saved[day] = True;
    }


    void
    EditExitCB(w, day, call_data)
        Widget w;
        caddr_t day;
```

```
        caddr_t call_data;
{
    XtUnmanageChild(w);
}


void
EditChangedCB(w, client_data, call_data)
    Widget w;
    caddr_t client_data;
    caddr_t call_data;
{   int day = (int) client_data;
    text_saved[day] = False;
}


/*
**      Edit Day CB
*/
void
EditDayCB  (w, editor, call_data)
    Widget    w;            /*  widget id         */
    Widget    editor;
    caddr_t    call_data;    /*  data from widget class
*/
{
    /* parent is the scroll bar, its parent the
       unmanaged selection box
    */
    XtManageChild (XtParent(XtParent(editor)));
}


/*-----------------------------------------------
**      FileSaveCB              - callback for quit button
*/
void
FileSaveCB (w, client_data, call_data)
    Widget    w;
    caddr_t    client_data;
    caddr_t    call_data;
{   int day;

    for (day = 1; day <= 28; day++)
        if ( ! text_saved[day])
            SaveFile (day);
}


void
```

```
modal_dialog_loop (w, dialog_over)
    Widget w;
    Bool *dialog_over;
{   int n = 0;

    XtSetArg (args[n], XmNdialogStyle,
                XmDIALOG_FULL_APPLICATION_MODAL); n++;
    XtSetValues (w, args, n);
    XtManageChild (w);
    while (*dialog_over == False)
        XtProcessEvent (XtIMAll);
    XtUnmanageChild (w);
    XtDestroyWidget (XtParent (w));
}

void
ExitSaveCB(w, dialog_over, call_data)
    Widget w;
    Bool *dialog_over;
    caddr_t call_data;
{   int day;
    caddr_t data;
    int n = 0;

    /* find which day it is */
    XtSetArg (args[n], XmNuserData, &data); n++;
    XtGetValues (w, args, n);
    /* convert back from pointer type */
    day = (int) data;

    SaveFile (day);
    *dialog_over = True;
}

void
ExitDontSaveCB(w, dialog_over, call_data)
    Widget w;
    Bool *dialog_over;
    caddr_t call_data;
{
    *dialog_over = True;
}

void
ExitAnywayCB (w, client_data, call_data)
    Widget    w;
```

```
          caddr_t     client_data;
          caddr_t     call_data;
     {
          exit(0);
     }


void
DayUnsaved (day)
     int day;
{    Widget warn = NULL;
     char message[512];
     XmString xmmessage;
     int n;
     Bool dialog_over = False;

     n = 0;
     warn = XmCreateWarningDialog (popups[day],
                    "warning", args, n);
     XtAddCallback (warn, XmNokCallback,
                         ExitSaveCB, &dialog_over);
     XtAddCallback (warn, XmNcancelCallback,
                         ExitDontSaveCB, &dialog_over);
     XtAddCallback (warn, XmNhelpCallback,
                         ExitAnywayCB, NULL);
     sprintf (message, "Day %d\nnot saved", day);
     xmmessage = XmStringCreateLtoR (message,
                         XmSTRING_DEFAULT_CHARSET);
     n = 0;
     XtSetArg (args[n], XmNmessageString,
                         xmmessage); n++;
     /* store the day value in the widget's user data */
     XtSetArg (args[n], XmNuserData, (caddr_t) day); n++;
     XtSetValues (warn, args, n);
     XtManageChild (warn);
     XmStringFree (xmmessage);

     /* make the dialog modal */
     modal_dialog_loop (warn, &dialog_over);
}


/*-----------------------------------------------------
**     FileExitCB                 - callback for quit button
*/
void
FileExitCB (w, client_data, call_data)
     Widget     w;
```

```
    caddr_t     client_data;
    caddr_t     call_data;
{   int day;

    /* modal dialogs to query about unsaved days */
    for (day = 1; day <= 28; day++)
        if ( !text_saved[day])
            DayUnsaved(day);
    exit (0);
}
```

Let us examine this program, stopping at the more interesting or new parts. The function `main()` holds nothing new. `CreateApplication()` has a call that we have not seen before: `XmMainWindowSetAreas()`. A main window is set up to manage a menu bar, a command widget, vertical and horizontal scroll bars and any other kind of widget that is generically called a 'work area.' Here we have just a menu bar and the row column. Although they are parented from the main window, this alone does not tell the main window which is which. For this, the call `XmMainWindowSetAreas()` is used to inform the main window how many widgets it has, and in what roles. The `CreateMenu()` call is identical to previous ones apart from the client data in the callback for the File Exit button. This will be discussed later. The call creates File and Help menus, with Save and Exit buttons on the File submenu, and About and Application buttons on the Help submenu.

In `CreateCalendar()` most of the work of creating the application is done. A row column is created with packing, orientation and number of columns set. We want all children to take the same size. For this the packing is set to `XmPACK_COL-UMN`. We want to add the widgets by rows, so orientation is set to `XmHORIZONTAL` instead of the default vertical. If you want to have a calendar with the labels down the side, with days running in columns, or if it you desire to leave it to user control, this resource can be omitted, so that it can be set in resource files. The number of rows is set to five—one for the labels and four for the numbers. It would be preferable to set the number of columns to seven instead of the number of rows, but this is not possible unless we change the orientation to vertical, which makes adding in the widgets more messy, as we would have to add them by columns:

```
for (col = 0; col < 7; col++)
{   label = XmCreateLabel (rowcol, daylabel[col],
                              args, n);
    for (row = 0; row < 4; row++)
    {   sprintf(day, "%i", row * 7 + col + 1);
        button = XmCreatePushButton(rowcol, day,
                                      args, n);
    }
}
```

(Real calendars typically have five rows for the numbers, with 'overflow' numbers being placed back in the first row.)

The seven labels along the top are now created. The widget name is set using the array of day names with values 'Mon,' 'Tue,' etc. However, the `labelString` resource is not set. The label displayed will default to the widget name, but could be set by the user in a resource file. This would allow the user to set any day labels they want, such as French ones.

The day buttons are then created. For these, the name is set to the number of the month, using `sprintf()` to create the ASCII string for each number. This time, though, the `XmNlabelString` is set to `NULL`. This forces the widget to use the name as the label, ignoring any user-set value. (This feature is not clearly documented in Motif 1.0.) Essentially we are being a little lazy here, by making the label widget do all the work of creating the label as an `XmString`. Otherwise we would have had to do:

```
sprintf(daystr, "%i", day);
xmday = XmStringCreateLtoR(daystr,
                XmSTRING_DEFAULT_CHARSET);

...

XtSetArg (args[n], XmNlabelString, xmday); n++;
button = XmCreatPushButton(...);
XmStringFree(xmstr);
```

The callback is added to each button of `EditDayCB()`. It is the same callback for each button widget, although of course it has to invoke a different pop-up for each. The callback function needs to find the editor widget for the pop-up. The simplest way is to use the method we have used several times before and pass in the editor widget as client data to the callback function. Then, when the callback is invoked the editor widget will be passed in to the callback function as the second argument.

The `CreateHelp()` call is basically the same as before. It creates a pop-up message box with an OK button. This function differs from the previous pop-up help in that the help message string is given as a parameter rather than being hard-coded into the function. A callback has been added to this message box so that when the OK button is pressed it destroys the message-box parent (the pop-up shell) and all of its children. This reclaims memory that otherwise might build up steadily each time help is called.

The function `CreatePopupEditor()` is similar to the earlier version. It differs in that instead of being passed input and output strings, it takes the integer value of a day. This is used in the call to `ReadFile()` which reads in a text string from the corresponding day file (or `NULL` if there is no file) and sets the text from that. In the callback functions, this integer is also passed around as client data instead of an output sink for the text. Note the type casts: client data is a pointer type, so to send it an integer value it has to be cast first. On retrieval it will have to be restored to an integer.

The function `ReadFile()` is all new. Its purpose, as mentioned in the last paragraph, is to read the text from a file into a string and return the string. This is done by standard Unix calls to open and read a file.

Three virtually identical functions follow to create the Help pop-ups. They differ in the text string to be shown in the help-message box and in the label to be used for this box. The similarity suggests that a tidier solution could have been found using only one function. This is left to the exercises.

By putting together pieces of programs that have already been discussed, a substantial amount of the calendar has already been built. Nearly all of the user interface has been done, with the array of buttons and labels, the menu, and all the help functions. The rest of the program is concerned with supplying application functionality so that when buttons such as Save are pressed, the right thing happens. We need to design the data types and fill in the callback functions.

Starting with the editor functions, there are three buttons to deal with. The Exit button is simple: just pop-down the editor window by unmanaging it. The Save button should get the text from the editor and save it in the appropriate file for that day. This means that the callback for the Save button must be able to determine both the text-editor widget and the name of the file. There is a variety of ways of doing this. The one adopted here is to pass the integer value of the day through to the callback via the client data field, and to maintain an array of pop-ups of the text widgets, indexed by the day[13]. The file name can be constructed from the day by turning the integer value into a string. The callback function `EditSaveCB()` retrieves the day index from the client data by casting it back to an integer, and then calls the function `SaveDay()` to get the text from the pop-up editor by `XmTextGetString()` and then writing it to the file. For convenience, the text is also saved in an array of text strings `text`. This just acts as a mirror of what is in the corresponding day file. Note that before a new value of the text is placed in this array, any old value is first freed by `XtFree()`. So that we can keep track of which editors have saved text, a Boolean array `saved` is also used. The value of the current day is set to `True` after the save.

The `EditCancelCB()` must cancel the current set of changes. The program restores the text to the last saved value. This is the string in the `text` array, so this function sets the widget text from this array. The value of `saved` for this day is also set to `True` as the text has been restored to a saved state. Note that no memory reclamation is done by the program: Text does its own memory handling each time its value is changed.

What sets the values in the saved array to `False`? Every time a change is made to the text in a Text widget the callback `EditChangedCB()` is called. This just sets the saved value to False. This function is on each Text widget's `XmNvalueChangedCallback` list.

---

[13] The array is indexed from 1 to 28 for simplicity. The zero'th element of the 29-element array is wasted.

Under the File menu are two buttons: one to Save and one to Exit. The Save button is to save all currently unsaved editors. The `FileSaveCB()` function only needs to do a pass through the `saved` array and for each day marked as unsaved, to call `SaveDay()` for it. The Exit button should terminate the application. However, it should ensure that if any days have unsaved entries, the user is prompted to save or discard the changes. For each unsaved day, this should be a modal dialog so that the program does not exit before the dialog has been completed. This leads to the `for` loop:

```
for (day = 1; day <= 28; day++)
        if ( !text_saved[day])
                DayUnsaved(day);
exit (0);
```

where each call to `DayUnsaved()` is modal. The `DayUnsaved()` function creates a warning dialog with three buttons 'Save', 'Don't Save' and 'Exit Anyway.' The last button causes an immediate exit (which terminates the application) but the other two need to terminate the modal dialog. They are passed the flag `dialog_over` in the callback function. Unfortunately, the Save callback also needs to know *which* day to save. Previously client information such as the day has been stored in the client data, but this has just been used for the modal flag. However, each widget has a resource `XmNuserData` that can be used for any purpose, and the program stores the day value in this resource.

Finally, what are the application defaults for this program? The following file contents should be stored in `/usr/lib/X11/app-defaults/XmCalendar`:

```
XmCalendar*applyLabelString:        Save
XmCalendar*okLabelString:           Quit
*XmText.width:                      300
*XmText.height:                     200
XmCalendar*warning.okLabelString:       Save
XmCalendar*warning.cancelLabelString: Don't Save
XmCalendar*warning.helpLabelString:   Exit Anyway
```

This just sets the labels in the various buttons and sets a height and width for the editor widgets.

10.3.1 Summary

This section has considered a simple but realistic Motif program. It uses a MainWindow to contain the major application areas which in this case are a Menu and a Row-Column of Labels and PushButtons. Additional visual components are a number of modeless and modal dialogs. The application behavior is controlled by resources and through the functions attached to callbacks.

Exercises

1. Some errors (such as being unable to open a file) are reported by the calendar to the standard error output. Replace these with warning dialogs.

2. When the editor for a day contains information, that is, is not empty, show this by inverting the colors in the corresponding day button.

3. Add extra buttons to allow the user to move backward and forward to the previous and next months.

4. Fix the day/month mechanism so that the calendar shows the correct days for this month. (This has nothing much to do with Motif.)

5. Replace the multiline text editor for each day with a set of one-line time-slot fields so that entries can be made for the periods 9.00 to 10.00, 10.00 to 11.00, etc.

Chapter 11

Intermediate techniques

In this section some techniques are presented that are not necessary to begin Motif programming, but need to be absorbed relatively early.

11.1 Translation tables

Each widget defines a set of actions that it executes, documented for each widget in the Programmer's Reference Manual under Behavior and Default Translations. For the arrow widget these are `Enter()`, `Leave()`, `Arm()`, `Disarm()`, `Activate()` and `ArmAndActivate()`. These actions are triggered by events or sets of events. The Enter action is triggered by the pointer (mouse) entering the window, and the Arm action is triggered by a press on the left mouse button.

In Motif 1.0, the Default Translations section documents the relation between events and these actions. For example, pressing button one down (the left one) invokes the function `Arm()`, which calls the callbacks on the `XmNarmCallback` list. Similarly, pressing the Return key invokes the function `ArmAndActivate()`. The Motif 1.1 documentation states essentially the same thing under the Translations section. This unfortunately has adopted another level of abstraction using a system called 'virtual bindings' in which BSelect is the left button (button one), and KSelect is the Return key (this correspondence is documented in VirtualBindings). If the attachment of actions to keys and buttons were left like this it would smack of hardcoding and this is against the X philosophy. For example, a person who uses the mouse on the left side may prefer to click on the right button instead of the left one.

The correspondence is actually managed via a *translation table* and the documentation lists the default translation-table that results if nothing else is done. However, either the user or the application can modify this table. This can be done in a number of ways. New key/button combinations can be added to invoke the functions; an existing key/button combination can be made to invoke a different function; the default table may be replaced entirely. The most common mechanism just adds new combinations.

11.1.1 User translations

The user may override the translation table entries by using the normal resource database mechanisms. The translation resource is set to a new string with the new event/action binding. For example:

```
*ArrowButton*translations: #override\n\
                           <Key>Q: Arm()\n\
                           <Btn2Up>: DisArm()
```

means that pressing the 'q' key (in either upper or lower case) will invoke the `Arm()` action and releasing button two will invoke `DisArm()`. Neither the key nor the button is attached to any actions in the default translation. If they had been, the old action would have been overridden. Note the mechanism to continue the table onto the second and third lines: the '\n' stands for the new line character in the string, and the second backslash escapes the immediately following new line. The full syntax is described in an appendix to the 'MIT X Toolkit Intrinsics—C Language Interface.' It allows a full range of modifier keys (shift, etc.) plus keys and button descriptions, for example:

```
Ctrl <Key>A, <Btn1Down>
```

stands for simultaneously pressing Ctrl–A and pressing the left button.

11.1.2 Programmer translations

The programmer can override or augment the defaults by defining a translation table in the application and then adding this to the widget's translation table. The syntax of the string used in the translation table is the same as in the resource file:

```
char myTranslations[] = "<Key>Q: Arm()\n\
                         <Btn2Up>: DisArm()";
XtTranslations trans_table;
trans_table = XtParseTranslationTable(myTranslations);
XtOverrideTranslations(arrow_widget, trans_table);
```

This overrides any previous translations attached to key Q and button two up, and adds any new ones. The call `XtAugmentTranslations()` would add new key/button combinations, but use the old values in cases of clashes. Note that this is independent of the callback attachment mechanism. If this is added to the arrow program after the widget has been created but before `XtMainLoop()`, both the default of pressing button one and also pressing the key 'q' or 'Q' will invoke the `Arm()` action.

How useful is this? It allows configuration of widget responses to user actions. The default response covers many situations but cannot cover all requirements. For example, consider the text widget. This can be used as the basis for an editor. Most editors have a common subset of actions, such as delete to end of line, move to the start of the text, etc. Editors regrettably differ vastly in the key/button combinations they use for each action and people have strong preferences for their favorite editor. The Motif text widget has a large number of actions, such as `delete-to-end-of-line()` and `beginning-of-file()` (many of these were unfortunately not documented in Motif 1.0). The user can set preferred key bindings for them. For example, to get emacs-style bindings for the common functions, place this in `.Xdefaults`:

```
*XmText.translations:   #override\n\
    Ctrl <Key>b:            backward-character()\n\
    Meta <Key>b:            backward-word()\n\
    Meta <Key>[:            backward-paragraph()\n\
    Meta <Key><:            beginning-of-file()\n\
    Ctrl <Key>a:            beginning-of-line()\n\
    Meta <Key>>:            end-of-file()\n\
    Ctrl <Key>e:            end-of-line()\n\
    Ctrl <Key>f:            forward-character()\n\
    Meta <Key>]:            forward-paragraph()\n\
    Ctrl Meta <Key>f:       forward-word()\n\
    Ctrl <Key>d:            kill-next-character()\n\
    Meta <Key>BackSpace:    kill-previous-word()\n\
    Ctrl <Key>w:            key-select()kill-selection()\n\
    Ctrl <Key>y:            unkill()\n\
    Ctrl <Key>k:            kill-to-end-of-line()\n\
    Meta <Key>Delete:       kill-to-start-of-line()\n\
    Ctrl <Key>n:            next-line()\n\
    Ctrl <Key>p:            previous-line()\n\
    Ctrl <Key>l:            redraw-display()\n\
    Ctrl <Key>osfDown:      next-page()\n\
    Ctrl <Key>osfUp:        previous-page()\n\
    Ctrl <Key>space:        set-anchor()\n
```

11.1.3   Translations and Text in Motif 1.0

Translations work as described in Motif 1.0. However, in one particular circumstance there is an unfortunate situation which requires the programmer to correct erroneous behavior. In a dialog, a BulletinBoard container is used. This expects a number of buttons in the dialog, such as OK and Cancel buttons. We have not said much about keyboard mechanisms for buttons, but pressing the Return key while a button has the focus will normally execute the button's `Activate()` action. BulletinBoard intercepts the Return key for its own purposes: if the user presses Return, it is 'clearly' a signal that they want the `Activate()` routine of a default button executed.

One case where this is clearly wrong is where a multiline Text widget is a child of BulletinBoard, where the Return key should not activate the default button but really be a Return key for the Text widget. The BulletinBoard behavior must be removed and replaced by the default Text behavior. This has been done whenever we have had a pop-up editor. Collecting the relevant pieces of program gives:

```
#if XmVersion == 1000
#define MOTIF_1_0
#endif

#ifdef MOTIF_1_0
/* to fix a "feature" of a bulletin board in a dialog */
char transLine[] = "<Key>Return: newline()";
#endif

#ifdef MOTIF_1_0
    /* edit_text is a child of a selection box
        in a dialog.
        A form is a subclass of a bulletin board which
        "redefines" the return key in this context.
        Fix the return key back to what it should be:
      */
    transTable = XtParseTranslationTable(transLine);
    XtOverrideTranslations(edit_text, transTable);
#endif
```

11.1.4   Translations and menus

The Motif style guide determines what the keys and buttons do in menus, and this is quite different to what happens outside menus. For example, pressing the up arrow key on a button inside a menu pane moves up one menu item, whereas pressing the same key on a button outside the menu pane has no effect. To implement this, some distortions were made in the normal translation-table mechanism. The effect is that the user cannot do anything to override, augment or replace translations, but the programmer can. What happens if the user sets a translation table for say a button in the menu is this: the user's translations are ignored but also the PushButton translations such as pressing the button to activate it are ignored. Only the menu-traversal actions, such as the use of the arrow keys, are left in. So the user only makes things worse by trying to set translations in menus. On the other hand, the programmer can augment/override translations quite happily after the widget has been created.

11.1.5   Summary

Translation tables add a level of configurability by allowing either the user or the programmer to call widget actions by their own key or button combinations using the functions:

```
XtParseTranslationTable ()
XtAugmentTranslations ()
XtOverrideTranslations ()
```

or the resource:

```
translations
```
Two cases where translations work 'incorrectly' (Text in a Motif 1.0 dialog, and Menus) have also been discussed.

11.2 Adding resources

We have seen extensive use of the resource database for control of widgets and applications. However, the resources so far come from the widgets although there have been times when it would have been useful to have resources specific to the application. For example, in the Motif version of the noughts and crosses program, 'nought' always started. A more configurable version of the program would allow either 0 or X to start. It should default to say '0' but the user should be able to override that with either a command-line option or resource-database value:

```
xmcrosses.starter:    X
```
in a resource file, or by:

```
xmcrosses -starter X
```
as a command-line option.

It is not difficult to create new resources for an application. It is really a matter of letting the resource-management system know all about the resource and then querying it when needed. The first part to look at is command-line parsing. An array of option descriptions is created, one entry for each option. This is later used by `XtInitialize()` to extract the options from the command line and store them in the resource database. Command-line options come in many forms. The three most common are where the option is the value (like the `-l` in `ls -l`) where the value immediately follows the option (like the line number 70 in `pr -l70 file`) or follows as the next argument (like the file name in `mail -f file-name`). These three are respectively described by `XrmoptionIsArg`, `XrmoptionStickyArg` and `XrmoptionNextArg`. The resource system also has to be told under what name to store the resource in the database. To get an additional command line of `-starter X`, with the value stored under the resource name `starter`:

```
XrmOptionDescRec myoptions[] =
{       {"-starter", "starter", XrmoptionNextArg, NULL}
};
```
The array is of the structure `XrmOptionDescRec` which is a record with four fields. The first is the command-line string, the second the resource name, the third the type of option. The last one is generally `NULL`.

This array is passed as the third argument to `XtInitialize()` with the fourth being its size:

```
app_shell = XtInitialize (NULL, Class_name,
                    myoptions, XtNumber (myoptions),
                    &argc, argv);
```

Intermediate techniques   203

This extracts all known command-line options from the command-line vector `argv`. This includes all the standard ones such as the foreground `-fg color`, geometry, etc. and in addition any starter. If `argc` is greater than one after this, a command-line error has probably occurred and should be reported. In addition to command-line options, all resources in resource files are also loaded into the resource database.

To extract values from the resource database, a structure and an array must be defined. The structure is used to store the values from the database and consists of one field for each of the new resources. There is only one new resource, so there is only one field in the structure. The type of this field is an `unsigned char` since that is the type of the option. This structure should be constructed using a typedef, because its type is required later:

```
typedef struct
    {unsigned char starter}
MyResourceType, *MyResourceTypePtr;
```

```
MyResourceType myresources;
```

The address of the variable `myresources` will later be given to a function that will fill in the value of the field starter.

There is one last step, but it is a little complex. Resources have an instance name, like 'width,' a class name, like 'Width' and a type. The names are clearly needed by the resource manager because it will need them to find their values. We tell the resource manager about this in an array of structures of type `XtResource`. An array is needed because more than one resource may be defined. Here the array only has one element because only the one resource 'starter' is being defined. The first two fields of the structure are the instance name 'starter' and the class name 'Starter.'

Both in the resource files and on the command line, the value of the resource is an ASCII string. In fact, we know that it can only be a single character (in fact, an X or 0). We could perform the conversion from string to character in the program (by looking at the first element of the string) but the resource manager does such conversions (to integer, to Boolean, to Position, etc.) automatically for a large number of types. By specifying the required result type of the resource, the manager will do the appropriate conversions. The type is given as the next field of the structure. Symbolic names are used rather than actual types, such as `XmRString` for Strings, `XmRInt` for integers, and so on.

Next the resource manager needs to know where to find the field to place the value in the variable `myresources`. A macro is used to help: `XtOffset (MyResourceTypePtr, starter)` returns where the field `starter` is in the structure. Finally, we need a default value, in case the resource is not actually in the database.

The default value should be of pointer size (e.g. a pointer to `char`). It may be possible to fit in the actual default value, as happens when the type is an `unsigned char`. `XmRString` says it is a pointer to a string; `XmRImmediate` says the actual value is given (coerced to pointer size if needed).

All these components add up to give the definition of the array 'resources':

```
XtResource resources[] =
{    {"starter",               /* instance name */
     "Starter",               /* class name    */
     XmRUnsignedChar,         /* type          */
     sizeof(unsigned char)    /* type size     */
     XtOffset (MyResourceTypePtr, starter)
                              /* field offset  */
     XmRImmediate             /* default value follows */
     (caddr_t) '0'            /* coerced value */
     }
};
```

After that rather complex step, all the hard work is done. The resource manager does all the rest; reading the resource files, parsing the command line, converting the type and storing the values in the resource database. Finally the program makes a call to `XtGetApplicationResources()` to extract the values. This call should be placed anywhere after `XtInitialize()` and takes the arrays we have just constructed:

```
XtGetApplicationResources (app_shell,
            &myresources,        /* where values
                                    are put */
            resources,           /* resource description
                                    array */
            XtNumber (resources) /* size of array */
            NULL,
            0);
```

(The last two arguments are for the resources which are *not* to be set by the user.) From now on, the resource values are available for use. We could now hard-code whose turn it is to start, since we have looked in all the places a user might put its value.

```
if (myresources.starter == '0')
    turn = 0;
else    turn = 1;
```

Exercises

1. Add the resource day number to the Calendar so that it can be started showing a particular day.

2. If you have made a version of the Calendar that can find the current date, add a resource mechanism that will also allow the application to be started by:

```
calendar -day today
calendar -day +3
```

11.3 Adding actions

There is a major problem in object-oriented systems: how and when should an object be closed off? When an object is closed off its internal operation becomes inaccessible and cannot be modified by a programmer. This is a good thing for any completed object as it then becomes stable for any user. Inheritance requires that the programmer, in designing new objects, have access to the internals of an object to modify them (override methods) and to use the internal data structures to extend them. This requires objects to be open, which, for inheritance, is a good thing. These are incompatible.

Xt objects are closed but extendable. That is, there is no access to internal data structures. However, message types can be added to an object and then both how these messages can be invoked and the callback functions to be invoked by them, can be specified.

For example, suppose we wished to leave the arrow button behavior to the default, but wished to augment it by having a means of exiting the program by pressing 'q', independent of the existing callback mechanism. This is a somewhat contrived example; a much more realistic one is given in the exercises. We would require a means of 'opening up' the widget to add an action, application code invoked by it, and an event to trigger the action. The only new part is the addition of an action, which becomes associated with an action function. The action function is defined by the programmer. This is done by an extension of the actions method of the last section, adding in an 'actions table.'

The first component of this is a string by which the new action can be known for use in translation tables. The next component is the address of a C function which contains the actual code of the action. By convention, this is a capitalized version of the action string. An array of such string/address pairs is set up:

```
XtActionsRec actionsTable[] =
{
    {"quit", Quit}
}
```

This defines 'quit' as the name of the action, which can be used henceforth by quit( ) in translation tables and associates this with the C function `Quit()`. Note that the declaration of this function must appear before the table is defined, because otherwise the C compiler will be confused, unable to figure out the address and type of `Quit()`.

This new table is installed into the application by a call to XtAddActions() some time after initialization. This may look a bit odd: we are only going to use the new action in the arrow button, but nevertheless it is installed in an action table for the application rather than the arrow button.

The new action is invoked by a key/button combination by attaching the combination to the arrow widget using a translation table, exactly as in the last section. This may be done either by the programmer in the code, or in a resource file such as /usr/lib/X11/app-defaults/ClassName, or in .Xdefaults. The only remaining component is the definition of the application function Quit(). This is called with four parameters: the widget invoking the action, the X event causing this and two other rarely-used parameters which can be used to carry information into the function from the invocation. The program is called arrow_actions.c.

Program 22: arrow_actions.c

```
#include <Xm/Xm.h>
#include <Xm/ArrowB.h>

char Class_name[] ="Arrow";

static char defaultTranslations[] = "<Key>Q: quit()";
static XtTranslations trans_table;

void
quit(w, event, params, num_params)
    Widget w; /* widget that invoked this function */
    XEvent *event;  /* last event that triggered
                        the action */
    String *params;
    int num_params;
{
    printf("Key Q was pressed\n");
    exit(0);
}

static XtActionsRec actionsTable[] =
{
{"quit", quit}  /* name of action and  function above */
};

main(argc, argv)
    int argc;
    char **argv;
{
    Widget toplevel, arrow_widget;
```

```
        toplevel = XtInitialize(NULL,
                                Class_name,
                                NULL,
                                0,
                                &argc, argv);

    /* Create a widget, with the toplevel as manager;
        its class is ArrowButton
    */
    arrow_widget = XmCreateArrowButton(toplevel,
                            "an_arrow",
                            NULL,
                            0);

    XtManageChild(arrow_widget);

    /* register the new actions */
    XtAddActions(actionsTable, XtNumber(actionsTable));

     /* compile the translation table */
     trans_table = XtParseTranslationTable(
                        defaultTranslations);

    /* augment the existing translations */
       XtAugmentTranslations(arrow_widget, trans_table);

    /* display all of the widgets */
    XtRealizeWidget(toplevel);

    /* enter the main processing loop */
     XtMainLoop();
}
```

Exercise

1. Add actions 'left,' 'right,' 'up' and 'down' to the arrow program so that pressing 'l', 'r', 'u', 'd' will change the direction of the arrow.

11.4 Memory usage

Programs built using Motif are often large. Worse, they have a tendency to grow, the longer the program executes. Programs often *leak memory*. The end result, of course, is that an application may simply run out of memory and die. Whose fault is this and what can be done about it?

In one sense the fault lies with the C language since it has no inbuilt garbage-collection mechanism. Any application is responsible for getting memory from the heap by `malloc()` and, when it no longer needs it, releasing it with `free()`. (Xt uses `XtMalloc()` and `XtFree()`, which have some additional checks, but do not resolve the problem.)

Some *servers* leak badly. There is no solution to this but to switch to another X server, preferably a later one. The Xt libraries had a bad leak in Translation Table management. Again the solution is to switch to a later version of Xt. The Motif libraries leak, particularly in `XmString` handling. This has improved with each release, so again, use the latest release of Motif available.

Finally, many applications leak by failing to reclaim memory themselves. Each time a widget is created, it uses memory. When you have finished with one, reclaim the memory by destroying it and its children using `XtDestroyWidget()`. If you use `XtMalloc()` to get space from the heap, reclaim it when it is no longer needed by `XtFree()`. If an `XmString` is no longer needed, reclaim it by `XmString-Free()`.

A major source of memory leaks in an application is resources. When a resource is *set*, Motif usually makes a *copy* of its value. This is simple protective programming: if a widget had to rely for its internal workings on something that it had no control over, it would not last long. This means that *after* a resource has been set, there are two copies of its value present—the one the application has, and the copy that the widget has. You should reclaim space for the application's copy if it no longer needs it.

If you *get* a resource, things are more complex. For some resources, Motif gives a copy, but for others it does not. So it is not always clear whether you can reclaim the space after the application has finished with it, because the widget may still be using it. The rule of thumb is that if the resource value is a table (an array) you get a pointer, not a copy, whereas if it is a simple value such as an integer or string, you get a copy. This is to reduce computation time. So the rule of thumb is that the application *cannot* reclaim space for tables from a widget, but can for simple values. Unfortunately for this rule, not all widgets obey it. Some widgets do not return a copy, so the value cannot be reclaimed. Examples of this in Motif 1.1 are; BulletinBoard does not return a copy of its dialogTitle, FileSelection Box does not return a copy of either its directory or its noMatchString; RowColumn does not return a copy of its labelString; Scale does not return a copy of its titleString. These are fairly obscure resources, so in general, follow the rules. Motif 1.0 had more bad cases. Later versions should have less.

11.5   Using Xlib within Motif

We have seen that quite substantial applications can be built with Motif, scarcely using Xlib. However, there are occasions when Motif does not supply enough functionality by itself, and Xlib calls have to be used.

Many Xlib routines take a display and a window. Motif and Xt do not deal with such terms although most widgets have windows and of course they all have to show on a display. Xt gives routines to extract these values for any widget:

```
Window   XtWindow (widget);
Display *XtDisplay (widget);
```

Some of the Xlib calls discussed in Part II used the screen number. This is not accessible from Xt. What is accessible is a structure of type `Screen` (the screen number indexes into an array of these). Analogous to calls such as `BlackPixel()` are ones that take such a `Screen` structure:

```
Screen *XtScreen (widget)
BlackPixelOfScreen (screen)
WhitePixelOfScreen (screen)
```

There is one potential problem that should be watched for: a widget does not have a window until it has been realized. Attempts to do anything to it before then will produce an error. An example is creating a different mouse cursor for a widget, which was set as an an Xlib exercise in Section 4.5. The changes are minor:

```
#include <X11/cursorfont.h>
Cursor cursor;

cursor = XCreateFontCursor(XtDisplay(widget),
                           XC_sb_right_arrow);
XDefineCursor(XtDisplay(widget),
              XtWindow(widget), cursor);
```

Motif gives one widget in which it is expected that Xlib calls may be made and this is DrawingArea. Management of DrawingArea is kept to a minimum. This widget has callbacks for input, expose and resize events so that the widget can invoke callbacks for Xlib events of interest. Lines and text can be drawn in DrawingArea without any problems. In fact this (and DrawnButton) are the *only* Motif widgets that should be drawn into. The following program is a version of the Xlib `hello.c` adapted to Motif: its only purpose is to illustrate how to combine Xlib drawing calls with a Motif program. It does all drawing in the expose-callback function.

Program 23: motif_hello.c

```c
#include <stdio.h>

#include <Xm/DrawingA.h>

/*------------------------------------------------------
**      Forward Declarations
*/

void main ();
void CreateApplication ();
void display_somethingCB ();

/*------------------------------------------------------
**      Global Variables
*/

#define MAX_ARGS 20
#define Class_name "Draw"

Widget  draw_area;    /* Drawing Area widget */
Display *display;     /* the display device   */
Screen  *screen;      /* the screen on the display */
Window  draw_window; /* the drawing area
                         widget's window */
GC      gc;

/*------------------------------------------------------
** Create a graphics context using default values, and
** return it in the pointer gc
*/
GC
getGC ()
{   GC gc;

    gc = XCreateGC (display, draw_window,
               (unsigned long) 0, NULL);

    XSetForeground (display, gc,
               BlackPixelOfScreen (screen));
    XSetBackground (display, gc,
                WhitePixelOfScreen (screen));
    return (gc);
}
```

```
/*----------------------------------------------------
** Write a string
** and draw a circle
*/
void display_somethingCB (w, client_data, call_data)
Widget          w;
caddr_t         client_data;
caddr_t         call_data;
{
    /* the proverbial string */
    XDrawImageString (display, draw_window, gc,
                      10, 10, "Hello world",
                      strlen ("Hello world"));


    /* and a world (circle) to go with it */
    XDrawArc (display, draw_window, gc,
              30, 30,
              100, 100,
              0, 360*64);
    XFlush (display);
}
/*----------------------------------------------------
**    main          - main logic for application
*/
void main (argc,argv)
    unsigned int    argc;
    char            **argv;
{
    Widget          app_shell;

    app_shell = XtInitialize(NULL,
              Class_name,
              NULL,
              0,
              &argc, argv);


    /* set up all the sub-widgets */
    CreateApplication(app_shell);
    XtRealizeWidget (app_shell);


    /* Now get info about windows, etc
    ** The XtWindow() _must_ occur after XtRealize() has
    ** created the Drawing Area's window
    */
    display = XtDisplay (draw_area);
```

```
        draw_window = XtWindow (draw_area);
        screen = XtScreen (draw_area);
        gc = getGC ();

        /*    Get and dispatch events.
        */
        XtMainLoop ();
}


/*----------------------------------------------------------
**      CreateApplication    - create main window
*/
void CreateApplication (parent)
Widget          parent;
{

        Arg           args[MAX_ARGS];
        register int    n;

        /*    Create Drawing Area
        **    Make it a reasonable size
        */
        n = 0;
        XtSetArg (args[n], XmNwidth, 300); n++;
        XtSetArg (args[n], XmNheight, 300); n++;
        draw_area = XmCreateDrawingArea (parent, "an_area",
                                        args, n);
        XtAddCallback (draw_area, XmNexposeCallback,
                                display_somethingCB, NULL);
        XtManageChild (draw_area);
}
```

Exercises for Part III

The following can be set as a major exercise in Motif programming. It contains most of the elements seen before but also makes use of the List widget.

Create a program to act as an address book for up to, say, one hundred people. It could have an appearance similar to Figure 46, where clicking on a person's name from the scrolled list displays information on them. The address book should allow modification of existing entries, in case the information changes (the person may change address) and it should also allow the addition of new entries. The address book should have a help system and full error-reporting mechanisms. Some extensions to this might be:

1. Display short information such as name and email address, with a 'More information...' leading to the other details.

2. Add a utility function such as a mailer which will allow the user to compose mail messages and then send them off using the stored email address.

3. Add a utility such as letter-address creation, which will create a file with appropriate address, salutation and complimentary close. It could do so in particular word-processor format (e.g. `nroff`) if desired.

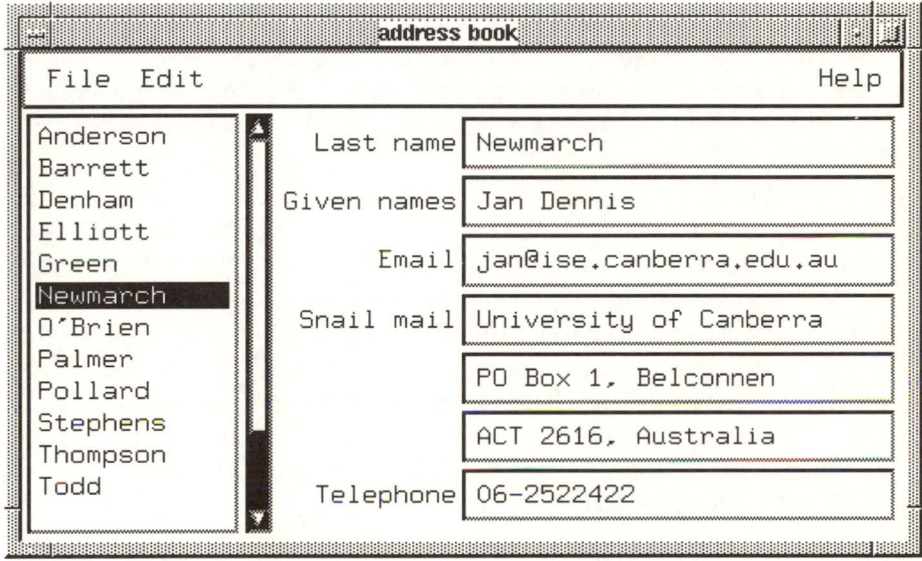

Figure 46: The address-book program

Summary of Part III

Programming for graphical user interfaces (GUIs) is a complex matter. As the quality of the interface improves, the difficulty for the applications programmer increases. New styles of programming also become necessary, with modeless, event-driven programming required, and an object-oriented approach.

Xlib provides an event-driven applications environment with mechanisms to handle keyboards, mice and a large number of graphics displays. In itself, it is a large system. However, it does not supply the structure of objects,and the Xlib programmer has to rely on traditional C methods for structuring and dealing with complexity.

The Xt library provides a framework for a particular style of object-oriented programming above Xlib. Xt does not supply the objects itself but gives the mechanism for the creation, destruction and manipulation of objects.

Motif is a library of objects within the Xt framework and an additional set of C routines for manipulating data structures such as XmStrings. It also contains a particular look-and-feel, and comes with a style guide to promote this look-and-feel. Motif programming is a matter of both using the library of objects, and using them in a manner consistent with this look-and-feel.

This book has attempted to give an overview of Xlib, Xt and Motif programming. The serious GUI programmer in this environment will have to go to a much deeper level, but what we have given should be enough to give the flavor, and show the power, of this approach. Good luck, have fun, and build applications that your users enjoy using!

Bibliography

This list of books on the X Window System and Motif is not complete. The list gives a selection of books that you may wish to explore for further information.

Asente P.J. and Swick R.R. (1990) *X Window System Toolkit, the Complete Programmer's Guide and Specification*. Digital Press (distributed by Prentice-Hall).

Barkakati N. (1991) *X Window System Programming*. Englewood Cliffs N.J.: Prentice-Hall.

Berlage T. (1991) *OSF/Motif: Concepts and Programming*. Wokingham: Addison-Wesley.

Heller D. (1991) *Xlib Programming Manual*. Sebastopol CA: O'Reilly and Associates.

Johnson E.F. and Reichard K. (1989) *X Window Applications Programming*. Salt Lake City, Utah: MIS Press.

Jones O. (1989) *Introduction to the X Window System*. Englewood Cliffs, N.J.: Prentice-Hall.

Kobara S. (1991) *Visual Design with OSF/Motif*. Reading, MA: Addison-Wesley.

Mansfield N. (1991) *The X Window System: A User's Guide*. Amsterdam: Addison-Wesley.

Nye A. (1990) *Xlib Programming Manual*. Sebastopol CA: O'Reilly and Associates.

Nye A., ed. (1990) *Xlib Reference Manual*. Sebastopol CA: O'Reilly and Associates.

Nye A. and O'Reilly T. (1990) *X Toolkit Intrinsics Programming Manual, Motif Edition*. Sebastopol CA: O'Reilly and Associates.

Open Software Foundation (1991) *Motif Style Guide*. Englewood Cliffs N.J.: Prentice-Hall.

Open Software Foundation (1991) *Motif Programmer's Reference*. Englewood Cliffs N.J.: Prentice-Hall.

Open Software Foundation (1991) *Motif Programmer's Guide*. Englewood Cliffs N.J.: Prentice-Hall.

O'Reilly T., Quercia V. and Lamb L. (1990) *X Window System User's Guide*. Sebastopol CA: O'Reilly and Associates.

O'Reilly T., ed. (1990) *X Toolkit Intrinsics Reference Manual*. Sebastopol CA: O'Reilly and Associates.

Young D. (1989) *The X Window System: Applications and Programming with X, OSF/Motif Version*. Englewood Cliffs N.J.: Prentice-Hall.

Index